*f*P

SPOILS OF WAR

The Human Cost of America's Arms Trade

JOHN TIRMAN

THE FREE PRESS
New York   London   Toronto   Sydney   Singapore

THE FREE PRESS
A Division of Simon & Schuster Inc.
1230 Avenue of the Americas
New York, NY 10020

Designed by Carla Bolte

Manufactured in the United States of America

10 9 8 7 6 5 4 3 2 1

Library of Congress Cataloging-in-Publication Data

Tirman, John.
    Spoils of war: the human cost of America's arms trade / John
Tirman
        p.   cm.
    Includes index.
    ISBN 0–684–82726–3
        1. Defense industries—Moral and ethical aspects—United States.
    2. Arms transfers—Moral and ethical aspects—United States.
    3. Military assistance, American—Moral and ethical aspects.
    I. Title
    HD9743.U6T57   1997   97–13522
    382' .456233' 0973—dc21   CIP

To, for, with

N.Z.T.

Contents

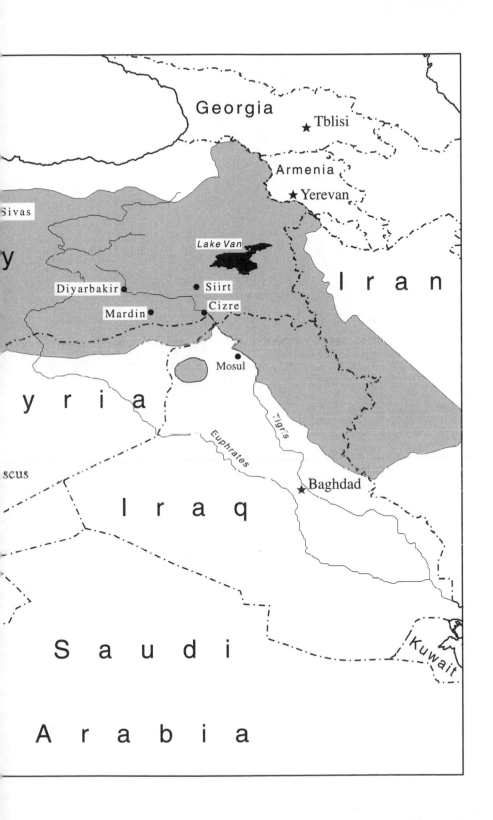

PART ONE

1

THE TRAJECTORY OF TRAGEDY

The landscape is rugged, with small villages nestled into valleys and along the slopes of the jagged mountains. A formation of helicopters swoops between the peaks, looking for small convoys and campsites of the rebel forces. Soldiers in the choppers' cabins are outfitted for a fight; one of them surveys the terrain through the sights of a machine gun mounted in the aircraft's hatch, ready to fire thousands of rounds per minute at the hostile encampments. The squadron leader spots a hamlet he suspects may harbor insurgents, and orders the pilot to hover over a pasture nearby. From a hundred feet above the ground, the helicopters frighten the sheep and the shepherd, then open fire on the confused animals as they scatter in panic. Incendiary explosives are hurled into an adjacent forest, setting it ablaze in an instant. Two of the rotorcraft descend into the village schoolyard. An officer steps out and with a bullhorn summons the townspeople to the school. An interrogation must take place, he screams. Rebels must be found. Collaborators must be punished.

The villagers obey. They have heard from cousins of this same horror besetting other villages not far away. They gather in the hot, sundrenched yard, standing for hours as the men are taken inside the school, one by one, to be questioned, accused, beaten, and humiliated. Are you a terrorist? Have you given bread to the terrorists? Do you stash guns for the terrorists? Isn't your uncle in prison, a convicted terrorist? When were they last here?

Soldiers from the helicopters ransack the now-empty homes, looking for "evidence" and seizing the few valuables—a clock, a gold trinket—

3

they may happen upon. When the interrogations are finished, the officer in the schoolyard accuses the villagers *en masse* of complicity with the rebels. You are aiding the terrorists! We will not tolerate enemy villages! You must leave—where you go we don't know and don't care. The soldiers then pour a white powder on the fifty small houses and set them on fire. Livestock are shot. A few bloodied men are roughly loaded into the helicopters.

As the black smoke of the villagers' homes, homes to countless generations of their families, rises into the air, so too do the helicopters. A few spurts from a machine gun cut down a stray plowhorse. Then the big steel birds fly away as suddenly as they came. The village men inside the aircraft are never seen again. The villagers are bereft, dazed, angry. Nothing of their way of life remains. The village is destroyed. They will that very night begin the long trek to the city where they'll join a million other villagers made homeless.

The notorious "special teams," the men and their helicopters, have struck again.

The scene could be Vietnam thirty years ago or El Salvador ten years ago. But the men of the special teams are not Americans; only the helicopters are. The place is in Turkey, in the southeastern mountains of Anatolia, which Kurds inhabited long before the Turkish tribes of Central Asia swept in to dominate the region, and where America's stout ally, the Turkish military, is waging a campaign of terror against the Kurdish people. The war with the Kurds has already lasted thirteen years. It is a war rooted in Turkey's obsessive nationalism but supported by the United States out of a misbegotten fear of Islamic radicalism and a mistaken definition of American interests.

The story of Turkey's Kurds is one of the world's massive human-rights violations. Some two and a half million villagers have been displaced and thousands have been killed by Ankara's fitful attempt to defeat a small rebel army. This war has accelerated an Islamic revival in Turkey that now threatens to usher in precisely what U.S. policy was so determined to prevent—a Muslim leadership hostile to the West. It is eerily reminiscent of the catastrophic failure of America's fervent support of the Shah of Iran in the 1970s, and may foreshadow the collapse of pro-American regimes in Saudi Arabia and Egypt as well.

The currency of the policy is weaponry, lavish supplies of military hardware, training, intelligence, and strategy. The hardware is among America's best: Black Hawk and Cobra helicopters, F-16 fighter jets, tanks and armored combat vehicles, missiles and land mines and guns. As America's political will to wage war diminished with the disaster in Vietnam, Washington's brain trust supplied allies to do the fighting for us; and as the end of the Cold War diminished America's ability to stock its own arsenal, Washington's brain trust supplied allies to keep our own arms factories running. The two policies seemed to fit each other so neatly: protect our interests by containing Islamic fundamentalism, protect our interests by arming the countries surrounding the fundamentalists.

The policies have gone awry, wastefully and tragically. The very act of militarily supplying the Shah's repressive regime led to his downfall and the triumph of the Islamic revolution. To "contain" that disaster, the United States then shored up the repressive regime of Saddam Hussein in Iraq; two wars and hundreds of thousands dead were the result. Many factors were at work in these catastrophes, of course, not just the eager conveyance of U.S. weapons. But the pattern was unmistakable. Arm our Muslim friends to confront our Muslim enemies. Keep the arms factory humming, the weaponmaker's profits flowing, and the defense worker's job secure. And protect American interests abroad.

These "interests" are something of an embarrassment to the Washington brain trusts. Democracy and human rights have rarely been at stake during the quarter-century that the policy has been pursued. No pretense of democracy existed in the Shah's Iran, Saddam's Iraq, or the oil sheikhdoms of the Arabian peninsula. Human rights are derisively ignored in Turkey and Egypt. No, the stakes are summed up in one word: oil.

Black gold was the linchpin of American involvement in the Persian Gulf for a half-century; it was the bottom line of every calculation of U.S. politicians. When the oil embargo of 1973–74 rocked the world's economy, Americans widely agreed that such vulnerable reliance on foreign sources of oil was a dire threat to economic security. Fifty percent of those imports came from the Persian Gulf, a frightening reality confirmed again by events in 1979 (the Iranian revolution and another doubling of prices) and the two Gulf wars. But agreement on a strategy for America's "energy independence" was subverted by ingrained habits of consumption and the influence of the oil corporations. As successive occupants of the White

House encountered America's exposure to instability in the Gulf, they reached for that most ready instrument of presidential power: the military. U.S. armed forces would be called upon only once—in Desert Storm—but other militaries could be strengthened, encouraged, and borrowed for the essential task of ensuring the flow of petroleum to America, Europe, and Japan.

Other concerns animated American policy in the Middle East—shipping lanes, stability in the eastern Mediterranean, and the sovereignty and safety of Israel. Dominating them until 1989 was the containment of the Soviet Union, whose clumsy meddling in the region was also carried out through military power—supply of Syria and Iraq, war in Afghanistan, support for insurrections in Muslim Africa. The U.S.-Soviet rivalry was the backdrop for American policy in the Islamic world, a ready justification for huge exports of weapons. When a few scattered Soviet inroads were made in the late 1970s in the Horn of Africa, when regimes in Libya and Syria and Iraq sided with Moscow, when leftists engineered vocal or violent protests in Iran or Turkey, the United States reinforced its military support for its surrogate rulers. For Muammar Qaddafi or Hafez al-Assad or Saddam Hussein, the links to the USSR were matters of convenience, born of their hatred of Israel and their pretensions of following a socialist path. But the Soviet Union, while a constant menace and as irresponsible a military supplier as the United States, was not the principal threat to American interests in the region: that threat was Arab nationalism, which sought to eject Western dominance—and after 1979 the Islamic revival, which, more rooted than socialism could ever be, posed a mortal danger to the hegemony the West had long enjoyed.

Because the response to this Muslim challenge was backed by military power, it reverberated within the United States as well. A fresh buildup of military strength that began in the late 1970s, while largely aimed at the Soviet Union, was fueled by American anxieties over the oil crisis, the fall of the Shah, and other setbacks in the region. And this buildup, accelerated when Ronald Reagan became president, created hundreds of thousands of new jobs in the defense industry to build missiles, aircraft, and the other instruments of warfare. By the mid- to late 1980s, the Reagan rearmament was employing seven million people, directly or in related industries. As the Soviet threat began to fade with the ascendancy of Mikhail Gorbachev, the arms industry was facing a crisis similar to that of the U.S. withdrawal from Vietnam: suddenly the Pentagon contracts were drying up, workers were being laid off, whole corporations dependent on the war footing were in jeopardy of bankruptcy. The pressure on U.S. politicians, especially those with constituencies enriched by the arms buildup, became enormous.

The end of the Cold War was supposed to produce a "peace dividend," a cut in defense spending that could then be applied to other national needs. While there was much talk about beating swords into plowshares to provide jobs for the bloated defense workforce, little of that was actually in store. For defense contractors, the strategy of survival had little to do with "conversion" to commercial products. Instead, the major military manufacturers competed to gain a larger slice of the smaller defense budget, as the procurement of weapons for the U.S. military shrank by 56 percent between 1987 and 1994. Major corporations merged to stay alive: Lockheed with Martin Marietta, Grumman with Northrop. Workers were laid off in droves—two million lost their high-paying jobs in the 1990s.

And the weapons so central to the Cold War were exported with a fervor not seen since the salad days of the mid-1970s, when the oil monarchies of the Middle East eagerly traded petrodollars for American arms. The United States soon dominated the world's commerce in weaponry, accounting for as much as 70 percent of the trade to the Third World in the mid-1990s, and will export more than $200 billion worth of weapons by the end of the 1990s. This astonishing surge seemed to run counter to the recent historic settlements of longstanding conflicts; not only had the Soviet Union collapsed, but bitter conflicts were ending in southern Africa, in Central America and, most remarkably, between Arabs and Israelis. Yes, wars still festered in places like Bosnia and Rwanda; confrontations with rickety communist regimes in North Korea and Cuba were sustained. But the potential for exports for those beleaguered venues was small.

Where, then, could America's technological wizardry be sold? The answer lay in that cauldron of unrest, the Persian Gulf. The noxious regimes of Iran and Iraq, against all odds, remained in power. New policies of "containment" were fashioned, "requiring" vast quantities of arms to bolster our friends in this rough neighborhood. The arms industry in the defense communities of Connecticut, Massachusetts, Texas, and California would, it seemed, be given a new lease on death.

The fresh emphasis on arms exports to Turkey, Saudi Arabia, Kuwait, Jordan, Egypt, and Israel in the 1990s was engineered virtually without public comment. Dissent was expressed in intellectual circles, in editorial comment in newspapers, in the liberal advocacy groups. But that outcry rarely registered on the scale of the nation's major political concerns.

The stakes, however, remained exceptionally high. Imports of oil from the region were as high as ever. The costs in U.S. military deployments in Turkey (to protect Kurds in northern Iraq from Saddam) and Saudi Arabia (to protect its monarchy from Iran and Iraq), the aid dollars soaked up by Israel and Egypt, the political and economic capital squandered in attempting to isolate Iran, Iraq, and Libya, all signaled the primary importance and extraordinary price of U.S. policy in the Middle East. Without their arms exports into the region, several American arms makers would collapse, with tens of thousands losing their jobs. And the order in the region remained crucial to the prospects for peace, stability, and economic growth of the nations on its periphery, especially the newly independent states of the former USSR, many of which were Muslim. Nowhere in the world, not in Russia, not in China, is there more attention from American government and business than in the Middle East, and nowhere has American engagement been more consistent, and more consistently a disaster.

The following chapters unfold the tale of this calamity. The story is told in three interwoven threads: in the world of Washington policy making; in the Middle East, particularly Turkey; and in a key venue of American arms manufacturing, Connecticut. The three places have combined uncannily to produce one of the world's great human-rights catastrophes, the village-by-village destruction of "Kurdistan," the unsovereign homeland of perhaps 20 million people.

The story begins in different historical eras. To grasp the evolution of the Middle East and its relations with the West, we reach back more than a thousand years; to understand the politics of American intentions, we reach back to Richard Nixon's presidency; to see how Connecticut's prosperity became so dependent on the military, we reach back to the American Revolution. By the 1970s, the three are interacting forcefully: Washington is exporting weapons to Iran, Turkey, and elsewhere in the region—weapons often made in Connecticut—with uncommonly mortal consequences.

The interwoven stories demonstrate, among other lessons, the sheer complexity of the American–Islam confrontation in the late twentieth century; they also show the utterly destructive role that U.S. military largesse has played. The story encompasses not only folly and miscalculation, but the authentic "Hobson's choice" of how to gracefully wind down the military-industrial complex from its Cold War excesses. The story is told not simply to blame the avaricious or amoral posturings of American leaders but, more significantly, to lay out how their embrace of specious ideas about the Muslim world and American power has led to one failure after another in the region, with staggering human costs at home and abroad.

Our story argues for a new *modus vivendi* with Islam and a reorienting of America's 30-year habit of projecting military power through the conveyance of high-tech weaponry. The transfer of military goods to Iran, Iraq, Saudi Arabia, Egypt, and Turkey has brought no net benefit to the United States. At home, it merely puts off harder choices about economic growth and industrial jobs. It can confidently be said that no such shipments would be needed, either there or here at home, if more sensible and readily available policies of diplomacy and economics were embraced.

That theoretical assertion, however, is less compelling than the tale that follows.

2

THE WEST'S ENCOUNTER
WITH ISLAM

The vitality of Islam has for centuries been a source of troubling anxiety for the West. For most Europeans before 1917, the Muslim world was manifest in the Ottoman Empire of Turkey: its militant origins, its expansiveness, its religious fervor, and, finally, its instability challenged Europe's strength repeatedly. At the same time, Turkey was the gateway to the Orient, just as it had been for millennia before. As such, it served as the conjugal chamber for the complex liaison between Europe and Asia, the place where cultures, religions, empires, armies, and myths of the two continents clashed and conjoined.

The importance of the place itself was evident long before nomadic tribes of Central Asia swept into the high plains of Anatolia in the eleventh century A.D. to establish the several successive dynasties of Turkish rulers. The small Greco-Roman city of Byzantium became Constantinople in 330 A.D. and Istanbul in 1453. It has always provided a symbolic passageway between East and West across the narrow Bosporus that links the Black Sea to the north with the Sea of Marmara, the Dardanelles, the Aegean, and the Mediterranean to the south. And the Anatolian peninsula itself juts into the Aegean, toward Greece and the West, a perfect seaward launch or landing for adventurers and generals.

The linkages, rivalries, and mutual fascination between East and West began long before Byzantium arose. The brief, mysterious civilization of the Hittites, believed to be invaders from the Caucasus, thrived in the central plain of Anatolia two thousand years before Christ. Some tribes from

Anatolia may have migrated across the Bosporus to settle in Greece. The Greek influence grew and returned eastward soon after. Along the southern shore of the Sea of Marmara lay Troy, then the great Greek trading city of the Dardanelles. Just at the time the Hittite empire disappeared, Troy was the site of the story of Homer's *Iliad*—the first recorded clash between armies of Asia and Europe. Eight centuries later the vast Persian armies of Darius and Xerxes crossed from Anatolia to their defeats at Marathon and Salamis in Greece. Alexander the Great, the young king of Greece's northern neighbor Macedon, led his armies across the Hellespont in 334 B.C. to conquer all of Anatolia and the modern Middle East, bringing down the Persian Empire and extending the Hellenic cultural and economic world into North Africa and Central Asia.

The military might of imperial Rome overwhelmed the world Alexander had left in Asia Minor—by the final century of the pre-Christian era, Roman vassals controlled all of Anatolia—and, more significantly, brought to the Greek city of Byzantium a "New Rome," a new capital of the Empire, in 330 A.D. This extraordinary act symbolized the transformation of the Empire itself under its first Christian emperor, Constantine. As a rejection of the old, corrupted pagan Rome, and as a sign of a new beginning, Constantine I moved the seat of power from Rome to Byzantium, lavishly expanding and adorning the city with palaces, arenas, and fortifications. The capital came to be known as Constantinople, and its domain the Byzantine Empire. Under Justinian in the sixth century it ruled an expanse nearly as great as that of Rome under Augustus half a millennium earlier. It stretched from eastern Europe across the Mediterranean and into Asia, encompassing Araby, the Balkans, the Caucasus, and North Africa. Culturally, Byzantium was distinctly Greek and Christian; its achievements—built on the Roman past and aspiring to Hellenic idealism—were overshadowed by the constant ebb and flow of military exigencies: threats from the Slavs to the north, Goths in the west, Arabs to the south, Persians from the west. The Persians were permanently defeated at Nineveh in 627, but Slavs and Arabs proved more resilient, their attempts to take Constantinople barely repulsed. More troublesome to the aging empire were unending palace intrigue, excruciating doctrinal tempests, and declining populations in once-vital outposts, such as the port at Ephesus.

The decisive challenge to the Byzantines came from the central Asian steppes far to the northeast. The Turks' many tribes originated throughout the enormous central plateau of Asia and the Altaic range near Mongolia. The Seljuq Turks, the tribe that first expanded into the provinces of Persia, Araby, and the Caucasus, derived from a group of Oghuz tribes that were converted to Islam by wandering holy men and dervishes. The Seljuqs were quickly embraced as standard-bearers of the Faith. One of the first Turkish conquerors, Tughrïl Beg, took Baghdad in 1055. He then got the caliph of Baghdad, Islam's ecclesiastical head, to anoint him secular protector, or sultan (the first recorded use of that title). That act of anointing, symbolizing the transfer of power from the soft cosmopolitan theocrats to a warrior caste, was a decisive moment for the Turks and Islam, joining them inseparably for the next eight centuries. The Turks immediately provided Islam with a refreshed militancy and martial skills that helped defend the Faith from the assaults of the Crusades; and the evangelistic quality of Islam combined neatly with the Turks' restless military prowess.

The Seljuq Turks moved north to Armenia and defeated the Byzantines in a momentous battle at Manzikert in 1071. The battle was the first military confrontation between Turks and Christians, and the defeat at Manzikert initiated the decline of the Byzantine Empire; it also heralded the rise of the Turks in Anatolia and the Balkans, replacing Christian rulers, a gradual but violent cultural shift that endured for four hundred years. The Turks easily swept through Asia Minor and into the Balkans, but Constantinople again resisted the conquerors. By the time of the final triumph of the Turks over the Byzantines—the Turkish siege of Constantinople in 1453—the nature of both adversaries had changed markedly.

The Byzantines were in a perpetual state of crisis, buffeted most profoundly by Western Europeans who sought to "reclaim" Orthodox Christian Constantinople for the Roman Catholic faith. Thus, they were often challenged from within Christendom—by would-be conquerors from France, Venice, and Serbia, among others. Many of the challengers took parts of the remaining Byzantine lands and so their revenues. The Crusades, which began just after the defeat at Manzikert, were among these challenges, presenting for the Byzantine emperors a dilemma which they never adequately resolved: they had to support the Western Christian invaders against the encroaching Turks, but they still lost their imperial domains—if not to one, then to the other. The most noteworthy humiliation was the sacking of Constantinople in 1204 by the Fourth Crusade, a bloody and infamous affair that left the Latin invaders in power there for

50 years. Near the end, Byzantium was, in one historian's reckoning, "a shrunken remnant of former greatness, its naval and commercial supremacy lost to Genoese and Venetians, its structure weakened by the same processes at work in the West—feudal service inadequately replaced by a money economy, Black Death, economic disruptions, religious dissent, workers' uprisings, warring peoples." Nearby kingdoms once loyal to the Patriarchate, notably the Serbs and the Bulgars, cabaled with Latin princes against Byzantium. The final insult was a promise of military defense if the Orthodox Church bowed to Rome; Constantine XI, the last Byzantine emperor, acquiesced to this reunification, but the defense was never mounted and Constantinople fell to the Turks six months later.

The Seljuqs also fell on hard times. Mongolian successors to Genghis Khan overran Anatolia and drove the Seljuq tribe toward gradual obscurity. They were replaced, after a series of internecine wars and rivalries, by one of the smallest fiefdoms of the Turks, led by 'Osman, and this 'Osmanli tribe finally gained ascendancy in Anatolia by the early fourteenth century. Decades of rivalry and cooperation with the Byzantines ensued. The 'Osmanli sultans rallied the disparate tribes of Turks by a call to *jihād,* holy war against the infidel, and as the *ghāzī,* the conqueror of infidels, the sultan amassed formidable armies to send against the fractured remains of Byzantine rule. The 'Osmanli Turks, known in the West as Ottomans, quickly captured lands surrounding Constantinople and drove westward into the Balkans. Sultan Murad, grandson of 'Osman, defeated the Serbian-led forces in the battle of Kosovo in 1389, and a few years later he imposed a bloody humiliation on a major Christian coalition at Nicopolis. These victories assured the Ottomans control over southeastern Europe just thirty years after their first incursion onto the continent—an event that startled Europe into a deepening and abiding fear of the Islamic threat.

The Turks whittled away at the remains of the Byzantine dominion, encroaching, through political demands, on Constantinople itself, but the final assault was delayed by internal strife (controlling the many tribes of Anatolia troubled the Ottoman sultans for centuries) and the meteoric, rampaging reign of Tatar prince Tamerlane. Over the first half of the fifteenth century the Ottomans regained control of Anatolia—Tamerlane, like his Mongol cousins before him, was better at warring and pillage than at settled administration—and continued to extend their reach into Europe, defeating the last Crusade of the Hungarian king Sigismond. When the young Mehmet II became sultan in 1451, Constantinople seemed ripe for conquest; this would assure him first place among the many Turkish factions and within Islam (the conquest of Constantinople having been a vision of the Prophet himself), and would dissuade Europeans from mounting yet another offensive to save Byzantium for Christianity. In fact, Constantinople was overripe. After a 54-day siege in the spring of 1453 Mehmet finally breached the great walls surrounding the city, and some 250,000 Ottoman troops overwhelmed 17,000 Greek defenders, ending a thousand-year Christian dominion. Mehmet II marched triumphantly into his new imperial city, henceforth known as Istanbul.

It is said that Mehmet II went on a pilgrimage to Troy before the final conquest of Constantinople. Alexander the Great, after first landing in Anatolia, also went immediately to that epic site, "where the most famous, most foolish, most grievous war of myth or history, the archetype of human bellicosity, had been played out." The Ottomans went to pay homage to the legendary warriors, but their visits to the place of the first East-West battle symbolized not merely their own confrontation with the "other," but those of centuries past and centuries to come. The bridge between East and West was also their battleground.

The reach of the Ottoman Empire was astonishing: larger and richer than the Roman Empire at its height, it was the seat of a rapidly expanding religion and boasted unmatched military technology and tactics, encompassing the superior intellectual achievements of Arab culture. The sultans of Istanbul had every right to believe they occupied the center of the universe. Their dynamic expansion coincided with a period of unprecedented ferment in Europe—the emergence of nation-states, the Renaissance, the Inquisition, the Reformation—which both aided the Ottomans' success in dominating southeastern Europe and produced a series of complex responses to that success. At the same time, the Ottomans' hegemony over the Arab world tied the vitality of Islam to that of the Sublime Porte, the seat of power in Istanbul.

The Ottoman Empire was a mixture of an enlightened despotism, a clever architecture of vassal states that nearly ringed the Mediterranean, an insular trading empire, and the fiercely dedicated defender-cum-proselytizer of Islam. The sultans' despotism was notably prenationalistic. The Ottoman Turks thought of themselves first and last as Muslims; ethnic identity, though occasionally revived during the Ottoman period, was subsumed in devotion to the Prophet Mohammed. And this devotion was not exclusionary. Istanbul, reflecting the Empire as a whole, was an exquisitely multicultural city, with Arabs, Slavs, Greeks, and Italians occupying crucial posts in the government, in commerce, and in the intelligentsia. (This openness is sometimes cited as a source of the Ottoman decline, because it took place after power passed from the Turkish aristocracy to the "slave" classes.) But it was also an empire of conquest; its wealth, administration, alliances, and ethos were dependent on expansion—a vestige of its roots in the marauding tribal culture of Central Asia, in which wealth was acquired by seizing it from the next town on the frontier. The intricate web of fiefdoms, which were the sources of soldiers, loyalty, and tribute, corroded as the limits to empire were reached in the seventeenth century.

At the same time as the empire was losing its momentum, it was faced by challenges from a Europe that was innovating technically and economically while the Ottomans were stagnating in their medieval ways. Western Europe began to dominate global trade, for example, by innovating its industry and its shipbuilding. One of the results of Columbus' voyage to the New World (itself driven partially by fear of Turkish control over the old silk route to India and East Asia) was the flooding of the Old World with silver and gold, disastrously undermining the Sultan's currency. Holding to a rigid system that could not match Europe's dynamic industrial rise, the Ottomans lost their military edge, fell further behind in trade, and altogether were drained of vigor. The imperial court, led by men of daring and vision for the Empire's first three hundred years, became riven by faction and incompetence. The ingenious matrix of administration ossified into a stultifying, corrupt bureaucracy. The dashing *ghāzī* became a horseless infantryman retreating from the infidel. The Ottoman wealth of plunder and land dissipated and was devalued by the trade, manufacture, and colonialism of Europe. It was a slow decline for the Sublime Porte, not complete until the 1920s, but the ongoing decay was visible for two centuries.

That decline slowly became apparent to Europeans, but throughout the period of Seljuq and Ottoman ascendancy—which lasted more than 800 years after the battle at Manzikert—the Turks appeared to them to be a very real menace. It was not just their military skill that prompted this perception, because the West's fear and loathing appeared well before the

Turks demonstrated their prowess in their Balkan campaigns of the fourteenth century. Sermons, folk tales, and fantastic reports of travelers cen-
tering on Islam itself began to appear in the West in the twelfth century. In
these, the Prophet Mohammed was depicted as a sorcerer, promoting sexual licentiousness and blood lust; the individual Muslim was seen as a bar-
barian. One chronicler of that time claimed, "It is safe to speak evil of one
whose malignity exceeds whatever ill can be spoken." The growing horror
at the "satanic" presence of Islam, and most especially of the Muslim occupation of the holy sites of Jerusalem, led the European aristocracies and
clerics to devise and execute a series of campaigns to capture the Holy
Land and vanquish the Turk and the Saracen. These campaigns, the first
military confrontation in the "near east" between the Christian West and
the Muslim East, were the Crusades.

For the Europeans who instigated the Crusades, the objects of their
restless ambition were many: the capture of the Holy Sepulchre, Gethse-
mane, and Bethlehem, to be sure, but also adventure, plunder, conquest,
and sheer antipathy to the "Mohammedan." The Crusades were, in origin,
a holy war not much different from the Islamic concept of *jihād*. In fact,
the concept of divine salvation through fighting the infidel was already set
in the *Chanson de Roland,* the epic poem depicting Charlemagne's ninth-
century campaign against the Arabs in Spain. In November 1095, Pope
Urban II called for a united Christendom to seize Jerusalem and protect
the Faith in the East; those who took up this duty "from devotion only,
not from advantage of honor or gain" would earn eternal salvation. Some
100,000 answered the call, and by the end of that century the Crusaders
did indeed capture Jerusalem; as one historian notes, "on 15 July 1099,
amid scenes of hideous carnage, the soldiers of Christ battered their way
into Jerusalem, where they slaughtered all the Muslims in the city and
burnt all the Jews alive in the main synagogue before, in the Church of the
Holy Sepulchre, clasping their bloodstained hands together in prayer and
thanksgiving."

Several other "crusades" of various princes, priests, and plunderers followed, including the infamous sack of Constantinople in 1205, but none
could unseat the growing power of the Turks. And this repeated failure left
its mark on the European mind. The humiliation of one defeat after another—virtually every military campaign against the Ottomans in the
Balkans was glorified as a "crusade"—left two indelible legacies. The first

was a further demonization of Muslims, often by way of romanticizing the Crusades; the second was a persistent desire to defeat the Turks and dominate Islam.

The depictions of the Turk and the "Saracen," or Arab, were not universally denigrating; at times they were accurate, and often romanticized, as in the paintings of Delacroix or in Rimsky-Korsakov's *Scheherazade*. But more often the European's view of Islam was dark and foreboding. "The West's image of Islam fashioned in the Middle Ages," a French historian notes, "was an attitude that was, for the most part, contemptuous and uncomprehending, and it continued basically unchanged." The Prophet was "the famous imposter Mahomet, author and founder of a heresy," proclaimed an influential seventeenth-century history, the *Bibliothèque orientale*. In another biography of Mohammed of the same period, entitled *The True Nature of Imposture,* his supposedly violent expansion is underscored: "He raised up the Saracen to be the instruments of his wrath, who taking advantage of weakness . . . overran with a terrible devastation all the eastern provinces of the Roman empire." The manifestation of Satan was a recurring theme: one of Sir Walter Scott's Crusader heroes in *The Talisman* told the famed Kurdish warrior Saladin that "[Y]our blinded race had their descent from the foul fiend, without whose aid you would never have been able to maintain this blessed land of Palestine against so many valiant soldiers of God." The French writer Chateaubriand insisted in the early 1800s that the "Crusades were not only about the deliverance of the Holy Sepulchre, but more about knowing which would win on the earth, a cult that was civilization's enemy, systematically favorable to ignorance, to despotism, to slavery, or a cult that had caused to reawaken in modern people the genius of sage antiquity, and had abolished base servitude?"

These typical examples of hostility were born of competition and fear. The competition derived from two concrete challenges. The first was the Arab rule of much of Spain, the long tutelage over Jerusalem, and, most threateningly, the Ottoman domination of the Mediterranean and southeastern Europe, which twice took the Turk to the gates of Vienna. This threat was painfully real. The Ottoman took lives and treasure in endless battles *in Europe*—in Italy, Hungary, Poland, Russia; it for a time choked off the trade routes to Asia; it dominated the Maghreb and much of Africa; and it lasted for centuries. An Elizabethan historian, in commonly expressed alarm, excoriated the Ottomans as "the present terror of the world." The impact on the European mind of the collective memory and folklore of thirty generations can scarcely be overstated. It contributed significantly to European self-identity, and was thereby an ethnically unifying influence.

The second challenge was religion. Islam and Christianity both claimed to be world religions, built upon the same foundations. Islam believed itself to be a successor to Christianity, which it regarded as an incomplete revelation. Each saw the other as an infidel, an impostor, and naturally a mortal threat. No less a figure than Martin Luther charged Islam with being "a movement of violence in the service of the Antichrist; it cannot be converted because it is closed to reason; it can only be resisted by the sword." Later, as Europe came to dominate the Middle East in the 1800s, religious fervor was reawakened, now taking on a conspiracy phobia: Muslim resistance to Europeans was seen as an attack on, or hatred of, civilization, and any expression of pan-Islamism was seen as stemming from satanic influences.

Other cultural factors also came into play during the millennium of the rivalry. Prominent was the Europeans' fear of a culture more advanced than theirs, which Arab civilization certainly was in the centuries before the Renaissance. In philosophy, medicine and science, technology (including the techniques of warfare), and art, the Muslims far outdistanced Western Europe—but much less so Byzantium. As the West gradually caught up and surpassed the Ottomans in these arenas, Christians' fears shifted to the alleged sensuality of the Muslim, at once an inspiration to the romantic (and Romantic) imagination and another pretext for scorn and accusation.

By the nineteenth century, much had changed. The Ottoman Empire was clearly in retreat. Europe, vitalized by the Enlightenment and empowered by industrialism, could be patronizing toward the Muslim, but remained essentially contemptuous. The ease with which Europe colonized much of the former Ottoman and Persian lands had turned its perceptions of threat and superiority around. European imperialism was now the order of the day, as it would be through much of the twentieth century.

Europe had an impact on the Middle East, too, even before the age of Western imperialism. The Ottomans were particularly receptive to European weaponry. Long before the capture of Constantinople, the Turks were using European-made artillery. They also adopted European shipbuilding techniques and navigation, and Muslims bought Western weapons of all kinds, possibly as early as the Crusades. As one scholar observes, "European powers never seem to have had the slightest compunction in selling weapons of war to enemies who were determined to destroy them." The welcomed military technology frequently required European teachers of various kinds to inhabit Istanbul, which to the Turks was a distasteful necessity.

European imperialism was not confined to the gradual consuming of the Ottoman and Persian empires, of course. Russian influence in Central Asia was growing throughout the eighteenth century, and by the middle of the nineteenth century Britain had secured its grip on India. Such ambitions raised the importance of Turkey and Iran in an entirely new way: they were lifelines between London and Delhi, the grounds of competition between imperial Russia and imperial England. The most arcane maneuvers and blunt military campaigns in the "Great Game" took place in Afghanistan and Iran. But the tottering Ottoman sultan also had a role: Britain's need to secure its routes to the East and to control the Black Sea (thereby controlling the Russian navy) led it to a lengthy relationship with the Sublime Porte in which Queen Victoria provided certain guarantees in return for unfettered naval access through the Dardanelles and the Bosporus. But religion again intervened. Supposed "atrocities" of the sultan against Christian minorities created such a stir in England that William Gladstone, upon succeeding Benjamin Disraeli as prime minister in 1880, severed those ties to Istanbul. That event was only another in a dizzying series of shifting alliances and bids for influence in the Middle East, but it would have consequences for the course of history in the region. The sultan, seeking a European ally to counterbalance Russia, turned to Germany, newly united and strong under Bismarck. The Berlin-Istanbul partnership remained sturdy right up to the ignoble demise of both parties in the debacle of World War I.

By 1914, the Ottoman Empire was routinely described as the "sick man of Europe," a weak and ineffective government that nonetheless held on to a sizable domain in the Levant and Arabia, including the provinces of Mecca and Medina along the Red Sea; Mosul, Baghdad, and Basra, to the southeast; and Syria and Palestine to the south. The gradual loss of its European holdings was concluded by the bloody Balkan war of 1912, in which it was ejected from all but Thrace. Bulgaria and Romania had been lost decades before. Russia had virtually surrounded the Empire to the north-east, starting with the taking of the Crimea in 1774. Ottoman suzerainty over North Africa was eroded as well; Algeria was taken by the French in 1830, Egypt a half-century later by the British. The sultan was ready to be toppled, but the issue of precisely how the Ottoman Empire would finally be laid to rest would shape the Middle East for decades to come.

In 1918, at the end of the Great War, Britain and France effectively controlled all the Muslim lands from the Mediterranean east through India. Until the next world war some two decades away, Europe's dominance would be nearly complete; only the Saudis and the successor Turkish state maintained some independence, and they were gradually drawn toward the Western orbit as well. Even the bloodbath of World War II did not bring down the European colonial dominion. The West's encounter with Islam at last seemed to be a decisive and durable military triumph.

3

NIXON'S "NEW DIPLOMACY"

Richard Nixon flew west one fine July morning just six months into his presidency, west across the Pacific where he would spark a new American dynamo that would affect East Asia little but would recast the politics of war and peace in Western Asia more than anything had since World War I.

The occasion on Guam was celebratory, a break–open–the–champagne moment for world history: Neil Armstrong, Buzz Aldrin, and Jim Lovell were returning to earth from the moon, and the president of the United States was there to greet them. The excitement of that July 25, 1969, splashdown in the Pacific Ocean infected even the hardened political warriors of the new Republican administration. Oddly enough, the president made news that day, news having nothing to do with outer space. Buoyed by the astronauts' daring, perhaps, or by his first visit to the Pacific as president, Nixon began to speak to gathered reporters off the record about a new foreign policy. He articulated, in this almost casual manner, a "doctrine" to relieve the United States of its increasingly unpopular role as global cop. Intended as part of Nixon's plan to escape from Vietnam, the new policy actually reshaped other conflicts more powerfully, creating a legacy with greater impact than virtually anything else Nixon did. As a measure of the significance of that remarkable day, the doctrine more attuned to Ares than Apollo outlasted humanity's journey into the heavens.

The Nixon Doctrine was rooted in the topsoil laid down by Henry Kissinger, Nixon's national security advisor and later secretary of state. The war in Vietnam had become a millstone around the neck of the United States. The American public was bitterly divided about fighting for a corrupt South Vietnamese regime, and the toll of American lives and money was staggering. Inheriting this dreadful situation from Lyndon Johnson and his inept blundering, the new administration was forced to cope not only with the morass of Southeast Asia but with the political debris of the war at home. The American public seemed poised to reject the Vietnam disaster itself as well as the longstanding proclivity in Washington to enforce foreign-policy wishes through military intervention. "For two centuries," Kissinger later remarked of that time, "America's participation in the world seemed to oscillate between overinvolvement and withdrawal, between expecting too much of our power and being ashamed of it. . . . I was convinced that the deepest cause of our natural unease was the realization—as yet dimly perceived—that we were becoming like other nations in the need to recognize that our power, while vast, had limits."

For Kissinger and Nixon, the goal was to maintain American power and prestige while finessing a retreat. As long as power and prestige were defined as military values, which was the conventional definition, then the terms of the withdrawal were indeed pivotal. Americans' opposition to the war, which grew dramatically from 1965 on, was not a demand for isolationism so much as a sustained outburst of moral disgust. Shaped by the civil rights movement, the antiwar fervor challenged the very foundation of U.S. foreign policy, particularly reliance on military prowess to enforce the always ill-defined concept of "U.S. interests." So where Kissinger saw a widening gap between isolationism and engagement on the global stage, the dissenters regarded the difference as morality versus an ideology of national security run amok. As historian and activist Howard Zinn wrote in *The Nation* at the time, "It is only by discussing the root questions of means and ends—questions such as violence, revolution, and alternative social systems—that we can understand what it means to say there is 'a moral issue' in Vietnam." The war had broadly stirred a radical reevaluation of American globalism and the nature of the state that spawned it. Against this, something had to be done; even Nixon later acknowledged that his escalation of the war was tempered by the mounting protest. The "something" was fitful and imperfect, leading as it did to additional decades of bloodshed throughout Indochina. But a perception of *something* different from the Kennedy-Johnson war policy was urgently needed to quell the power of the antiwar activists.

The result was the Nixon Doctrine. Kissinger wanted to reorient American foreign policy toward the Europe-Japan-U.S. trilateral axis, while Nixon simply wanted to find some "peace with honor" in Vietnam. The doctrine articulated at Guam fulfilled both impulses.

Kissinger began to formulate the new policy during the summer, and crystallized most of its concepts in a memo to Nixon just one week before the trip to Guam. A parallel study at the National Security Council (NSC), the White House advisory team that Kissinger headed, had also advised a "surrogate strategy" for the Persian Gulf. That became National Security Decision Memorandum 92, read by the president just prior to his Asian sojourn. That same month, Kissinger and his military aide, Alexander Haig, also formulated a plan for a savage attack on North Vietnam, one which envisioned massive bombing and options for tactical nuclear weapons. The veneer of statesmanship coating the doctrine about to be revealed on Guam was hiding a far darker intent. Still, the doctrine had an effect; how closely it conformed to its intent was more difficult to gauge.

At the Top o' the Mar Officers' Club in Agana, Guam, Nixon gave his press briefing. His remarks about a new presidential policy surprised everyone, including Kissinger and chief of staff H. R. Haldemann. His top assistants wanted him to make a formal policy speech some time that summer, not an impromptu set of remarks like this. But Nixon, looking toward a lengthy trip through Asia, exhilarated and exhausted by the day's events, was keen to redirect attention to himself. He chose to speak, for 50 minutes and without notes, about the U.S. position in Asia and his intention to redress the politically vulnerable position of deep military involvement. "Asia is for the Asians," he told the reporters gathered at the naval officers' club. "We should assist, but we should not dictate. . . . We must avoid the kind of policy that will make countries in Asia so dependent upon us that we are dragged into conflicts such as the one we have in Vietnam." In response to a hypothetical question posed by a reporter, Nixon went on: "If any nation desires the assistance of the United States militarily in order to meet an internal or external threat, we will provide it."

His remarks, which the press could report without direct quotation, caused a sensation: a clear change was taking place in the thinking of the American leadership, one finally recognizing the brutal facts on the ground in Vietnam. It was dubbed the Guam Doctrine by the news media; the president took pains to revise it into the Nixon Doctrine.

At the United Nations two months later, Nixon again spoke to the issue. "Now we are maturing together into a new pattern of independence," he told the opening of the General Assembly. "It is against this background that we have been urging other nations to assume a greater share of responsibility for their own security." Instead of direct U.S. intervention, our friends, amply supplied with weapons by the United States, would have to take responsibility for themselves—that was the essence of the policy. It drew from the pain of the Korea and Vietnam experiences, and a lack of confidence in the alliance system created after World War II to contain Soviet imperialism, alliances which—with the singular exception of the North Atlantic Treaty Organization (NATO) in Europe—possessed little coherence or vigor. Mostly, the doctrine was the precursor to "Vietnamization," Nixon's hope for a "peace with honor" that brought neither peace to Vietnam nor honor to America.

While Nixon's press conference reverberated through the political quagmire of Indochina, it did not have much impact on arms sales immediately. But a groundwork was being laid for a more ambitious worldwide program of military assistance. Kissinger's NSC staff was preparing studies of arms transfers to the Middle East, among other related issues. The Defense and State departments were ginned up for expanded weapons aid. A shift from grants of arms to sales of arms was also engineered, which had the added benefit of greatly weakening Congress's funding authority. In 1971 a new mechanism in the Pentagon, the Defense Security Assistance Agency, was created to evaluate and promote arms sales and giveaways. In contrast to the Eisenhower and Kennedy administrations, which had supplied or sold ample amounts of arms to advanced Western democracies, the Nixon team explored the arming of Third World regimes friendly—or potentially friendly—to the United States. Well before the explosive growth in arms trade in the 1970s, the Nixon Doctrine had in effect energized the bureaucracy to set the charges. Since all sales of weapons must be approved by several layers of officials in the State Department and in the Pentagon, the orientation created by appointments and presidential directives is fundamental to the eagerness with which the arms trade is pursued in Washington. The White House in 1969–71 was sending an unambiguous message.

The new policy contained an additional seed of change from past practices that blossomed quickly in the hothouse climate of the 1970s. As Nixon himself put it in a foreign policy report to Congress in February

1971, "We are encouraging countries to participate fully in the creation of plans and the designing of programs. They must define the nature of their own security and determine the path of their own progress." This he called "the new diplomacy." It invited foreign governments to write their own defense prescription and then request the United States to fill it.

The theory and mechanisms of the Nixon Doctrine were in place by 1971; events in Vietnam and the Middle East made it flourish. In Vietnam, Nixon was withdrawing gradually, and this meant a rather sharp reduction in military spending and weapons procurement. In the Middle East, Libya and Iran were agitating for higher oil prices, the beginnings of a rebellion among oil producers that drastically altered the political landscape of the vast Muslim region from Morocco to Pakistan.

When the oil monarchies of the Persian Gulf, with their windfall of profits, wanted to purchase weapons at a startling rate, the Nixon administration was ready and willing to sell. Its doctrine or "new diplomacy" had already passed muster with the opinion elite in New York and Washington: the policy change, after all, apparently fulfilled the popular desire for less direct engagement. So the table was set for an epic economic feast. Oil would pay for it. And the post-Vietnam drawdown would provide the cooks and waiters—the defense workers who otherwise would go begging in the street. Before 1971, the total of the major U.S. arms transfer program, Foreign Military Sales (FMS), stood at less than $2 billion annually; by 1973, it reached $5 billion; and by 1975, it nearly topped $15 billion. The major recipients were Saudi Arabia, Iran, and Israel, whose combined total far outstripped the rest of the world. The FMS program was not the only mechanism of U.S. arms exports, either; there were outright give-aways and commercial sales, among other devices, but FMS was preferred in those days, providing maximum leverage for the Pentagon, less congressional intrusion, and a favorable impact on the trade balance.

While that trade incentive was not uppermost in Nixon's formula, it tempered congressional alarm during the first surge of arms exports. In the Vietnam drawdown, procurement spending dropped from $24 billion in 1969 to $15 billion in 1974. The aerospace companies were hard hit— Grumman, the New York manufacturer of fighter jets, nearly went bankrupt until sales to Iran saved it. But the arms makers were also adroit lobbyists and lavish supporters of Nixon's political campaigns. The Nixon Doctrine, the surplus of petrodollars abroad, and the crying needs and influence of American defense contractors combined neatly. The executive branch began to argue that exports would also help keep the assembly lines open and the costs of U.S. procurement down. But exports scarcely hindered the enormous job losses in the defense industry in the early 1970s: from 4.6 million workers in 1969 to 3.5 million in 1972. The 700 percent increase in exports did not solve the defense-layoff crisis as much as a resurgent Pentagon budget in the mid-1970s did, but that lesson apparently was absorbed by few over the next two decades. In fact, all the arguments for exports that appeared as the Cold War ebbed fifteen years later—jobs, trade balance, "warm" production lines, and aiding allies abroad—were articulated time and again in the mid-1970s.

When public and congressional opposition to the lavish exports began to mount in 1974, the horse had already left the barn. Companies were increasingly dependent on foreign sales. The oil crisis and balance-of-payments deficit were powerful monetary spurs to arms trading. The bureaucracy was at full gallop, not least the military brass, who saw sales as a way of keeping their own per-unit costs down. The Nixon Doctrine, constructed as political cover for the president's desperate search for a way out of Vietnam, was within five years the engine of the defense-industrial complex and a key element of American globalism.

Oddly, the "new diplomacy" didn't much affect the region for which it was designed. Nixon's view, expressed at the Guam briefing, that East Asia was the world's most volatile powder keg but could be dampened by the supply of weaponry to America's friends there, turned out to be wholly mistaken. Peace in Asia was maintained in the ensuing decades by noncoercive diplomacy (notably with China in the 1970s and North Korea in the 1990s), bilateral military alliances (with Japan and South Korea), democratic movements (in the Philippines and elsewhere), and the efforts of nonaligned nations (India especially). The principal conflict of the region, apart from Indochina, was that between Pakistan and India in 1971, which the United States directly tried to manipulate. Even in Southeast Asia, the Nixon Doctrine was a chimera: he fitfully escalated the war in Vietnam and widened it to Cambodia, with immensely shameful results.

But the policy, with a life of its own, had spread its wings and flown to the other end of the vast Asian continent. Nixon's doctrine found its epicenter in Iran, where it caused an earthquake that still reverberates from Pakistan westward to the Mediterranean Sea.

4

THE IRAN PRECEDENT

The earthquake was slow in coming, and it was preceded by thousands of tremors. The Iran that America suddenly awakened to in the 1970s was a country that only gradually took shape in the Western mind, and even then as a plaything of the great powers. This view, so deeply grooved into the history of Iran's tense relationship with Europe and America, was at odds with more than one strong and abiding tradition of that ancient civilization.

The empire of Cyrus, Xerxes, and Darius was the dark counterpart of the Hellenistic ideal that became the self-image of Europe and the new world of the Western Hemisphere. Complex and vibrant, imbued by cosmology—first Zoroastrianism, then Manichaeism—the Iran of Cyrus divided the world into forces of light and darkness. Successive dynasties were occasionally challenged by the dispossessed, and these sturdy cultural forms of good versus evil and class warfare persisted into the Islamic period. The faith of Mohammed spread through Iran like wildfire within decades of the Prophet's revelation, and it readily fed on the brittle remnants of the old order. Like smaller polities around the Arab world, Iran was ripe for radical change. The weakness of the old religion and state made for easy conquest by the newly energized tribes of the Arabian peninsula. The Iranian reign of the Arab Muslims lasted briefly—only for the years 632 to 651—but Islam quickly took root. Iran was ruled by a string of invaders and dynasties—Seljuq Turks, Tamerlane, Mongols, and Safavids among them—but was dominated to a greater or lesser degree by tribal leaders and their armies.

Throughout Iran was Muslim; it became the principal outpost of Shī'ī Islam. The Muslim world fractured soon after Mohammed's death along competing lines of succession. The Sunnī, ruled by caliphs, claimed to be the rightful heirs of the Prophet and extended control through most of Arabia, the Levant, and North Africa. The caliphate, a spoil of conquest accruing to the Ottoman sultans, was established in Istanbul. The so-called Twelver Shī'ī, while rarely challenging Sunnī hegemony, attained primacy in Iran and much of Iraq by the sixteenth century. The differences between the branches of Islam were centered on the succession and some doctrinal matters, including a messianic vision and a belief in the divinity of the imam, the spiritual leader of Shī'īsm. But the differences between the Twelver Shī'ī and Sunnī took on political overtones during decades of wars between the Safavids, the first Shī'ī rulers of Iran, and the Sunnī Ottomans. The promotion of a distinctly Shī'ī Iran by the Safavids served to instill the requisite faith in the righteousness of their cause and the necessity of sacrifice. Twelver Shī'īsm and the national identity of Iran became nearly one and the same.

Temporal power passed into the hands of the Qajar dynasty and remained there through the nineteenth century, the period of keener interest in Iran on the part of the Western powers. The British were determined to protect access to their great colonial prize, India, while the Russians looked upon their southern neighbors with increasing covetousness. The Great Game between the two imperial powers was one of intrigues, interventions, commercial appeals, and diplomatic maneuver. In Iran, the foreign influence was at times the object of popular uprisings against the ruler, the Shah, fomented by the *'ulamā'*, the Shī'ī clergy. Foreign dominance not only was anathema to national pride, but undermined local economic activity, as Iran's crafts, agriculture, and natural resources increasingly served the British, Russians, and other Europeans. Iran was an independent state only in name; it would not dare make any decision on commerce, political reform, or diplomacy without the approval of Russia or Britain. This dual tutelage, and the resentment it fostered, persisted into the twentieth century.

The discovery of oil in Iran in 1908 lent new urgency to the Great Game and naturally multiplied Iran's value to the West. The British Royal

Navy converted from Welsh coal to oil in 1911, a decision made by Winston Churchill based on the Iranian source. ("Mastery itself," he said, "was the prize of the venture.") By then, Russian troops occupied five provinces in the north, and the British, already established in the south, moved into a previously "neutral zone" that was the site of oil production. Rounds of political turmoil, including direct challenges to the Shah, were largely subsumed or manipulated by the foreign occupation. The onset of World War I created more turmoil: the growing influence of the German Kaiser, the Bolshevik revolution in Russia, the defeat of the Ottomans, the toll of the war in Iran itself—all hastened a further weakening of the central government and outright dominance by the British. The war was followed by a dizzying series of machinations by the British to maintain control, driven by the oil wealth of the Persian Gulf and accelerated by the West's determination to keep Bolshevism out of the area. With the help of the British, a strongman emerged who could establish a stable central authority and maintain British interests—Reza Khan, a general who crowned himself Shah and founder of the Pahlavi dynasty in 1925. The new government was less obviously beholden to foreign influence than the Qajar shahs, but British interests were safe all the same.

Challenges to the new despot came from two sources, as they had since the late nineteenth century and would throughout the twentieth: from the Shī'ī 'ulamā' and from social-democratic reformers. The latter were particularly strong in the northwest, in Azerbaijan, where local leadership had been virtually autonomous for many years; their policies emphasized land reform, more equal distribution of wealth, and the like. The 'ulamā' represented the traditional society, which had been wracked by war, foreign commerce, and urbanization. They despised Reza Shah's modernizing ways; together with the democrats, they spoke for the increasingly impoverished peasants and urban working classes. Reza Shah dealt with both groups of dissidents harshly.

His own sense of his authority betrayed him fatally following the outbreak of World War II. Iran would again be a vital resource of war, not least because it provided a route for the Allies to supply the Soviet Union. The Shah's obvious sympathy with the Nazis made him unreliable, and the British and Soviets occupied the country in August 1941 and immediately deposed him, replacing him with his young son. The first Reza Shah died in exile three years later.

Postwar Iran suffered the sorts of turmoil that had repeatedly made central governance difficult. Competing claims for autonomy—there were, in addition to Persian-speaking Aryans, large groups of Turks, Arabs, and Kurds, each divided into many tribes—and demands for reform, both from left and right, buffeted the essentially conservative government that emerged from the war. Owners of agricultural land (the country was mainly agrarian well into the 1960s) were politically dominant; the government was the largest landlord of all, owing to Reza Shah's aggressive expropriation to himself and his supporters. The landlords and oil producers had new backing, moreover, as American interests were for the first time exerted in Iran. The Cold War was starting, and Soviet challenges were seen in every leftist movement. But the reformers were at root nationalists, not communists, and the issue that galvanized them above all others was the control of oil.

The national parliament—the Majlis—became a hotbed of opposition to foreign oil interests, in particular the Anglo-Iranian Oil Company (later called British Petroleum), which had held the main "concession" to produce and sell oil from Iran since 1909. Gaining a foothold in the Majlis in 1950 under the leadership of the populist Mohammed Mossadegh, the reformers opposed a new agreement with Britain signed by the premier, General Ali Rezmara. The long-standing configuration of Iranian politics—a Western-oriented head of state opposed by nationalist reformers and Islamic militants—was careening toward a new crisis. Rezmara was assassinated by Islamic extremists in 1951. The Majlis turned to Mossadegh. As premier, Mossadegh made good on a key tenet of the populist agenda: he nationalized the oil industry, promising the British compensation and a 50/50 sharing of revenue. The British reaction was vitriolic. They demanded a reversal in the World Court; getting no satisfaction, they initiated a worldwide boycott of Iranian oil. Mossadegh appealed to the United States, even visiting Washington to plead his case—and warning that he was a hedge against communism—but he was rebuffed. The United States backed Britain.

The boycott produced a sharp decline in oil exports that crippled Mossadegh's government. Some new reforms were implemented, and the political climate was liberalized; once banished political forces, such as the Marxist-oriented Tudeh party and the staunchly Islamist Ayatollah Kashani, became significant players in Iran's politics. The Western oil boycott took its toll, however, and the fragile economic conditions eroded popular support for Mossadegh. By 1953, the change of governments in the United States and Britain, both shifting to the right, made feasible a long-dormant British plan to oust him.

The plan was British, but the action was American. The removal of Mohammed Mossadegh from office was engineered by the Central Intelligence Agency; it was not a particularly difficult undertaking. Mossadegh's collapse as political leader of Iran had been preordained by the boycott and the havoc it wreaked, and by Iran's political isolation, fostered by Whitehall and Foggy Bottom. The coup d'état was actually a coup de grace. With a relatively small amount of money distributed to key political operatives, massive demonstrations were mounted against Mossadegh after the Shah had fled in the face of antiroyalist riots. The army, control of which had been a prime bone of contention between Mossadegh and the Shah, intervened against the premier. Key political leaders—the Tudeh party and several ayatollahs—deserted him. This array of enemies was too much for Mossadegh to bear, and he submitted. He was tried and narrowly escaped a death sentence; some of his allies were less fortunate. The Shah returned, his power vastly enhanced. He never willingly permitted such a rival to challenge his power again.

For the next 20 years Iran moved fitfully toward "modernization," but the social dynamics of the country changed little: power and wealth were accumulated by a small elite around the royal family. Lower economic classes gained little. Dissent against the mounting repression of the regime was dealt with summarily. Protest came from several quarters, and not least from a leading cleric, the Ayatollah Khomeini, who repeatedly challenged the Westernizing, corrupted ways of the regime; he was jailed several times in the 1960s for condemning the Shah's heresies. Unfailingly loyal to the United States, the Shah desperately wanted to build a formidable, well-equipped army to match the grandeur befitting him as the successor to Cyrus the Great, but each U.S. president was leery of his stated needs for military hardware. The threats to Iran, even those from the neighboring Soviet Union, did not warrant such a massive supply. Both Eisenhower and Kennedy, the most ready of cold warriors, dismissed the Shah's requests for military hardware, for their strategy of containment simply did not warrant them.

Oil again changed the landscape. The Shah's oil minister was among the first to agitate for higher oil prices for the petroleum-rich Middle East producers, and he did so four years before the 1974 crisis. The Shah broke the 20-year collaboration in which revenues were split evenly between the Western oil firms and the exporting countries by insisting on a higher share for Iran *and* annual price increases. The new pact, the Teheran Agreement, opened the floodgates to price hikes and ever-greater shares of the wealth for the cartel called the Organization of Petroleum Exporting Countries, or OPEC. Said one insider of the Shah's gambit: "It was the real turning point for OPEC. After the Teheran Agreement, OPEC got muscles." The ready acceptance of the new arrangement by the United States set the table for the main course—the embargo and the quintupling of oil prices in 1973–74 after the October 1973 war between Israel and its Arab neighbors.

The gargantuan windfall of petrodollars blown Iran's way by the price explosion afforded a new and larger geostrategic role for the Shah. In 1967, Britain announced it would in 1971 withdraw from the policing role in the Gulf that it had maintained for a century; the responsibility for protecting Western interests now fell on the shoulders of the United States. The dependence on OPEC oil of Western Europe, Japan, and the United States was quite severe: nearly 40 percent of their consumption. The Arab states of the Gulf, while friendly to the West (with the notable exception of Iraq), were not reliable. Arab embitterment over the Israelis' six-day romp in the June 1967 war and Israel's occupation of the West Bank, Gaza, and the Sinai placed the United States in opposition to the Arabs on that emotionally charged issue. The Shah, with friendly ties to Israel and scant pretensions of Islamic fealty, was by far the most suitable candidate to be the U.S. anchor of the region.

From Washington's perspective, a newly enhanced role for the Shah also made sense because of the U.S. war in Vietnam. The limits of American power were painfully evident in Southeast Asia. New military commitments, such as an increased deployment in the Persian Gulf, were untenable. The Shah presented a seemingly elegant alternative: supply Iran with state-of-the-art military technology, training, and logistical support in exchange for the oil dollars that were flowing into Iran, and bestow the title of regional gendarme on the Pahlavi regime. The agreement was sealed in a 1972 meeting in Teheran between the Shah, Nixon, and Kissinger, when Nixon said to the Shah, "Protect me." Protect me from the burden of policing the Gulf and protecting Western interests by accepting this offer to be America's military surrogate in Western Asia. The Shah eagerly agreed.

From that moment on, Iran had access to any and all American weapons apart from the nuclear arsenal: Iran was to be the paragon of the Nixon Doctrine. Kissinger issued a directive to the bureaucracy—the departments of State, Defense, and Commerce—that Iran was to be sold anything it sought. Immediately after the price of oil quadrupled, the Shah ordered the equivalent of a large and sophisticated air force: 80 F-14 fighter jets manufactured by Grumman; 100 F-16 fighters just starting to be made by General Dynamics; 108 F-4 fighters made by McDonnell-Douglas. Over the next few years, Iran's orders of U.S. weaponry reached into the tens of billions of dollars. Per-capita spending on arms in Iran increased tenfold from 1970 to 1978, reflecting the economic burden on the average Iranian of the Peacock Throne's status, by 1975, as the largest importer of weaponry in the world.

The unprecedented flow of weapons fulfilled what became known as the "twin pillars" strategy for the Persian Gulf region. As one policy aide describes it, the strategy "relied on Iran and Saudi Arabia to serve as the two key protectors of U.S. interests in the Persian Gulf. Although the policy statement suggested that the two were to be treated equally, it was apparent that Iran was the more important partner. This importance resulted from Iran's geostrategic location adjacent to the Soviet Union, Iraq, Pakistan, and Afghanistan; its physical control of the Strait of Hormuz; its proven oil reserves, daily production and Organization of Petroleum Exporting Countries leadership; its large population; and the stated willingness of the shah to act aggressively on behalf of American interests wherever they might be threatened."

The effect on Iran was not appreciated in Washington. The Shah was known to be a dictator, a stereotypical oriental despot, one of the world's worst violators of human rights. The commonplace view in American policy circles was that "he's a bastard, but he's our bastard." The depth of the discord within Iran was not widely appreciated outside, however, nor was the singular contribution to that unrest made by the arms sales themselves.

The weapons did not arrive in Iran quietly or cleanly. They were accompanied by thousands of U.S. technicians, arms merchants, new embassy personnel, advisers, and assorted camp followers whose public behavior outraged many Iranians. The competition between weapons manufacturers was fierce—this was the biggest arms-sales gold rush in history—and it stirred a flurry of bribes. The regime, those close to the royal family and at the top of the military hierarchy, readily gave into temptation. Stories circulated of this elite's sexual excesses. The gap between rich and poor grew, a gap that was cultural as well as financial. At the same time, the spending on the military drew skilled labor and resources away from domestic needs such as housing, while spurring inflation and even food shortages. American businesses began to take hold of several sectors of the Iranian economy, not just oil and arms, and they brought their own laborers and managers. A cycle of exploitation spun furiously, alienated most of the population, fueling anti-American feeling. "The militarization of Iran," writes one scholar of the Islamic revolution, "deepened the country's dependence on the United States and became a rallying point for the Shah's opponents, who considered so expensive an initiative a plunder of a precious natural resource."

The Shī'ī mullahs were the main pole of opposition to the oil-and-arms phenomenon, the leftist parties being ruthlessly suppressed by the Shah's infamous internal security force, SAVAK. Many leftists joined the Islamic militants as the only way they could oppose the regime. Because they were the one traditional locus of Iranian society that possessed greater moral authority than the state, the Islamists became ever more powerful as the conspicuous Westernization of the elite gained momentum throughout the 1970s.

Washington's ignorance of these impacts was so deep that when Jimmy Carter assumed the presidency in 1977 Iran received very little special attention beyond the routine questions of arms sales, oil, and, less importantly, human rights. The primary focus of the State Department and National Security Council staff was the sale of seven "flying radar" planes, or AWACs, and approval of 160 F-16s. No significant review of U.S. policy toward Iran took place in 1977. Despite the new president's emphasis on curbing the arms trade and promoting human rights, Iran was simply embraced, as it had been in previous administrations, as an anchor of the region. "Recognizing Iran's strategic centrality, we chose to continue that [Nixon-Kissinger] policy, approving major sales of arms to Iran in the course of 1978," recalled Zbigniew Brzezinski, Carter's national security advisor, while "the longer-range strategic and political implications of the Iranian crisis came to be appreciated in Washington only gradually."

The foreign-policy bureaucracy took little note of the mounting opposition to the Shah, even after a noisy demonstration in Washington during his November 1977 visit. Dissidents were seen as nettlesome but insignificant; riots in the holy city of Qom in January 1978, opposing the Shah and supporting Khomeini, went unreported by the U.S. embassy in Teheran. What mattered were the weapons, the price of petroleum (the stabilizing of which was rewarded by less pressure on human rights), and, oddly enough, the sale of nuclear reactors to the oil-sodden country. The Shah had, after all, upheld his end of Nixon's bargain: he had served as a loyal friend in policing the Gulf. He helped quell rebellions in Oman and Pakistan and supported a Kurdish rebellion in Iraq at Kissinger's behest. (He also seized islands belonging to the United Arab Emirates, with no protest from Washington.) Carter saw no reason to upset this relationship, and the American policymakers' willful ignorance extended to the profound opposition building in Iran.

Throughout 1978 the Shah's position became increasingly untenable. Riots and demonstrations, some provoked by police brutality, became frequent. The Shah was both keenly aware of the turmoil and oblivious to its character and magnitude: he saw himself as beset by both "the red and the black," but the black—the *'ulamā'*—were infinitely more formidable than the red, the left opposition. Responding to a pro-Moscow coup in neighboring Afghanistan, he requested a monumentally large influx of U.S. weaponry. He vacillated on political reform. His health was deteriorating. By November, U.S. policymakers began to consider life after the Shah, and to a man they expressed a preference for a military government, perhaps with a disempowered Shah as a figurehead, over any substantive concessions to the Islamic clerics. But the Shah, mortally ill, fled Iran in January 1979. The rickety government he left behind lasted only a few days before the Islamic revolution, led by Khomeini, easily took power.

The jubilation of the masses of Iranians who took to the streets after the Shah departed was a jolt to Western observers. A first-hand account by Jim Atkins, the head of Bell Helicopter, shows the turbulence of the time. Bell had contracted to manufacture 1,000 choppers near Teheran for the Shah's military, which helped Bell's prospects after "the phasing down from Vietnam." Atkins sensed trouble in the fall of 1978 and began to evacuate Bell's American employees (while, he says, the U.S. ambassador "told us to bring in more people"). But 2,000 workers were still there when the Shah left the country; they were moved in a matter of hours from their housing complex to the Hilton hotel, where "revolutionary mobs shot the hotel up, with many Bell people lying on the floor to escape the rain of bullets." Khomeini granted them safe passage to the airport, where they were flown home by special Pan Am crews. Other, similar stories were told of hasty and perilous evacuations by American corporations, befuddled by the seemingly sudden outbreak of Muslim radicalism.

The reading of the religious ferment in Iran was being undertaken in Washington by illiterates. The reasons for the discontent of the *'ulamā'* were, if described at all in policy discussions, laid to the encroachments of the Shah's modernization. In this, policy professionals saw Iran in the widely accepted idiom of the social sciences: "modernization" meant growing economic development, penetration of useful technologies, the maturing of a political system based on law, and the like. It also meant the waning of "superstition," including religion, and the triumph of rationalism; in such a process, the charismatic authority of traditional leaders had been eroded and replaced by the bureaucratic state. This process was viewed approvingly by most Westerners and virtually everyone in power. When the Shah undermined the power of the clergy and severed the traditional ties of the *'ulamā'* to the small merchant class of the bazaar, Western policymakers saw this as an inevitable trend. They also regarded the mullahs' opposition as the cry of a dying caste, and the exhortations of the *'ulamā'* to reject the corruptions of the West as a veneer for their self-interest or simply reactionary. That more modern reformers were also beginning to couch their opposition to the Shah in Islamic terms tended to reinforce this miscalculation.

The self-interest of the clergy and the disingenuous partnership of the leftists with the clergy were real. But they alone could not make a revolution. At work—invisibly to American political and opinion leaders—was a resentment, a wounding, many decades in the making. Foreign dominance of the country's finances, resources, and diplomacy stretched back to the eighteenth century. Now, the wholesale revamping of Iranian society to serve the interests and tastes of an elite modeling itself in every way on European secular (and often decadent) culture and explicitly subservient to Western security interests was a sheer insult to Shī'ism and its uniquely nationalistic character and was intolerable to the Iranian people. It was this set of grievances that animated the revolution and swept the Shah from power and into exile.

The recriminations for the "loss" of Iran were savage in the United States. President Carter's seeming vacillation over support for the Shah was widely blamed. The hand of Moscow was seen in the demise of this pro-Western stalwart. Carter's rhetoric on human rights, the poor performance of the intelligence agencies in predicting the Shah's collapse, the perceived weakness of the U.S. military presence in the Gulf—all of these apparent weaknesses and errors were brought to the court of U.S. public opinion. But none was the real explanation. It was virtually impossible for most Americans to grasp the allure of militant Islam and quite impossible to swallow the Ayatollah Khomeini's depiction of the United States as the Great Satan. The 444-day hostage ordeal that began in November 1979, ten months after the Shah left Iran, reinforced the U.S. view that America itself was a victim of irrational and sinister forces. After all, hundreds of years of European conditioning made it easy for European-Americans to demonize the Muslim clerics.

More dispassionate postmortems led to a different conclusion about Iran. As Gary Sick, a key participant in the policy making of the Carter period, put it, "[T]he decision by President Nixon and Henry Kissinger in 1972 to subordinate U.S. security decision making in the Persian Gulf to the person of the Shah was unprecedented, excessive and ultimately inexplicable." Doubts about the freewheeling arming of Iran in that period were raised by bureaucrats as high as the secretary of defense, but such qualms never affected U.S. policy. The theory was clear: identify a pro-U.S. government in the turbulent Islamic world, destroy his opponents on the left, arm him to the teeth, draw him into the circle of Western interests, and he will do our bidding.

That bidding, moreover, was not a Cold War imperative. In practice, it had everything to do with the protection of U.S. economic prerogatives. The notion that the excesses of American policies in Iran were necessary elements of U.S. containment of the Soviet Union was and is a convenient fiction. Oil was America's primary strategic concern from the early 1900s onward. That the oil trade and the arms trade became deeply intertwined drove all parties to greater depths of desperation when the scheme began to unravel, for the Shah's importance was elevated by the "sensitive" CIA listening outposts, squadrons of high-tech aircraft, and burgeoning nuclear capability with which his special relationship to the United States endowed him.

There was precious little thought given to the potential consequences of such militarization, and even less understanding of how the traditional political and cultural currents of Iran would give shape to those consequences. "Iranians see foreign powers, which recently meant mainly the Americans, as using them for their own purposes: always for Iran's strategic role, with the hope of scoring gains and stopping gains by others," wrote a prominent analyst of the Islamic revolution. It was this dynamic perspective that escaped policymakers in Washington throughout the 1970s, the idea that using a proud Islamic society for its own narrow security goals was unacceptable, indeed, a profound and mortal challenge to the foundations of that society itself. The Iran precedent, however vivid, would be repeated time and again.

5

CONNECTICUT, SIKORSKY, AND THE RISE OF THE MILITARY HELICOPTER

O f all the venues producing the military goods used in Iran and the rest of the Middle East, none were more important than Connecticut. Its reputation as the "arsenal of democracy" was earned at the very beginning of the American republic, and through the decades of American expansion into a global power Connecticut's guns, submarines, and aircraft were at the forefront of America's wars and of American industry's ties to the military. A continuum of brilliant inventors, from Eli Whitney to Igor Sikorsky, assured this unique stature. The state's fortunes ebbed and flowed with the requirements of war, a pattern that remains unchanged to the present day.

During the Revolutionary War, when imports were no longer acceptable or sufficient, master craftsmen began to make muskets, handguns, and cannon in New England. In Connecticut alone some 200 arms companies sprang up to serve the military's needs. These implements of war formed the bedrock of Connecticut's industrial economy, especially in the southwest of the state, from New Haven to Bridgeport and along the Connecticut River north to Hartford.

The most familiar names of American gunnery were Connecticut originals—Colt, Winchester, Remington Arms, Smith & Wesson, and Sharps—and each contributed some dynamic feature to the evolution of lethal force. The most novel was the change wrought by Eli Whitney. Whitney is remembered for the invention of the cotton gin—which he created in ten days but profited little from, while altering the destiny of the

American South—but his more influential legacy was a revolution in manufacturing technique. A descendant of the first John Whitney, ancestor of
the many remarkable members of that family (John Hay Whitney, Harry
Payne Whitney, Cornelius Vanderbilt Whitney, and Jock Whitney among
them), Eli Whitney stumbled into a career as an inventor in 1793, after law
studies at Yale, when he was alerted to the desperate need for a mechanical
way to extract seeds from cotton. Within a year of his invention, the
United States had increased its cotton exports more than twelvefold, and
within eight years by 120 times. His frustrations in the business of cotton
turned him toward the making of firearms, about which he knew virtually
nothing, and in this, too, he excelled quickly. In 1798 he obtained a contract from the federal government for a thousand muskets, which he would
make through a new means of production: instead of each gun being made
by a single craftsman, Whitney insisted that each part of the weapon be
made in a standard, uniform way and then assembled into the whole. Machines largely replaced craftsmen, and production greatly accelerated. This
innovation, which came to be known as the American system of manufacturing, swept quickly through other industries, notably farm machinery,
and was adopted throughout Europe.

This singular achievement, as important as any in American industrial
history, set another precedent: the pivotal value of a military contract in
stimulating innovation. The government could afford to invest in new
technologies, especially large projects, more readily than private capital
could, and while there were less pressing demands for such public investments in civilian enterprise (railway lines, waterways, roads, dams, et
cetera, notwithstanding), the military had an added incentive: it would
purchase the consequent inventions. So Whitney's benefactors were to
play the same role time and again, enabling innovations not only in the
technique of manufacturing (which the Pentagon continues to fund) but
in the products themselves—for example, nuclear power, electronics, information processing, aviation, and genetic engineering. Nearly every
leading technology in the late twentieth century was affected by the military's research and development monies, an effect not every observer
would see as beneficial, but an indelible effect all the same. And this relationship began with Eli Whitney at his Whitneyville armory and village
just outside New Haven, Connecticut.

A few decades later another such relationship would be forged between

Washington and Connecticut, this time in the person of Samuel Colt. A roué of sorts with a flair for self-promotion, Colt began making pistols at a young age and soon set up a company to supply the army's campaign to subdue the Seminoles in Florida. The company failed, but fortunately Colt had also sold firearms to the Texas Rangers. The Texans used the early Colt pistols in a savage encounter with Comanches in 1844, and the triumphant Rangers, led by Captain Sam Walker, extolled the new gun's precision and reliability. Walker was so enamored of the weapon that he encouraged Colt to reenter the business, securing a contract for one thousand pistols. The new sidearm, nicknamed the "Walker," had a scene of the battle with the Comanches engraved on the cylinder. Colt had no factory, so he commissioned Eli Whitney, Jr., to manufacture them at Whitneyville. The success of the Walker enabled Colt to build a vast armory on the Connecticut River in Hartford, and by the outbreak of the Civil War he employed 1,500 men.

Samuel Colt perfected the formula for military contracting success: technical innovation and political guile. He advanced the reliance on machines in production, and was a tireless tinkerer—the Colt pistols and rifles consistently outpaced those of his rivals. But he also understood the value of self-promotion. He made lavishly decorated pistols for Generals Zachary Taylor and Franklin Pierce, both of whom became president, and for Czar Alexander II and other monarchs. (The landmark blue onion-shaped dome atop the Colt armory was reputed to be an appreciative gift from the Ottoman Sultan.) Colt's well-placed presents were not forgotten when the time came to award contracts. He opened a factory in England, becoming the first major U.S. arms exporter, and he sold guns to the Confederacy right after Fort Sumter. The Civil War was a boon for all arms makers—the Hartford factory was humming day and night during those years—but Colt was also insightfully expedient in profiting from the expanding military mission of "controlling" indigenous populations. In America, most notably, that meant amply supplying the Army's cavalry. And the company's most renowned product, the Colt .45 "peacemaker," became known as "the gun that won the West."

The Colt armory nurtured other inventors who would go on to play a role in arms making, among them Francis Pratt and Amos Whitney, whose Pratt & Whitney company would in the next century become the state's largest. Connecticut's armaments industry attracted other legendary inventors: Oliver Winchester, whose New Haven factory made 450,000 Enfield rifles for the two world wars, and Remington Arms of Bridgeport, which produced more ammunition than any factory for World War I. The nation's submarine fleet was also inaugurated at Bridgeport, the USS *Holland* being the invention of John Holland, who later teamed with Simon Lake to create Electric Boat, the eventual builder of the Trident nuclear submarine at Groton.

The common quality of all these Connecticut enterprises, linking the eighteenth century to the twenty-first, is technical mastery—a Yankee ingenuity that could be translated into military utility. Such mastery became the engine of innovation in the twentieth century as the pace of invention and its military applications accelerated with the two world wars. The process of pushing a technique toward greater refinement and usefulness depends not only on the availability of scientific knowledge or materials or corollary inventions; it also hinges on precisely *what uses* are envisioned and how much money can be supplied to the engineering talent required. No invention so symbolized this symbiosis, this joining of talent and opportunity, as did the helicopter. And no place contributed more to this high-tech marvel than Connecticut.

The evolution of the helicopter is closely interwoven with the life of Igor Sikorsky. One of the greatest inventors in the history of aviation, Sikorsky is often described as a man of three careers. The first was as a premier airplane designer in Czarist Russia. Then as an émigré in New York and Connecticut he earned an enthusiastic following as an inventor of "flying boats." In the third phase he took crude notions about helicopters and refined them into a uniquely valuable aircraft. Each career was remarkably ingenious. He stands with the Wright brothers and a handful of others as a titan of the golden age of flight.

Born to an educated family in Kiev in 1889, Sikorsky from an early age displayed the qualities of engineering acumen and fanciful imagination so vital to world-class inventors. His mother, Zinaïda, was a physician and an admirer of Leonardo da Vinci. His fascination with human flight was stirred by da Vinci's famous drawings and by popular writers like Jules Verne. Ivan Sergeyevich Sikorsky, his father, was a successful psychologist. Even in the increasingly liberated atmosphere of late nineteenth-century Russia, such a household was unusual, and unusually nurturing for Igor's ambitions: a family steeped in science and learning and readily able to bankroll his early aviation experiments.

At the age of fourteen he was sent to the Imperial Naval Academy in St. Petersburg, returning to Kiev three years later to enroll in the Polytechnic Institute. Each level of study fed his enthusiasm for flying. In 1908 his father took him to Germany for summer study, and there he found the aviation world gripped by the achievements of Wilbur and Orville Wright, then on a triumphant tour of the Continent. He immediately set out to design a helicopter. In his studies in Kiev—now dedicated to aeronautics—and visits to leading aviators in Paris, he began to fashion rudimentary ideas for vertical flight.

The state of the art was oriented to fixed-wing aircraft, and there was little encouragement in Paris to build helicopters. The technical difficulties were enormous, and no remotely successful experiments had been done. Sikorsky persisted, purchasing a 15-horsepower engine in Paris and returning to Kiev to put his ideas to the test. But his first attempts—ungainly contraptions with sprawling blades and wires—would not lift off the ground. He was convinced that a working helicopter could be designed and constructed eventually, but the nearly total absence of well-fitted hardware of consistent quality was too much to overcome in 1910. He quit the project and committed his energies to airplanes.

His success was nearly instantaneous. Within two years he built six flyable planes, beginning with a biplane that stayed aloft for four minutes. His early inventions earned him a major aviation prize in Moscow and the position of chief aviation engineer at the Russo-Baltic Wagon Company in St. Petersburg. By 1913 he had designed and piloted two enormous, four-engine airplanes with enclosed cockpits and even a luxury cabin. He flew the second of these, the *Il'ya Muromets,* the 700 miles from St. Petersburg to Kiev in August 1914. The unprecedented flight established Sikorsky as a leading figure in world aviation. The Great War began virtually at the moment when *Il'ya Muromets* touched down in Kiev, so his burgeoning career soon became entwined—as all aviation did—with the growing demands of the military.

Imperial Russia was one of the main antagonists of the war, and Czar Nicholas II mobilized all his industry for what was to be a three-year effort. The *Il'ya Muromets* became a bomber, and Sikorsky built 70 like it for the Russian air corps. The aircraft also served reconnaissance missions. These two tasks were aeronautical engineering's contribution in the 1914–18 conflict, and though they did not appreciably affect the outcome it was apparent to all that the future of aviation as an instrument of warfare was assured.

Those crude aircraft may not have influenced the war, but the war profoundly affected aviation. Sikorsky's responsibility—to build as many aircraft as possible—enhanced both the technology of mass production and the engineering of the airplane. The pressure to produce, the resources of the national treasury, the close attention of science and engineering talent, the additional daily hours workers willingly contribute, the opportunity to tinker with so many aircraft, the testing under fire: such factors propel an infant technology far more rapidly than the weak force of the free market. War, or more precisely, the ways modern societies organize for war, has always driven its manifold techniques forward quickly, most dramatically the new inventions that need a little more of everything—money, engineering, experiment—to advance briskly.

In Russia, the progress of the airplane was abruptly ended in 1917 when the monarchy fell and the provisional democratic government of Alexander Kerensky followed suit a few months later. V. I. Lenin came to power in a relatively simple coup in October and immediately withdrew Russia from a war he saw as an acquisitive contest between capitalists in their final death throes. Igor Sikorsky, being bourgeois by birth and having years of associations with czarist enterprises on his record, thought it was time to leave Bolshevik Russia. He moved to Paris and set out to design a new bomber for the French, but the war ended before it went into production. The armistice meant that Sikorsky was out of a job as well, and it was then that he began to see his future in America. Years later, he recalled that "the United States seemed to me the only place which offered a real opportunity in what was then a rather precarious profession. I had been inspired by the work of Edison and Ford, the realization that a man in this country, with ideas of value—and I hoped that mine were—might have a chance to succeed."

The end of the war was no better for aviators in the United States, and Sikorsky, by then one of the recognized giants of world aviation, found himself teaching science to Russian immigrants in New York City. After four years, he put together a small group of like-minded émigrés to start an airplane company on Long Island, New York, using an old chicken farm as a flight-testing area. (Among the investors was Russian composer Sergei Rachmaninoff.) Using scrap metal salvaged from the town dump and similarly acquired parts, Sikorsky built a passenger plane, the S-29-A, which gained some attention—it flew a grand piano to Washington for Mrs. Herbert Hoover—but no sales. The plane was bought by a popular barnstormer and completed its career in the motion picture *Hell's Angels,* in a blazing crash staged by its director, Howard Hughes.

The next project of the Sikorsky Aviation Company made a stronger impression. Boosted by the new popularity of flying stirred up by Charles Lindbergh's transatlantic heroics, Sikorsky built two series of airplanes: those that could touch down on water, the so-called flying boats, and the amphibians, which could also touch down on land. The flying boats were an ingenious answer to the lack of airports, as they could land anywhere in calm water, and they virtually created worldwide air travel. Pan American Airways, with Lindbergh its technical adviser, was Sikorsky's eager client: the S-40, the largest airplane ever built, was launched by Pan Am in 1931 as the *American Clipper.* Others followed throughout the 1930s—record-breaking transoceanic craft—but by the end of the decade the flying boat yielded to land-based airports. The last of the flying boats, the S-44, was also the last fixed-wing aircraft built by Sikorsky. His second career was grinding to a halt.

Some years earlier, United Aircraft and Transport Corporation had purchased Sikorsky's company, an amicable arrangement that reflected Sikorsky's dislike of the business side of aviation. He was the quintessential inventor, an intuitive tinkerer who wanted nothing more than to work in the shop with his Russian émigré pals. He had already declined to head the company that bore his name, preferring instead to be its engineering manager. He moved the operation to southeastern Connecticut in 1929 to build the flying boats. He chose Stratford, a small town adjacent to the booming industrial city of Bridgeport. Stratford's principal physical feature was ideal for his flying boats—its perfectly broad and shallow Housatonic River estuary flowing into Long Island Sound. The partnership of Sikorsky Aircraft and Stratford, Connecticut, became one of the most enduring relationships in aviation.

Stratford is a mirror image of America," says the town historian—a small-town America of industriousness, community spirit, and growing problems. Stratford was settled early in the life of the nation. The English immigrants who created Connecticut as a colony of the Crown went to war with the Pequots in 1637 and decisively subdued the native people in Fairfield County, killing some 700 and taking others as slaves and servants. Stratford was founded two years later, partly by purchase from the Poquonock tribe, and was populated by England-born families who had landed in Massachusetts. By 1750, Connecticut had grown to more than 100,000 inhabitants (fewer than a thousand of them Indians), and Stratford had 3,500, including 120 black slaves.

Bridgeport was a creation of Stratford and was incorporated as a borough in 1810. It quickly became a center of commerce, prominent throughout New England for its whaling port. By the end of the Civil War it had grown to a city of 17,000 and was an economic success story, progressing from whaling and a carriage-making trade to an industrial center. Remington Arms was established in 1866 to make guns and ammunition. The year before, Bridgeport Brass set up shop with $150,000 in capital and became one of the durable employers in New England.

The industrial surge continued unabated for decades. American Gramophone, Basick Company, Bullard Machine Tool, Carpenter Steel, and General Electric, among many others, built factories in Bridgeport. Reflecting the trends of the time, the economy became more concentrated, with the large industrial plants dominating. Still, some 440 businesses employing 42,800 people were at work in the city in 1920. It had benefited, as had all of New England, from production for the Great War. More than 1.2 million rounds of ammunition—production unequaled anywhere in the world—were manufactured at Remington Arms. The General Electric plant was the largest in the United States, employing 7,000 men and women. Submarines were made there too, though that business was eclipsed by the naval arms control that followed the war, and hundreds lost their jobs. Workers were active in demanding better labor conditions throughout the war, and the city saw some seventy strikes by unions seeking an eight-hour day. It was a dynamic, tumultuous city, numbering nearly 150,000 in the early 1920s, and it continued to be a bastion of manufacturing through the ensuing half-century.

Stratford was a quiet little place by comparison; its major industry was a factory that made toilet paper, and when that burned to the ground in 1907 there was little left but a slaughterhouse and oyster fleets. Even that fishing business had moved on to Bridgeport by the time the Great War began. The town had for unknown reasons attracted a number of aviation buffs, however, and it became a center of the infant technology even before Igor Sikorsky landed there in 1929. Gustave Whitehead, a German immigrant, is reputed to have flown an aircraft before the Wright brothers, including a seven-mile flight over Long Island Sound in January 1902. A monoplane was later designed and built by Stanley Beech at his family's farm in Stratford; it was the first aircraft to use a gyroscope. He subsequently located his factory in Bridgeport. The Army flew aircraft operationally for the first time from a base in Stratford, using Curtis and Wright planes for observation missions to protect New York City. In 1929, and with a great amount of publicity, the Huntington Aircraft Corporation came to Stratford, but it collapsed into bankruptcy just two years later.

It was Sikorsky Aircraft that truly succeeded at Stratford, providing its industrial base and becoming a major presence in Bridgeport as well. The Chance Vought division of United Aircraft, Sikorsky's parent company, was temporarily merged with Sikorsky in the 1930s. Because of expanded wartime production the Sikorsky plant was moved to Bridgeport in 1943, where it remained until a new plant was constructed in Stratford, at its present site north of town, in 1954. (Vought was severed from Sikorsky and moved to Texas in 1948.) The company maintains a facility in Bridgeport, and many of its workers lived there over the years. As its business grew, particularly in the accelerated military production of World War II and the 1950s, as subcontractors sprang up to supply the main plants in Stratford and Bridgeport, and as other industries in Bridgeport began to decline in the 1960s, Sikorsky Aircraft became a mainstay of the local economy. It was soon to become the largest helicopter manufacturer in the world, and its impact on the cities and towns between New Haven and Stamford was equal to that stature.

The healthy growth of the company, however, was almost an accident. The end of the era of flying boats in the 1930s was nearly the end of the Sikorsky division of United Aircraft. The corporate headquarters in Hartford was ready to close down the Stratford plant. The clippers, while a public-relations triumph, had in fact not been profitable; their development costs exceeded estimates, and Pan Am was a tough customer. Losses totaled $600,000 on the S-40 alone. The Depression had its woeful effect, too, and by 1938 United had had enough. There was, said a corporate executive, a "limit to the contribution United Aircraft can make to Russian relief." United was a holding company, interested mainly in profits rather than aviation as such, and Sikorsky Aircraft's losses simply could not be sustained.

Eugene Wilson, United's man in Stratford, met with Igor Sikorsky, who certainly realized his untenable position. He proposed to Wilson a new line of aircraft from an old, cherished idea: the helicopter. Somewhat uncharacteristically for United, they went for it. They would provide a small amount of development money if Sikorsky would merge with one of its profitable aircraft divisions, Chance Vought. Sikorsky agreed. He wanted to build the helicopter, and in fact had been working on designs throughout the 1930s. The time was right, and Wilson's offer seemed like just enough to move ahead.

Attempts at vertical flight had advanced only slightly since Sikorsky had abandoned his work on helicopters more than a quarter-century before. The technical challenges were daunting. The early designs for helicopters, reaching back to drawings by Leonardo da Vinci and including attempts by Thomas Edison, had never received a practical demonstration. The problems encountered by Igor Sikorsky in his early experiments in Russia were shared by all who tried in the ensuing decades: configuring the rotor blades, supplying power to lift, and achieving stability in the air. Attempts to build an operable helicopter continued fitfully in Europe and the United States through the 1920s, with some minor advances but no breakthroughs.

The key to the kingdom of vertical flight was forged in the late 1920s by the invention of an odd hybrid called the autogiro, an aircraft that looked like an airplane with rotor blades above the cockpit. The creation of a Spanish aristocrat, Juan de la Cierva, the autogiro enjoyed a brief popularity—it was useful for getting in and out of difficult terrain—but it never quite caught on, in part because of the Depression and in part because it was a highly specialized vehicle requiring perfect wind conditions to operate. It was that limitation which turned away any military interest and doomed its prospects by the early 1930s. But the work on autogiros in the 1920s solved some of the early technical challenges of vertical flight, particularly those having to do with the rotor blades. More important, it stirred new interest in the helicopter itself, an interest pursued most avidly by Louis Breguet in France, Heinrich Focke and Anton Flettner in Germany, and Igor Sikorsky in America.

The aerodynamics of the helicopter appear simple, but matching the machinery to the physics was a decades-long task. The helicopter has one similarity to the airplane: the rotor blades on the helicopter and the wings on the airplane are both shaped to create lift. The cross-section of each roughly resembles a teardrop, with the fat end cutting the air. The wing or rotor blade is shaped to force the air passing over its top to travel further than the air flowing beneath it; because the top side is longer, the airflow above is dispersed more than it is on the short side beneath. As a result, more air pressure is created below, providing lift on the wing or rotor blade. There the similarity with the airplane ends, and the unique problems of vertical flight begin.

The principal obstacle faced by early inventors was "torque": when the horizontal rotor blade is spinning clockwise, the body of the helicopter is spun in the opposite direction. The pioneers of the technology tried to overcome torque in a myriad of ways, but it was Sikorsky who eventually hit upon the ideal solution. The most obvious fix—two rotors spinning in opposite directions—was tried for years and does work. Charles Kaman, a United Technologies engineer who founded his own company in Connecticut in the 1940s, successfully developed twin-rotor helicopters for years. But the single main rotor was generally preferred once the problem of torque was overcome. And overcome it was by Sikorsky's breakthrough, which was to place a small, vertical rotor on the end of a long tail behind and below the main, horizontal rotor. This idea, confirmed after many months of flight testing, and compensating for factors like the windy "downwash" of the main rotor, allowed the tail rotor or rudder to add maneuverability as well—such as turning the aircraft while hovering.

Hovering could be maintained simply by keeping the power steady, just as climbing was achieved by adding power—making the rotor blades turn faster—and descent by cutting power and letting gravity bring the craft down. But movement forwards, backwards, and sideways was more complex. Such movements were accomplished by changing the "cyclic pitch" or angle of each blade to tilt the rotor "disk"—the circle created by the rotating blades—so as to create thrust in the direction one wished to go. Tipping the disk forward in that way would move the chopper forward, with the fuselage also tipping in the same direction.

These basic functions were engineered successfully by Sikorsky by the flight of his VS-300, the experimental model that won over the Army in 1942 and stimulated production for the military through the rest of World War II. An array of technical challenges remained, however, and many were confronted during wartime production. The usefulness of the helicopter would depend on its ability to carry weight or bulk, for example, on its speed and dexterity, its range, and so forth. One of the early problems of the single-rotor copter was its center of gravity, making sure the load did not dangerously tip the craft, a particularly important issue when viewing the machine as a transport vehicle; engineers perpetually refined their craft to deal with it. Another constraint was the chopper's large piston engine and how that engine grew as the size and load of the aircraft were increased. Bell Helicopter's inventor, Arthur Young, said it was "the smaller power requirements of the airplane that were largely responsible for the fact that the airplane succeeded first." The big breakthrough came in the 1950s with the gas-turbine engine. Under development for many years for airplanes, it produced much more power for its weight than the piston engine, and its smaller size left more room in the fuselage for payloads. It was Charles Kaman at the firm bearing his name who first installed the gas-turbine engine in a helicopter, flying his K–225 in 1951. The companies producing the engines—General Electric, Pratt & Whitney, and Lycoming chief among them—became the steady partners of Sikorsky and the other copter makers. Lycoming, occupying Sikorsky's first factory in Stratford when Chance Vought moved to Texas after World War II, produced 17,000 turboshaft engines for the Bell Iroquois, or "Huey," the Army's main utility helicopter until the late 1970s.

Other innovations and uses followed. The size and speed of the helicopter, enabled by its new power plant, helped diversify its missions. New composite materials, lighter and stronger, enabled the choppers to withstand more extreme conditions. This desire of the military for invulnerability—the pressure to "ruggedize" technologies—would occupy R&D teams in many fields throughout the postwar period. Extremes of temperature and other weather conditions, enemy fire and "countermeasures," even nuclear radiation were among the conditions military technology was expected to withstand. In combination with the improving "performance characteristics"—speed, maneuverability, lethality, and the like—these military demands occupied the engineers and set the agenda for the path the technology would take, and continues to take. By the 1960s, most of the major innovations to the helicopter as such had been achieved. Its range of missions was set: transport, reconnaissance, search and rescue, attack, heavy lift. It could fly at altitudes of more than 20,000 feet, achieve speeds of more than 200 miles per hour, hover at 4,000 feet, range hundreds of miles, and maneuver like a hummingbird. Its complexity was such that very few countries outside the United States and Europe attempted to start a helicopter industry. Changes from then on were rather conservative; the military had what it wanted. What followed in the 1970s, '80s, and '90s were mainly variations on the theme, plus the on-board installation of advanced computers, avionics, and communications as those techniques became available.

L ike his flight of the *Il'ya Muromets,* Igor Sikorsky's invention of the VS–300 came at a propitious moment: its first flight occurred two weeks after Nazi Germany overran Poland, and the U.S. Army Air Corps soon showed markedly keener interest in the technology. The government awarded a contract to another company, Platt-LePage, but United Aircraft now saw the growing potential of the helicopter. Sikorsky continued to modify the VS–300, finally in January 1941 earning an army contract worth $50,000 (the unspent portion of the original $300,000 congressional appropriation), leaving a cost "overrun"—paid for by United Aircraft—of $150,000. The gamble was worth it: three months later, the VS–300 set a new world record for hovering—more than 90 minutes. By December 1941 the aircraft reached a point of genuine practicality, and the Army ordered flight tests. In the early spring of 1942 the Sikorsky helicopter flew the 761 miles from Stratford to Dayton, Ohio, achieving air speeds of 75 miles per hour—unheard-of achievements in the history of the helicopter, far surpassing the Platt-LePage prototype. Production on what the army called the XR–4 began soon after, and new, more capable versions followed quickly with the cost-plus army contracts. The British ordered 200 Sikorsky helicopters in January 1943, and by the end of the war the Stratford plant had turned out some 600 helicopters. The VS–300 had in its short life gone through more than eighteen major design modifications.

In World War II, the helicopter was used for search-and-rescue missions in addition to more mundane transportation chores. It was during the Korean War that the craft achieved broader uses, including the celebrated evacuations of wounded soldiers to MASH units that saved thousands of lives. The transition from one war to the next, less than five years apart, was not smooth for Sikorsky Aircraft. Within weeks of the victory over Japan in the Pacific, standing orders for helicopters were canceled, and the company laid off one-third of its workers. But the end of the war did not return Sikorsky and other defense manufacturers to the prewar status of commercial firms trying to find a place in an infant industry and having to cope with a depressed economy. Although many feared that demobilization would present them with precisely that prospect, the entire nature of military procurement had changed—from purely wartime production to a perpetual state of "readiness." Beginning in the late 1940s, a significant share of America's productive strength was devoted to this military readiness, a "permanent war economy."

This signal change in the economy and in the military establishment was embodied by Sikorsky Aircraft and most other aircraft makers. Before the war, Sikorsky Aircraft was nearly a pure commercial enterprise, albeit one whose main product, the flying boat, was quickly going out of fashion. After World War II, and particularly after the Korean War began in 1950, it was drawn into the growing military-industrial complex (as Eisenhower later called it) of Pentagon contractors. With a few notable exceptions, the company worked for the military. Its product, the helicopter, enjoyed brief flurries of commercial interest, as there was plenty of giddy talk about suburbanites commuting to work in helicopters, the postal service delivering mail in helicopters, intercity travel in helicopters, and the like. But the main customers—the *dominant* customers—were the Army, Navy, Air Force, Marine Corps, and Coast Guard.

With only one main client, Sikorsky Aircraft worked hand in glove with the Pentagon to develop its products. Success—profits, employment, stability—was measured in government procurement contracts. Fortunately for the company, for Stratford and Bridgeport, for the thousands of Sikorsky Aircraft workers, the growing enthusiasm for the helicopter in the armed services ensured the firm's prosperity. And, by all accounts, it did little to change Igor Sikorsky himself, who continued to lead and innovate the firm and the industry.

His reputation never wavered; he was always respected as the mild-mannered engineering genius he repeatedly proved to be. Sikorsky's devotion to his Russian friends was tellingly characteristic. Like him, they left Russia after Lenin's revolution took hold. Many of them he had met in naval academy days in St. Petersburg, and after October 1917 a few had borrowed Russian ships and used them as tankers, crossing to New York where Sikorsky took them in. Before computers, tests beds, R&D labs, and simulators, aeronautical engineers worked by trial and error, with "engineering judgment" as the most reliable instrument, and Sikorsky and his Russian émigré colleagues worked as a team in that seat-of-the-pants way. They lived in what was nearly a commune, and carried on with Russian ways. Although he was a peer and colleague of the Wrights, Lindbergh, Doolittle, Hughes, and the other aviation pioneers, Sikorsky personally gravitated to his Russian origins. He spoke Russian to the hundred or so émigrés he brought to Stratford; he founded a Russian Orthodox church in Stratford; he even dabbled in theology. He devised ways to keep his compatriots on the payroll even when the company was nearing bankruptcy. The Russians in the Stratford shop not only set a tone of joviality and élan, they were indispensable contributors to the success of the flying boat and the helicopter.

Sikorsky's strengths as an engineer were the necessary attributes of persistence, discipline, and hard work (in the intensive 1939–43 period of modifying the VS-300, he put in an *average* 16 hours a day), but what set him apart was a remarkable "mysterious faculty," as he called it, of intuitive insight that took him beyond the merely empirical but never veered off into the fantastic. This faculty continued to serve him well after his most creative years. In the early 1950s, for example, it was Sikorsky who first thought of using computers to perform the massive calculations required to advance the complex aerodynamics of the helicopter.

Vertical flight emerged from the Korean War stalemate as a fixture of military hardware. New companies entered the field, and while the Sikorsky company remained a major player, it was not alone at the top. Some emerged partly by simple good fortune. Larry Bell was drawn to the business in 1942 and hired the legendary Arthur Young to design new helicopters. Bell thought the machines so marketable that he produced 500 of them even in the postwar slump. It appeared to be a blunder until the North Koreans crossed the 38th Parallel in June 1950; Bell's warehoused 47-Bs were immediately scooped up by the military, giving him a strong market niche that lasted for more than thirty years. Others—Piasecki, Kaman, and Hughes among them—were prominent in the booming industry. All were military contractors, and their livelihood depended largely on that demand: by 1960, some 7,000 helicopters had been produced, 80 percent of them for the military, of which the army purchased half. Some 24,000 workers were employed in the industry.

Sikorsky Aircraft's evolution followed those contours in the 1950s, although it did manufacture a successful commercial craft (itself derived from the last of the World War II army helicopters) as well. But its bread and butter was, as always, the U.S. military, and when in the early 1960s the army began to embrace the chopper as an essential component of its war-fighting strategy, Sikorsky was ready. Studies were needed for the new requirements of mobility and firepower, so in 1960 a new unit within the design complex was created, a systems-and-operations analysis group. It marked another change from the old way of design, the trial-and-error methods of simple improvement in performance. The Sikorsky helicopters of the Vietnam-war era, when helicopters came of age, contributed a number of technical innovations and a few large transports like the Sea Stallion. The Bell Huey and the Bell Cobra were the most widely used in Southeast Asia, and Sikorsky Aircraft tried to emulate Bell's success by adapting its popular S-61 to an attack mission. It offered several technological advances, but it never won the military's affections and was shelved in 1974 after the crash of a prototype. It was called the Black Hawk.

Igor Sikorsky watched the company's growing military business with mixed feelings. His religious writings lamented the destructiveness of the two world wars, but he was, like many émigrés, devoted to the freedom and prosperity he had achieved in America. His view of Soviet communism was predictably disdainful. When President Eisenhower gave Nikita Khrushchev a replica of the presidential helicopter—a Sikorsky-made S-61—the inventor refused to meet the Russian engineers sent to Stratford to learn about it. In his final years as an aviation pioneer, Sikorsky, who officially retired in 1958, continued to work at the plant daily. There he pursued a civilian project, the flying crane, which became a reality in the early 1960s; more than 100 had been sold by the end of the next decade. His work continued in much the way it always had—he would, for example, rummage through hardware stores for gadgets to use in his designs—but the company's state-of-the-art research and development, largely funded by and devoted to the U.S. armed forces, were in important ways alien to his vision of aviation and his gentlemanly collegiality. After a day at the office in 1972, he died quietly in his sleep.

That same year, development began in Stratford on what would become the world's preeminent helicopter, a second version of the Black Hawk.

6

THE TWO CULTURES OF
WASHINGTON POLITICS

The work on the Sikorsky Black Hawk in those first years was not limited to the engineering rooms or test fields of Stratford. The modern aerospace giants conducted much of their work in the hearing rooms and playing fields of Capitol Hill. Nothing was especially new or startling about this, for the large industrial concerns of America had long found it easy to influence politicians. But when the arms trade began to flourish in the 1970s, the business of lobbying for special favors took on added urgency and new forms. The long-standing and lucrative procurement budget was suddenly jeopardized by the Vietnam drawdown and Nixon's détente with the Soviet Union. And in the great new game of the international arms trade, America's purveyors would need to engage foreign governments as well as their own.

Allied against this juggernaut was a nascent grouping of leftists and liberals who accused the U.S. arms trade of posing a mortal threat to world peace. By the mid-1970s the youthful "public-interest" community was feeling its oats: the antiwar activists had done much to turn the American public against the U.S. policy in Vietnam; the freshly minted environmental movement was growing by leaps and bounds; and the consumer-centered politics of Ralph Nader was already entrenched in the political life of Washington. Many other such movements were gathering steam. And amid those larger movements was a coterie of human-rights activists insisting that the lavish supply of arms to the Shah of Iran was more evidence that U.S. foreign policy was utterly bankrupt. In a predictable action-reaction dynamic, the skyrocketing sales of weapons to dicey dictators was spurring a rising alarm of public abhorrence.

They were, the lobbyists and the activists, two cultures of "internationalism," and they could not have been more different. Both believed in a certain American exceptionalism—that the United States played a special role in world politics—and both believed in the importance of foreign involvement. There the similarity ended. The aerospace companies, by far the most powerful lobbyists in Washington, combined a bottom-line culture with a technical can-do élan; many in its ranks were former military officers and engineers. No moral considerations about where weapons were sold entered into their thinking. "That's why we have a government," they'd say, "it's the State Department that makes those choices, not us." The activists may have agreed that the corporate decision makers were not legally responsible for their exports, but they insisted that moral considerations rather than hoary theories of national security should come into play. One culture based its arguments with lawmakers on the projection of American power, technological superiority, and jobs; the other held the national-security state responsible for the innocent people wantonly oppressed, silenced, imprisoned, and killed by U.S. "allies" empowered by American military aid.

Unlike the nuclear-arms debate, where the opposing sides could at least agree on what they were arguing about (e.g., the nature and level of weapons required for deterrence), the combatants over the arms trade never worked from the same premises. It was, moreover, a contest only in the abstract, for the size and scope of the pro-trade lobby was massive, the largest in Washington, while those opposed to trade were disunited, few in number, and capable of mounting only the occasional challenge to a particular sale. The human-rights organizations, notably Amnesty International and Human Rights Watch, had other fish to fry; for them the arms trade was only a *symptom* of another disease. Only later, after the second Persian Gulf War in 1991, did public interest groups dedicated to stopping the arms trade appear.

The human-rights revolution was nonetheless impressive. Few political phenomena in the twentieth century had such a far-ranging impact. Whereas, human-rights concerns had rarely surfaced in international affairs before the founding of Amnesty International in 1961, by the mid-1970s human rights were becoming a litmus test for U.S. dealings with other countries, and the influence of that outlook grew stronger still in the 1980s and '90s. That there were usually economic penalties for upholding human rights—the loss of trade in particular—makes it all the more remarkable that the movement succeeded. But when it came to arms trading, this Achilles heel of the human rights model—the money involved—consistently hobbled the effort to stem the flow of weapons. And when economics was elevated to the status of a "strategic interest," the voices of constraint could scarcely be heard. That was the landscape of the early confrontations between human rights and arms sales.

The corporate lobby for exports naturally thrived in the atmosphere created by Nixon's "new diplomacy." Although its persuasions were hidden from the public's view, a backlash was visible soon after the surge in exports began. "Sometimes you get the feeling that the whole world is against you," lamented the president of the Electronic Industries Association, a major player, in 1975. A colleague added plaintively, "Our buddies up on Capitol Hill have no concept of the hell we go through to make a sale." Despite these complaints, which became routine over the years, the weaponeers were riding high. "The arms lobby is huge, amorphous, and powerful," said one news report of the time. "Surrounding the White House and the Pentagon are offices of 221 companies producing weapons that have easy access to the White House and high members of the executive branch." Each manufacturer had its own phalanx of lobbyists, of course, and the industry also formed trade associations to exert additional pressure. "There are so many of these associations that a 'Council of Defense and Space Industry Associations' coordinates their activities," another report revealed. Campaign gifts were among their tools, and direct lobbying was a daily exercise. "When discussing defense appropriations," Les Aspin, then a Wisconsin representative, explained, "the talk isn't of the relationship between weapons and world defense, it's of jobs and what a specific project will mean to a congressman's district."

The defense industry did not completely forgo "strategic vision" as an arguing point, however. They instead helped to create and sustain a new class of right-wing intellectuals who did the big thinking for them. "The rise of Nader's Raiders and similar public-interest groups—which achieved remarkable results, considering how badly outgunned they were—brought a change in business thinking about money and public affairs," wrote journalist Gregg Easterbrook in tracing the growth of conservative think tanks. Suddenly in the mid-1970s a veritable deluge of new opinion mills, think tanks, and councils swamped Washington: the Heritage Foundation, the Center for Strategic and International Studies, the Committee on the Present Danger, and other such groups began to appear. Largely devoted to military strength and bitterly critical of détente, this new class was lavishly funded by or connected to defense corporations, among others, who felt that the foreign-policy debate had been dominated by liberals. Among their many contentions was that the United States *had* to confront Soviet expansionism with military power, our own and that of our allies, even those allies who ran authoritarian regimes. "Perhaps the most lasting contribution of the new think tanks," Easterbrook said, "is that they have transformed the terms of public policy debate. In politics, words are map coordinates that show on whose territory a battle is being fought."

The elegant complementarity between the weapons suppliers and the phalangist intelligentsia was burnished by the twin humiliations of Vietnam and the oil embargo. Such hard-to-swallow defeats became the perpetual heartburn of this partnership, and stirred the dire warnings of American weakness now being sounded repeatedly by the right-wing brain trust. Their influence spurred the infamous "Team B" intelligence assessment under President Ford's Director of Central Intelligence, George Bush. This alternative interpretation of Soviet strength and intentions, driven by the most marginal worst-case scenarios, called for the massive buildup of U.S. military power that did in fact begin within three years.

Part of the heartburn of the right wing arose from a certain self-loathing wrought by Indochina and other foreign misadventures. In the late 1960s, Congress began to exert some control over foreign policy in response to the Vietnam debacle, and the rounds of debate were often recriminatory: the military establishment was bashed time and again. Critics like Richard Barnett at the Institute for Policy Studies and Noam Chomsky at MIT unleashed a thundering critique of U.S. foreign policy, and activists on Capitol Hill mounted hearings, issued reports, and handcuffed the president's heretofore unchallenged supremacy in international management. It was an American Reformation, in effect, of the nation's global role. (The right-wing reaction, naturally enough, could accurately be dubbed a Counter-Reformation.) Congress's newfound boldness and its measure of influence were never relinquished. When the alarm over the explosive growth of arms supply to authoritarian dictators sounded in the early 1970s, the Democratic Congress felt compelled to act. Their assertiveness was channeled through two pieces of legislation constraining the arms trade—or, more accurately, providing Congress with a veto over certain sales.

The first was an amendment pushed through in 1974 by Senator Gaylord Nelson, a liberal maverick from Wisconsin. It was followed in 1976 by Hubert Humphrey's last hurrah, the Arms Export Control Act. The legislation, which drew strong criticism from Secretary of State Henry Kissinger, passed amid a torrent of industry lobbying, which managed to delete one of its strongest provisions—an annual ceiling of $9 billion on arms shipments. The lobbyists also attacked the human-rights criteria for sales, which centered on a legislative veto on weapons transfers to regimes engaged in a pattern of "gross violations" of human rights. William Hartung of the World Policy Institute described the lobbying pressure: "The industry argument boiled down to a simple assertion that if U.S. arms makers could no longer sell to Arab regimes that discriminated against American Jews or to Third World dictators who routinely violated the human rights of their citizens, they would be losing out on the fastest-growing segments of the arms market." Most of the veto power and the ceiling were excised from the bill to win President Ford's signature. A lasting provision, the right of Congress to disallow single sales exceeding $14 million, has never been exercised.

The advocates of constraint, a ragtag coalition of church activists, human-rights advocates, and the remnant of the noninterventionist radicals of the antiwar movement, worked hand in glove with congressional aides. They were joined on occasion by ethnic lobbies when a particular country was involved: Greeks arguing for an arms embargo on Turkey (for having invaded Cyprus); liberal Iranian students who chanted "Down with the Shah" in front of the White House; and, later, the Jewish-American groups that tried to defeat arms sales to the likes of Saudi Arabia. None of the ethnic lobbyists represented an authentic opposition to the arms trade as such; they were simply keen to punish their enemies and get more for their own kinsmen's regimes. Over the years, these groups generated more political influence than those specifically aimed at the arms trade, and such power could paralyze any comprehensive attempt to legislate restraint: consider the enormous sums given to Israel and Egypt after Carter's major foreign-policy triumph, the Camp David Accords, which set a very high standard for military assistance, triggered a Mideast arms race, and drained the foreign-aid budget of money for nonmilitary aid. But the opposition did endure, sustained by new anti-intervention and antinuclear fervor in the 1980s. It was unlike the austere, technically oriented professional class of arms controllers; the engine of its concern was in essence a pure moral outrage—which, outside the pulpit and the pew, is difficult to sustain as a political program. Its more practical side fostered local "plowsharing" activism to convert weapons plants from New England to California to commercial manufacture. But its influence was never greater than in the mid-1970s when Congress, also in a state of moral fury, acted to apply some standards to the international arms business.

Into this political milieu stepped a president who in his own person symbolized the duality of the two cultures flourishing in the Washington hothouse: Jimmy Carter. As a candidate and in his early months as president, Carter excoriated the arms trade. "We cannot be both the world's leading champion of peace and the world's leading supplier of the weapons of war," he told an elite audience at the Foreign Policy Association in June 1976. Once in the White House, he ordered a series of probing initiatives with allies and the Soviet Union to find means of constraint. His presidential directive (PD-13) of May 19, 1977, set out a sensible policy. It included, among other items, a ceiling below the 1977 level of U.S.-sponsored arms transfers, a vow not to introduce advanced weapons systems into particular regions, and the elimination of coproduction of weapons by recipient countries. The new policy, the first and last serious effort by an American president to curb the arms trade, earned him the scorn of the industry and its allies in the Washington policy mills. The president's moves toward arms restraint were belittled as idealism—or worse, weakness—a dangerous departure from Kissinger's *Realpolitik*. Human rights could not be the leading edge of American foreign policy, they insisted, in a world so dismissive of such sentimentality.

Carter's well-intended policy was beaten down not only by the bishops of the Counter-Reformation (and, of course, by the burghers), but by the federal bureaucracy itself. Here the legacy of the Nixon Doctrine was exceptionally sturdy. Delay and obfuscation in the arms-trade bureaus of the State Department, the Pentagon, and the Commerce Department created a bog in which the Carter policy could never get traction. The breadth of the bureaucracy's resistance was impressive. The Treasury Department, for example, in a report to Congress mere weeks after PD-13 was issued, wrote of how "production of exports helps maintain a warm mobilization base. . . . [and] makes it possible to avoid the dispersal of skilled and experienced labor teams."

But the president's fitful moves toward restraint were set back time and again by his own actions. A sharp rise in exports occurred almost immediately, with the Foreign Military Sales program climbing more than 30 percent from 1977 to 1978. Early in 1978, scarcely a year into his presidency, he approved the largest sale of U.S. hardware in the decade—200 advanced fighter jets to Saudi Arabia, Egypt, and Israel. Later, he would recommend sending the Airborne Warning and Control System (AWACS), the "flying radar," an exceptionally advanced technology, to Iran and Saudi Arabia. A negotiation with the Soviet Union on control of conventional arms transfers was scuttled by Carter's national security advisor Zbigniew Brzezinski when Moscow insisted on including the topic of U.S. supply of the Persian Gulf monarchies.

What did PD-13 in, finally, was the Middle East and the Islamic revolution. The oil-price shock of 1979, the Soviet occupation of Afghanistan, the abdication of the Shah, and the hostage crisis all electrified the climate of panic that seized the foreign-policy establishment. Virtually nothing of the early initiative remained by 1980, and Carter's successor easily buried the policy for good. Some historians credit Carter with putting human rights on the map of global politics, where even Ronald Reagan occasionally paid homage. And while it is true that Carter's rhetoric early in his presidency did much to raise the stock of human rights as a necessary dimension of international relations (and had tangible effects in Latin America and southern Africa), his vacillation and final abandonment of those principles dealt a harsh blow to the human-rights revolution. George Kennan, the venerable, uncanny seer of world affairs, put it bluntly: "Never since World War II has there been so far-reaching a militarization of thought and discourse in the capital," he said near the end of Carter's term. "An unsuspecting stranger, plunged into its midst, could only conclude that the last hope of peaceful, nonmilitary solutions had been exhausted— that from now only weapons, however used, could count."

It was an embittering moment for the advocates of restraint. Through the decade weapons transfers rose, retreated for a short interlude, and then catapulted to the top layer of readily used instruments of foreign policy. Over the coming years, fewer political fluctuations would disrupt the arms-export business; the future of the trade would mainly be marked only by its grisly results. By the late 1970s, too, the contours of the arms trade were grooved into permanent lines, with its advocates pressing forward successfully on the grounds of jobs and strategic interests, and its opponents digging their trenches in the looser soil of human rights. Carter's high-toned principles were no match for the Nixon Doctrine. And while Nixon's legacy in Iran gripped the Georgian's tenure, and the Iraq debacle still lay years ahead, Carter also set in motion another foreign-policy disaster, no less tragic in its outcome, which soon unfolded on the near perimeter of the Persian Gulf in the old Ottoman lands of Anatolia.

7

THE TURKISH OPTION

The defeat and dismemberment of the Ottoman Empire at the end of the Great War was the defining event shaping the Middle East for the remainder of the twentieth century. The Ottomans, even in their sickly condition, still reached as far the Persian Gulf, the Red Sea, and the Maghreb. In 1916–17 the British and the French drove the Turks from their six-centuries old possessions, aided by Arab uprisings (the famed desert raids organized by T. E. Lawrence) and the decrepitude of the Ottoman suzerainty. Their old lands were divided up among the European allies—Iraq, Kuwait, Palestine, and Jordan to the British, Syria to the French. By the armistice, what was left of one of the great empires of human history was a rump state in Anatolia with small holdings in Europe—Thrace, mainly—which the Sultan was perilously close to dealing away to cling to his disgraced throne. British troops occupied Istanbul, and the British prime minister, Lloyd George, was encouraging Greece to wrest control of the ancient Ionian precincts of western Anatolia, which were still ethnically Greek, away from the crippled Turkish nation.

The prospect of such a complete humiliation of the Turks—the virtual disappearance of a Turkish state—was unacceptable to a small group of patriots who despised the Sultan's backwardness and cowardice and envisioned a new sovereignty for their country. The vision and the action that converted it into a pivotal reality of the Middle East was the work of one remarkable man: Mustafa Kemal, later to be called Atatürk. A young general who was one of the only war heroes of Turkey—it was he who dealt the British (and Winston Churchill) their bitter defeat at Gallipoli in 1914—Kemal was the product of changing political attitudes in Istanbul that arose in the late nineteenth century. Seeing the decay of the Empire and attracted to European rationalism and culture, these few intellectuals, among them some military officers, rejected both the Ottoman and the Islamic past. They drifted toward a new conception of Turkish nationalism that did not rely—as the Turkish polity had for a thousand years—on sultan or caliph, but rather on a new, romantic view of the Turkish people. When the Ottoman Empire came apart at its seams, a tattered fabric of many nationalities ready to separate into fragments, this new vision of Turkishness as the basis of sovereignty came to be the sturdiest cloth of statehood.

Kemal's rise was due to a combination of fecklessness in the Sublime Porte, miscalculation in London, Paris, and Athens, and the extraordinary powers of the gifted Macedonian himself. Born in 1881 in Salonika (now Thessaloniki, then in Ottoman Macedonia), Kemal chose a military career and distinguished himself at an early age. His postings to far-flung corners of the Empire exposed him to its essential corrosion, just as his lengthy stays in Istanbul convinced him of imperial decadence. He harbored no illusions about the sultanate. Among educated Turks there had been for decades a growing disdain for the Ottoman rulers and the culture of the Court: they were centuries behind Europe and nothing less than radical surgery would do. The war provided the inescapable evidence of this; even in defeat the Sultan and his minions displayed a sickening desperation to retain some shred of authority. The victorious allies, huddled in the splendid conference halls of Europe to carve up the Ottoman lands, allowed the Sultan his petty powers and failed to occupy much more than Istanbul. Into this vacuum stepped Kemal, just thirty-eight years old when he was dispatched to central Anatolia as inspector general in April 1919.

Kemal turned history on its head by creating a new nation that stubbornly refused to acknowledge the victory of the allied powers and to accede to the capitulations of the Sultan. Within six months of his arrival in Anatolia, Kemal assembled a national congress, declared independence, established a new capital in Angora (now Ankara), and issued a National Pact setting forth the principles of what would become the Turkish Republic. These actions befuddled the British, who failed to see the connection between their insistence on humiliating their defeated wartime foes and the resentment and resistance such humiliation bred. The Treaty of Sèvres, forced upon the puppet government in Istanbul in 1920, left only a small rump state of the great empire: the Turks would lose virtually all of their European land, cede western Anatolia to Greece, forfeit claims to Armenia, and see a Kurdish state rise east of the Taurus Mountains. At the same time as the European victors were presenting this dead letter for Sultan Mehmet VI's signature, Kemal was obliterating British garrisons within sight of the Royal Navy in the Sea of Marmara. British Prime Minister Lloyd George decided, against the experienced voice of Lord Curzon, among others, to entrust the defense of the treaty's terms to the Greeks, who promptly attacked Kemal's forces and precipitated a brutal war lasting two years. Kemal proved his military mettle once again, defeating the invading forces, burning the Greek city of Smyrna in western Anatolia to the ground, and forcing a population exchange that removed from Turkey most of its once sizable Christian communities. "The catastrophe which Greek restlessness and Allied procrastination, division, and intrigue had long prepared now broke upon Europe," Churchill wrote of Kemal's triumph. "The re-entry of the Turks into Europe, as conquerors untrammelled and untamed, reeking with the blood of helpless Christian populations must, after all that had happened in the war, signalize the worst humiliation of the Allies." Kemal then presented to the British in London his terms, which were improved and codified in the 1923 Treaty of Lausanne: Thrace and part of Armenia to Turkey, no Greek sovereignty in Anatolia, no Kurdish state. The British signed.

Kemal then built his nation. He banished the Sultan and gradually reduced the power of Islam in the political life of the new republic. These actions, by no means easily accepted even within his inner circle, were unambiguous: There is no turning back, he was saying, and no standing still, either. We, this new Turkish nation, will look to the West, toward secular, industrial, progressive Europe for our future. Islam had served Kemal well, providing the fervor that defeated Greece: he was the *ghāzī*, the standard-bearer of Islam and conqueror of infidels. But the *ghāzī* used Islam only to fortify his troops and mobilize the peasant masses of Anatolia; it was a military strategy deftly employed. When the state was safe from further encroachments from without, the *ghāzī* discarded all vestiges of Islam in its precincts. Of the caliphate, he declared that the new Turkey would "cut out this tumor of the Middle Ages." Just six months after proclaiming the

Turkish Republic in October 1923, he did indeed perform the surgery. Other reforms would follow: banning religious sects and schools, forbidding Muslim headdress, Westernizing the calendar and the work week, and changing from Arabic to Latin script. Islam was not outlawed, but rather shunted aside from the center of society—and the political culture—to the private lives of believers, akin to Christianity's place in northern Europe.

In this new climate, the republic grew in Kemal's own image. When he adopted a surname—another bow to Western ways—he chose purposefully: Atatürk, "Father of the Turks." He was the father, the progenitor, of a new state shaped by principles of governance and philosophy at the core of his own life: first, the idea of the Turkish nation itself; second, a military ethos; third, the leading role of the central government in all matters. Turkey remained faithful to these tenets long after Atatürk's death in 1938, through the rest of the twentieth century.

The second of these principles, the pivotal position of the military, was built directly on Atatürk's shoulders. He set the tone for Turkey's political life and social outlook, which were imbued with his own military élan and discipline. (His private life was quite another matter; Kemal, unknown to most Turks, was a heavy drinker and sexually promiscuous.) Secularism was a military virtue, and the gap created by his rejection of Islam was partially filled in the political sphere by the conformist discipline, orderliness, and hierarchy of military life. Threats to the nation were, moreover, constant for the first few years. Among the intrigues Atatürk had to fend off was a sizable, if short-lived, Kurdish revolt by Sheikh Saïd in 1925, crushed mercilessly. The military remained at the core of Kemalism, its fiercest defender.

The central role of the state, the civil corollary to the military's preeminence, was expressed mainly in economic management, usually called "étatism." As Atatürk declared in his 1931 manifesto, "It is one of our main principles to interest the State actively in matters, . . . especially in the economic field, in order to lead the nation and the people to prosperity in as short a time as possible." It was not a collectivist model, like Bolshevism, and private enterprise was not discouraged. But the large industries—energy, transportation, steel, and the like—were deemed too vital to leave to the weak instruments of capitalism. The system of large state industries, despite poor results, remained entrenched in Turkey for more than a half-century.

But it was the idea of *the nation* that was most profound in Atatürk's revolution. The Empire was a classic dynasty based on the triumph of a clan—the family of 'Osman—and guided by religion. The identity of a citizen in the Ottoman Empire, whether in Istanbul, Cairo, or Baghdad, was first and foremost that of a Muslim. Fealty to a territory was shaped by the village or town, not a country or nation. The sense of a Turkish people of distinct character and destiny was largely absent until the closing years of the Empire. When building the republic, Atatürk embraced and nurtured this fresh concept of Turkishness. His state would encompass those people alone; it had no designs on the old provinces of the Empire. (Thus Atatürk could cede to Iraq—and the British—the nearby oil-rich province of Mosul.) He devised a powerful notion of statehood and patriotism that was at once *nationalistic*—extolling the Turkish nation or "race"—while rejecting the imperialistic urge of some intellectuals, who saw a Greater Turkey linking all the nomadic peoples that had spread across Asia and Europe over the previous millennium. This goal of extolling the virtues of nationality collided with ingrained habits: the very term "Turk" was used derisively within the Ottoman Empire to denote an uncultured peasant of Anatolia. Atatürk bullishly changed that perception: "Happy is he who calls himself a Turk," was his famous evocation of patriotism, and the state and political culture he forged over two decades aimed to reinforce that image. It sometimes took absurd forms, such as the claim (supported by Atatürk) that the Turkish people had founded the Chinese, Indian, and Middle Eastern civilizations, including those of the Hittites and Sumerians. The object of these foundation myths was to instill pride in what had been, in fact, a truly remarkable people. In more mundane ways, Atatürk was successful in his steady, unrelenting nation building. The change from Arabic to Latin script, for example, was part of a larger program to revive and enrich the Turkish language and give it a distinctly national form.

He was indeed a revolutionary: the transformation of the most important Islamic society in history assured him that place. In the Islamic world, Atatürk was at first celebrated for his astonishing military victory over the Europeans, turning a crushing defeat into a triumph in the name of the Prophet. Abolishing the caliphate and then turning to Western secularism earned him scorn from the same quarters. But his example was indelible. There would be no leaders like him in the Middle East until Nasser in Egypt in the 1950s, who was careful not to offend the *'ulamā'* but who was secular, étatist, and nationalist at heart. Nasser then became the model for later imitators—Ben Bella, Assad, Qaddafi, Saddam Hussein—but more than three decades before Nasser there was Atatürk. He was the original.

Kemalism was playing on a larger historical stage, and there too it was pioneering. Nationalism was hardly a new phenomenon. Its origins could be traced at least to the Napoleonic era. The growth and the intensity of nationalism are fed by a sense of exceptional worth and by a psychological wounding whose most virulent forms have sprung from the soil of victimhood. This peculiar mixture of *superiority*—the racial posturing, the belief in national destiny—and the *inferiority* stemming from a feeling of weakness, whatever vulnerabilities have led to the deep trauma of the people, makes a potent brew. It can, and does, appear in any sort of society—democratic, authoritarian, quasi-feudal, postindustrial—and may be the defining political feature of world politics since the French Revolution.

Kemal Atatürk's nationalism was in fact a version of fascism. The trauma was straightforward: the loss of a great empire. The loss occurred over many decades, not just in 1914–18, and was thus ingrained in the Turkish psyche. (Like other famous nationalists—Napoleon, Hitler, and Stalin—Kemal was born outside the center of his nation, in his case in Macedonia, and perhaps had the provincial's special desire to embrace the nation's "essence.") Little scapegoating attended this national trauma—no hysteria about fifth-columnists or Jewish bankers—and relatively mild resentment was directed at the Arabs for their desert uprising. (The Armenians escaped less easily, but the defining event in their modern history, their 1915 genocide at the hands of the Turks, took place before Kemal, under the Ottoman sultan.) This absence of virulence, as well as a commitment to rational nation building, kept Kemalism from devolving into the clownish nastiness of Italian fascism, or worse, into the depravity of German Nazism. Still, the new Turkish state was distinctly racialist: the massive population exchange with Greece in 1923, the continuous harassment of Armenians, and the denial of Kurdish identity altogether are characteristics of a vibrantly exclusionary nationalism. Turkishness was raised to the status of a special virtue; in this, Kemalism was primarily *nationalistic* rather than merely *patriotic*. And while he inherited the nationalism of the Young Turks, the modernizers of the late Ottoman period, Atatürk was far more positivist, far more ambitious in creating an entirely new image and foundation of statehood for his nation. So just as his lack of virulence set him apart from Mussolini and Hitler, his forceful insistence on nationalism as the core principle of his leadership set him apart from other authoritarians of the twentieth century.

However, the Turkish Republic bore a troubling likeness to fascism in other ways. Atatürk's exercise of political power was at times quite ruthless, based on military power and ethos. It was, until many years later, a dictatorship that employed terror and propaganda at will. Atatürk himself became a cult figure. The modernizing, centralized power of the state, a quasi-socialism, was upheld from the beginning. These characteristics combined to look very much like fascism. But what additionally set Kemalism apart from the disastrous experiences of Germany and Italy was its lack of territorial ambitions outside the borders set by the Lausanne treaty—Atatürk, indeed, was doggedly nonimperialist—and its gradual softening toward political liberalization and acceptance of democratic governance, however imperfectly employed.

Both attributes—isolationism and a slow gravitation toward democracy—marked the years immediately after the passing of Atatürk. His death in 1938 at age fifty-seven was a shock to the Turkish people, but his legacy was so sturdy that his passing scarcely affected the governance of the republic. He was followed as president by his military comrade, Ismet İnönü, a capable if uninspiring figure who presided over Turkey's avoidance of war duty against the Nazis and grudgingly acquiesced to free elections in 1950.

Turkey's studied neutrality during the Second World War was less the result of sympathy with Germany, its World War I ally, than it was a desire to stay clear of any such entanglements. The war had its impact, however: Germany used the Turkish straits, the waterway to the Black Sea, to attack the Soviet Union. After the war, the Soviets cited this fact in demanding some control over the straits, meaning a military presence in Turkey. This demand, made in August 1946, precipitated a profound crisis in the U.S. State Department and catapulted Turkey into the constellation of American strategic concerns.

The United States was just beginning to realize the scope of the Soviet challenge to Western interests and values the world over. A few key advisers, including George Kennan and Averell Harriman, both experienced in Russian affairs, advocated strong diplomatic pressure on Moscow. But arousing the bureaucracy and Congress to a new sense of urgency just as

American GIs were returning from Europe and Asia was difficult, if not impossible, as long as the threat remained abstract. The Soviets' hegemony over Eastern Europe was not yet a fact, and their meddling in Greece, Iran, and the Far East was worrisome but not alarming. Their demand for such influence over Turkey was another matter. Dean Acheson, then undersecretary of state, in a meeting with President Truman, General Eisenhower, and others in the Oval Office, presented the larger context: "Our report expressed the seriousness of the Russian moves against Turkey and Greece, which aimed at the domination of the Balkans and the eastern Mediterranean. They should be resisted at all costs . . . [and we should] be adamant against any interference with exclusive Turkish defense of the Straits." The Soviets backed off, but the crisis continued with the deterioration of the situation in Greece, whose incompetent royalist government was being pestered by guerrillas supported and harbored by Marshal Tito in Yugoslavia. Six months later, in its long retreat from global policing, Britain announced privately to the United States that it was withdrawing its postwar army from Greece and would no longer be able to support the Athens government financially. Foggy Bottom was astir again, seeing for the first time a vast new American commitment well beyond the Balkans, the Aegean, and the Dardanelles.

The policy that emerged rather quickly from these crises over Greece and Turkey was dubbed the Truman Doctrine, the first articulation of the U.S. strategy of halting Soviet expansionism. Again Acheson made the case: "Soviet pressure on the Straits, on Iran, and on northern Greece," he told the president, could lead to "Soviet penetration" of three continents. "The Soviet Union was playing one of the greatest gambles in history at minimal cost. It did not need to win all the possibilities. Even one or two offered immense gains. We and we alone were in a position to break up the play." The president went before Congress in March to request $250 million in aid for Greece, $150 million in aid for Turkey, and American military advisers for both. "I believe it must be the policy of the United States to support free peoples who are resisting attempted subjugation by armed minorities or by outside pressure," Truman declared. The doctrine of containment was born.

All this new attention to Turkey, which also was fending off territorial claims by Georgia and Armenia of the USSR, elevated it to a new, unknown status: important friend and ally of the Western powers. Soon its own political scene changed when İnönü in 1950 permitted free elections, including new political parties, and was surprised when the party of Atatürk was defeated. The new ten-year government, under the ill-fated Adnan Menderes, was in accord with the military (which in 1960 deposed and executed him) on at least one issue—the desire to pull closer to the West. The opportunity came in 1951, when the United States was attempting to establish a Middle Eastern command as part of its growing global commitment to military containment. Hoping to use Turkey as an entry point and platform for U.S. operations, Washington tried to conceive and form regional security pacts to protect U.S. interests from the eastern Mediterranean to the Indian subcontinent. Turkey (and Greece) saw this as an opening to demand entry into the North Atlantic Treaty Organization (NATO). The young alliance was having difficulty justifying the entry of Italy, much less countries further afield, but Turkey was unbending: they would not cooperate in any Western security schemes unless full NATO membership was granted. The United States, as always the first among equals in NATO, pushed hard, and in 1951 Turkey and Greece were voted full membership. It was a momentous decision for Turkey, not only gaining them new stature (and dreams of entering other European organizations), but providing a crucial flow of arms and training from the United States and Europe.

The events that landed Turkey in NATO were, in retrospect, rather minor and scarcely threatening. The Soviets were clearly testing U.S. and British resolve in their August 1946 note regarding the straits; Moscow immediately retreated when rebuffed, also rescinding its tenuous territorial claims. The Greek guerrilla activity was the doing of Tito, not Stalin. And entry into NATO resulted primarily from Turkey's geostrategic position in the Middle East, not from its front-line status as a bulwark of Europe against the Soviet Union. Certainly the Soviets wanted more influence in the eastern Mediterranean, but the titanic response to its meddling was not warranted by the actual threat. Apart from these minor forays, the Soviets never posed a military threat to Turkey again.

Despite its rather secure position—protected from Soviet mischief, at peace with other neighbors—Turkey's political climate was tempestuous. In 1960, 1971, and 1980 the military seized power, ostensibly to end chaos and bring order to a country incapable of functioning under civilian government. The first of the coups came when a restive officer corps, after several attempts throughout the 1950s, finally overthrew Menderes; several of the key plotters—including Alparslan Türkesh, who later headed the ultranationalist party—simply believed in military government. The requisite social turmoil was supplied by some student demonstrations, and Menderes, running a fiscally loose government, had also been employing questionable tactics to suppress opposition. Menderes was hanged after the coup and his party's leaders were imprisoned.

The military wrote a new constitution expanding political liberties, but it also dispersed political power—a reaction to Menderes' strongman tendencies—and provided a formal policymaking platform for the military via the creation of the National Security Council, which took over defense policy and never relinquished it. The "civilian" leadership was firmly in the same orbit: General Gürsel, the leader of the coup, was elected president, and the two presidents following him were also military officers.

Oddly, and unintentionally, the attempt to avert a civilian dictatorship led to a political pluralism that the military also found intolerable. The left in particular flowered in the 1960s—labor unions and student activism grew quickly—and this led to the formation of some far-left groups which committed acts of political violence in order to dramatize their demands for reform. At the same time, the political parties were unable to keep a steady hand on the government tiller; the dispersal of power intended by the 1961 constitution actually produced weakness and bickering instead. The generals stepped in again in March 1971—a "coup by communiqué" that decried the ineffective civilian leaders as "driving our country into anarchy, fratricidal strife and social and economic unrest." The military kept the constitution intact, insisting mainly that law and order be strengthened to deal with the challenge from the left.

From the military's standpoint, the results of the 1971 coup were unsatisfying. Martial law, more stringent laws on political expression, and an outright assault on the political left scarcely satisfied the hotheads in the officer corps. Political fragmentation persisted. The relatively liberal constitution of 1961 stood. The influence of the military was hardly diminished—and was quite evident in the foolhardy decision to invade Cyprus in 1974—but the parties were diversifying broadly. Civil unrest reappeared and grew throughout the remainder of the decade.

What mattered to Europe and America in these decades of on-again, off-again military juntas in Turkey was not the internal politics, but two festering problems in Turkey's foreign relations. The first was the growing American perception of Turkey as a supplier of opium and heroin, creating a backlash in U.S. aid programs. The second was Turkey's acrid confrontation with Greece over Cyprus, which caused a major rupture in U.S.-Turkish ties and which continues to shape Ankara's perception of American intentions.

The Connecticut-sized island off the southern coast of Turkey had been part of the Ottoman domain until the Sultan ceded control to the British in 1878 to counter Russian designs in the Levant. Cyprus was never part of Greece, but four of every five Cypriots were ethnically Greek, with the remainder mainly Turkish. When Britain gave up its crown colony in 1960—bending to a Greek Cypriot campaign of terror—it created an independent nation under the charismatic leadership of Archbishop Makarios III. A tripartite agreement, the London-Zurich Treaty of Guarantee, set up an ethnically balanced Cypriot government—providing for certain proportions of offices going to each community and forbade both *enosis* (union with Greece) and division into two entities. Both Greece and Turkey, signatories with Britain, were given vague powers to intervene if either *enosis* or partition was attempted.

The arrangement failed to work. Crises erupted in 1964 and 1967 that were dampened only by strong U.S. pressure. Greek nationalism in particular was ferocious, and escalated when the monarchy was overthrown by a junta of Greek colonels in 1967. Attacks on Turkish Cypriots, hate propaganda, and barely concealed maneuvering by the Greek junta kept the island in turmoil. The Turkish government repeatedly vowed to intervene on behalf of its Cypriot cousins. The Greek junta, displeased with Makarios' independent streak, engineered a coup against him in July 1974 that precipitated a Turkish military invasion. After a nasty, if brief, civil war in which 6,000 Cypriots were killed, the island was in effect partitioned. The sole benefit of the grisly episode was the collapse of the Greek military regime.

The reaction in the United States was thunderous—the Greek-American community, while generally ashamed of the junta, was outraged at the Turkish intervention, which was far more bloody than necessary to protect the Turkish Cypriots. President Nixon and Secretary of State Kissinger were blamed both for their unabashed support—including military supply—of the Greek colonels and for failing to avert the crisis. But the

Greek-Americans focused their ire on Ankara and its use of U.S. weapons in the invasion. Congressional critics were mobilized: House Majority Whip John Brademas, a Greek-American from South Bend, Indiana, demanded of Kissinger a U.S. embargo on aid to Turkey, which Kissinger and new president Gerald Ford rejected. Kissinger argued that an embargo was not warranted and that it would hurt negotiations. But through the persistence of Brademas, New York's Representative Benjamin Rosenthal, and Missouri's Senator Thomas Eagleton, all Democrats, Ford and Kissinger were forced to accept an arms embargo that went into effect in early 1975. Turkey retaliated by closing its U.S. intelligence bases—listening posts directed toward the Soviet Union—and hinted that it might leave NATO.

The impact of the crisis within Turkey was profound. Civilian government had been reintroduced only a year before the invasion. Bülent Ecevit, the new prime minister and the most liberal leader in Turkish history, had ordered the invasion, egged on by his coalition partner, Necmettin Erbakan, the head of the National Salvation Party (now the Refah Party), and endorsed by the military. Turks were particularly outraged by the longstanding neglect of the Turkish Cypriots' rights, which they saw as the root of the turmoil on the island; Europe and America, they believed, had sided with the Christians against the Muslims. Turkish leaders gravitated in foreign policy toward closer ties with Islamic states. But the invasion and occupation of one-third of Cyprus, while popular, further isolated Turkey and reinforced the military's self-image as the sentry of civil order.

While the Cyprus issue festered, it gradually faded as the main concern either of the Turks or of their relationship with Washington. The Turkish electoral system was seemingly incapable of producing a strong government to cope with the economic disarray and increasing political unrest. Ecevit vied for power with Süleyman Demirel, the leader of the center-right Justice Party, but neither enjoyed a clear mandate from the voters. Large provinces of the country, particularly the Kurdish southeast, came under martial law in the late 1970s to quell disturbances that made front-page headlines every day. The atmosphere of crisis was growing.

The arms embargo was just one source of turmoil in that climate. In the United States, a new strategic calculus was yielding an enhanced view of Turkey as an important protector of Western interests in NATO's southeastern flank. The embargo had not convinced Turkey to quit Cyprus, and critics of the embargo jumped on that fact to argue for its end. In the spring of 1978, just three years after the embargo was imposed, President Carter asked Congress to lift the sanctions. His special envoy on the Cyprus issue, Clark Clifford, argued before a Senate panel that "NATO is disintegrating" in that area, and that Turkey needed to be "beefed up" by lifting the embargo, which would also, he claimed, "make it easier to settle the Cyprus problem and accelerate the withdrawal of Turkish troops." Senator George McGovern offered a compromise allowing arms sales as long as there was positive movement toward a settlement in Cyprus, claiming, like so many other embargo critics, that the Turks would respond with more earnest negotiating.

The Turkish military was still being supplied by the United States and Europe through its partnership in NATO—the embargo applied only to direct U.S. shipments—but the sanctions hurt their sense of pride. Ecevit kept dropping suggestions of an independent Turkish foreign policy—a thinly veiled threat to leave NATO and draw closer to the dreaded nonaligned countries, which rejected the bipolarity of the Cold War (and which had been led by Archbishop Makarios). The Turks played the Soviet card with unusual finesse, using both their membership in NATO and the promise of reopening their U.S. bases.

Other factors were at work. First was the arms-trade dynamic itself. A State Department official stated it bluntly: "We make the point in dealing with other states that we are a reliable supplier, that the United States will supply follow-on support for the items that we sell. It's okay for people to sit in ivory towers saying, 'Don't do it,' but there are other factors to consider. Money's been spent; you've got a production line going; jobs are at stake." Turkey wanted to modernize its armed forces, and U.S. firms would benefit greatly. The second, unarticulated factor was what Zbigniew Brzezinski called the "crescent of crisis": the instability growing in the arc stretching from Ethiopia to Pakistan. Concerns about the Arab-Israeli confrontation and the health of the Shah's regime in Iran were the quiet subtext of returning Turkey to the fold. After a summer of wrangling in Congress, the embargo was lifted in September 1978.

The return to the *status quo ante* was short-lived. Turkey's prominence among U.S. allies suddenly became brighter when the Shah of Iran quit his throne in January 1979. In the idiom of American interests—containment of Soviet mischief, protection of the oil supply—the Shah's demise was

Turkey's rise: Washington needed another regional power to replace the reliably pro-Western Shah. Although the Camp David accords had drawn the Arab states somewhat closer to the United States, the gendarme role so faithfully executed by the Shah could not devolve as yet to the Saudis or another Arab state. The obvious choice, perhaps the only choice, was Turkey.

The need for these freshened Ankara-Washington ties was reinforced by the Soviet occupation of Afghanistan just one year after the Shah abdicated. However "defensive" the Soviet action was, it clearly justified the activation of Turkey's cherished but as yet unrealized role as a key player in NATO. The Turks adeptly parlayed the instability in Iran—then in the throes of Khomeini's revolution—and the Soviets' Afghan misadventure into a major new commitment from the United States: the Defense and Economic Cooperation Agreement (DECA), signed in March 1980. The United States gained access to 26 military facilities. In return, the accord opened the door to Turkey's acquisition, through either grants, loans, or purchases, of exceptionally capable U.S. military hardware, and $450 million to start buying it. The Turkish military, saddled with 1950s technology and NATO hand-me-downs, had long desired an ambitious modernization. But it had been foiled by the embargo just when the Nixon Doctrine was gathering steam. Now at last the arms pipeline was flowing freely.

Within Turkey, the political situation was deteriorating. Locked in a mortal rivalry, Demirel and Ecevit were unable to cope with rising political violence from the extreme right—the ultranationalist party led by Alparslan Türkesh—and the extreme left. The Kurdish provinces of the southeast were restive, and all were governed under martial law by late 1979. A new, militant organization, the Kurdistan Workers Party (*Partiya Karkari Kurdistan,* or PKK), had formed around a campus leftist, Abdullah Öcalan, and was making threatening noises. The urban Marxist group, Dev Sol, and numbers of other sectarian militants were mobilized. Political killings, bombings, and threats were commonplace; by summer, thirty fatalities a day were attributed to extremists of left and right. A sense of siege pervaded the society. The army chief of staff, General Kenan Evren, warned the political party leaders to end their squabbling and empower the military to deal more forcefully with the terrorism. The economy was suffering from 20 percent unemployment and 130 percent annual inflation; labor strikes were frequent and increasingly strident. Martial law was extended to İzmir (formerly Smyrna) and other Western provinces.

On September 5th, Parliament voted for a resolution of no confidence in Demirel's pro-Western foreign policy. The very next day, Necmettin Erbakan, the fiery leader of the Islamic party and the junior partner in the ruling coalition, led a rally in Konya, a city in central Anatolia with a long Muslim tradition—the home of a famous school for dervishes and a stronghold of Islamic feeling. The rally was boldly pro-Islamic and anti-Western. According to one account of the scene, "The rally was addressed by Erbakan, who called on Turkey to break with Israel and for all Muslims to 'liberate Jerusalem.' But Erbakan went further and proclaimed the start of a struggle to end 'the false Western mentality' that ruled Turkey. Banners in Arabic proclaiming the greatness of Allah and calling for the restoration of the *Shari'a* [Islamic law] were carried by the demonstrators, who ended the rally with the burning of the Israeli, American, and Soviet flags . . . the three 'Satans' which Islam had to confront."

Six days later, the military moved in. Positioning tanks at key intersections, taking control of the news media, rounding up the political leadership of the country for "protective custody," and imposing martial law for the remaining two-thirds of Turkey, General Evren declared yet another military regime. The constitution was suspended, Parliament sent packing. Some 1,700 mayors were ousted. A return to civilian government would come at the earliest possible time, Evren insisted, but first the "anarchy" had to be eliminated.

Naturally, speculation about the American role grew, particularly since the reaction in Washington was uncommonly forgiving. The coup leaders had informed the U.S. military command in Turkey at least 75 minutes before the coup; the suspicion that the generals asked permission of Washington before moving was plausible if wholly deniable. "Officials in Turkish military circles privately suggested recently that the armed forces would not intervene unless they received prior approval from Washington," the *New York Times* reported the day after the coup. Some analysts see a longer pattern of U.S. encouragement to the coup plotters—a persistent attitude of impatience with the civilian leadership, sometimes slow to do its bidding. When the DECA agreement was in the final stages of negotiation in January 1980, the State Department apparently found Demirel's attitude wanting, concluding "that Turkey under her existing government was incapable of playing the regional role that Washington had assigned her." Demirel failed to appreciate the U.S. obsession with Iran, which had just seized the embassy hostages in Teheran, and moreover was beholden to the Islamicist Erbakan for the survival of his ruling coalition. The generals had been planning the coup at least since December 13, 1979, when Evren returned from a NATO meeting in Brussels; in the ensuing months, the generals sought signals from the United States to proceed, and the signing of DECA in late March looked like such a nod to them. The U.S. officials of the period always denied foreknowledge or prompting of the coup, of course. Paul Henze, the former CIA station chief in Ankara who was responsible for Turkey on the White House national security staff during the Carter administration, stated flatly that there was no encouragement or prior approval of the coup. But he also said that "the Carter administration would not have discouraged the takeover if it had been informed in advance, but it preferred not to be. Given the fears that Turkey might go the way of Iran and that the entire Western security position in the Middle East would disintegrate, there was a great sense of relief throughout Washington when the change occurred." Carter signaled his approval by calling for generous increases in military aid in the next two years. Given how traumatic the arms embargo of 1975–78 had been for the Turkish military elite, it is unlikely they would have taken such a drastic step without some assurances from Washington that it would not earn retribution from the "human-rights president."

Certainly, the State Department's reaction to the overthrow of a democratically elected government was mild, and editorials in the *New York Times* and *Washington Post* also welcomed the action in the name of civil order. Invariably described as "bloodless," a "tremor more than an earthquake," the coup was widely praised, as were Evren's restraint and his commitment to a speedy return to democracy.

These tranquil images of the takeover were very much in the eye of the beholder. Thousands of people were arrested—labor leaders, political organizers, university activists, Islamic hardliners, journalists, teachers. When the coup occurred, the conventional wisdom was that it was regrettably necessary to restore order. But Evren's post-coup actions and statements indicated more sharply focused reasons: a determination to destroy Kurdish nationalism and a concern about the increasing stridency of Erbakan's Islamic followers. The timing of the coup just days after the Konya demonstration, the rising anti-U.S. sentiments among the political elite, the fears of Khomeini's influence, and the immediate prosecution of the Kurdish activists all signaled this dual purpose.

"What lies at the basis of the Turkish Republic," Evren said in a speech shortly after seizing power, "is the sublime Atatürk's philosophy that says, 'Happy is he who calls himself a Turk.' This philosophy includes every citizen who considers himself a Turk. . . . The integrity of the land and the nation finds its true expression and meaning in these words. . . . Atatürk's concept of nationalism is basically this. . . . The Turkish nation, based upon the principles of Atatürk, will survive by its unswerving adherence to the motto, 'a single state, a single nation' in the future, just as it has in the past. No power will be able to divide it."

The year 1980 was perhaps the most pivotal of all in U.S.-Turkish relations. The DECA agreement cleared away the underbrush of the Cyprus imbroglio and brought Turkey firmly into the American arms-supply fold. It also cleared the way for the military coup, and indeed DECA was undisturbed by the takeover. America's strategic interests were larger than its concern about democratic rights in a country where such rights had never taken root. The Carter administration embraced the military junta as a reliable ally in its design for the region; the incoming president, Ronald Reagan, would tighten that embrace throughout the coming years even more enthusiastically. The supply of arms had begun, aimed at restraining Iran and the USSR. But the arms, which never were needed for such containment, instead were used without restraint to suppress the perpetually beleaguered Kurds and to bolster the military internally against the Islamists who were threatening Kemalism. The Iran precedent, fresh from its opening act in Teheran, was already being followed in Turkey.

PART TWO

8

REAGAN REARMS

The year 1980 opened on a sour note for America, too, and its leadership would pay the price. Not only were Americans being held hostage in the U.S. embassy in Teheran, imprisoned by the strange new force of Islamic fundamentalism, but the Soviets had just marched into Afghanistan to prevent a similar fate for its puppet government in Kabul. The near-collapse of the détente of the 1970s sent a chill through the electorate, and most politicians responded in kind. America's helplessness to prevent two devastating oil price hikes in 1974 and 1979, the fall of the Shah of Iran, and anger left over from the humiliation in Vietnam had combined to set the stage for a fresh U.S. commitment to military power. The economy was in shambles, with interest rates at all-time highs as a result of the oil-price debacle. Jimmy Carter's desultory support for the Shah, his "surprise" at the Soviet invasion of Afghanistan, and his unwillingness to suffocate price inflation had combined ruthlessly against him. His initiation of an arms buildup—the MX missile, the B-1 bomber, Euromissiles—was too little and too late to satisfy the wolves at the electoral door, and he was soundly defeated at the November polls by that uniquely sunny militarist, Ronald Reagan.

Reagan's premise as candidate and president was straightforward: we were losing a battle with Soviet communism, we were being knocked about by Third World thugs, and only vast superiority in military strength would protect us. The ensuing debate about superiority—the United States, after all, had enormous technological advantages *and* the NATO partners—did not deter a new buildup, known as the "Reagan rearmament," which accelerated Carter's program in its rate of growth and outdistanced the Georgian even more in its rhetoric.

The new administration, which included hawks in every major post—Caspar Weinberger at the Pentagon, Alexander Haig at State, and William Casey at the CIA—revamped the military posture of the United States in four significant, though not unprecedented, ways. First, and most visibly, the president boosted defense spending across the board, with particular emphasis on nuclear capability and the procurement of big systems like aircraft. Second, the Reagan team refurbished and refashioned "counterinsurgency," the Vietnam-era tactics meant to fight terrorists, guerrillas, and other anti-American lowlifes, some of whom were now in power. Third, they took Carter's reins off arms exports. A fourth dimension—ferocious verbal assaults on the Soviet Union and its supposed surrogates in the Third World—also signaled a new attitude at the top.

The expansion was breathtaking. In the first Reagan term, from 1981 to 1985, Pentagon spending rose 40 percent (after adjustments for inflation). A large piece of that was added to the weapons procurement account. Government spending to research, develop, and purchase armaments rose from $42 billion in 1980 to $98 billion in 1985, increasing direct employment by more than one million jobs. Favorite states like Connecticut, Texas, and California eagerly reaped the windfall. In those prime states, the Reagan rearmament meant roughly 10 percent more jobs and an equivalent spurt in economic growth.

The nuclear issues got most of the attention, but the changes in the strategic rivalry with Moscow were wrought mostly by fierce rhetoric—Haig's threat to fire a nuclear "warning shot" in Europe, for example—rather than an actual change in policy. The big nuclear weapons systems were already in train, after all, and only the president's sponsorship of ballistic-missile defense research—"Star Wars"—altered doctrinal calculations. Even that, oddly enough, was a political reaction to the strength of the nuclear-freeze movement. Apart from Electric Boat, the nuclear-arms competition did not engage Connecticut as much as it did laboratory-rich Massachusetts and California.

The more durable change was reorienting the hidebound U.S. military toward a new tactical outlook. While the Cold War front in central Europe remained the pivot point of Army planning, a new emphasis on "low-intensity conflict" was gaining a foothold. The transformation of military thinking began when Reagan became president and a fresh accent on counterinsurgency was thrust on the Pentagon. "Today there seems to be no shortage of adversaries," intoned Secretary of Defense Caspar Weinberger, "who seek to undermine our security by persistently nibbling away at our interests through these shadow wars carried on by guerrillas, assassins, terrorists, and subversives in the hope that they have found a weak point in our defenses." A particular concern—one might even call it an obsession—was the fight against terrorism. The repeated instances of terrorist acts, epitomized by the Ayatollah's hostage taking, raised the specter of terrorism to unprecedented heights and allowed the West to isolate and stigmatize these renegades while unleashing covert and overt forces against them. The tactic of labeling violent insurgents we like *freedom fighters* and violent insurgents we don't like *terrorists* was well learned by regimes around the world and quickly entered the lexicon of global politics.

Mindful of this new threat, America would no longer be outmaneuvered in the "shadow wars." Instead, the Army would have "special forces" trained precisely for the skirmishes, night raids, covert action, and lightning-quick assaults that such low-intensity battle demanded, engagements that were not merely military but also psychological and political. It required innovations in training, even a new kind of soldier, and better weapons: light and mobile, with intimidating firepower, their users linked by high-tech communications.

The new emphasis immediately gained financial support, and the size of the special forces leapt: the troops available for special ops by 1987 totaled 60,000, twenty times their number at the previous peak in Vietnam. Spending on technology also kept pace. The Grenada operation in 1983 whetted the appetite of the new doctrine's enthusiasts for such confrontations with Third-World Marxists. The apparent popularity of the invasion of the Martha's Vineyard–sized island also accelerated the conceptual reform of army thinking. As a massive internal study in 1985 underscored, the emerging doctrine of low-intensity warfare required, above all, quickness and deadliness. And helicopters were tailor-made for the new fashion.

A parallel policy emerged in the early Reagan years that probably exerted the greatest impact worldwide of any military venture of the 1980s. Known as "the Reagan Doctrine" (a term coined by *Washington*

Post columnist Charles Krauthammer), the initiative sought to reverse the communist revolutions of the 1960s and '70s by supporting insurgencies *against* the Marxist regimes of Africa, Central America, and Asia. "We must not break faith with those who are risking their lives," Reagan declared in his 1985 State of the Union address, "on every continent from Afghanistan to Nicaragua, to defy Soviet-supported aggression and secure rights which have been ours from birth."

This policy differed from the Army's new infatuation with low-intensity warfare because U.S. troops would not be much involved. The Reagan Doctrine, like the Nixon Doctrine, envisioned other people doing the fighting with the support, advice, and sometimes the direction of the U.S. government. But where the Nixon Doctrine supplied shiploads of weaponry to defend friendly regimes, the Reagan Doctrine armed and guided (and often created) anti-Communist guerrillas to overthrow unfriendly regimes. The venues of the Reagan Doctrine were many: Nicaragua, Angola, Mozambique, and, most important of all, Afghanistan. There, in the chaotic trap Brezhnev had walked the Soviet Union into, the United States amply supplied the Islamic fighters, the *mujāhedīn,* with millions of Kalashnikov automatic rifles, Stinger antiaircraft missiles, and other technologies. It would be hailed as the great success of the Reagan Doctrine, a wrenching and costly catastrophe for the Soviets that embarrassed them at precisely the moment when their economic system was corroding toward collapse.

The introduction of the Kalashnikovs into Pakistan and Afghanistan was also in keeping with the Reagan team's aggressive export of weaponry. The new administration would worry less about the supposed evils of arming our friends. It would use this "essential element of our global policy" to avoid the "awkward result of undercutting the capabilities of strategically located nations in whose ability to defend themselves we had the most immediate and urgent self-interest." This reversal of Carter's policy included every one of his major points of restraint—all of which had been imperfectly applied, to be sure. Arms sales jumped accordingly: government-funded exports doubled during Reagan's first term. More foreign aid was directed to military ends. Instruments were fashioned to accelerate sales. And overall, both subsidized arms trade and commercial arms trade did increase—tripling, according to official figures, between 1979 and 1987.

The ostensible goal was the rollback of Soviet communism, but the

Reaganites had other game in mind, too. The chief humiliations America had recently suffered were in the Persian Gulf. Military might was thereby transferred with special urgency to the Gulf states, with Saudi Arabia by far the leading importer of weapons in the 1980s, outpacing even the warring Iran and Iraq. Turkey, Egypt, Jordan, and Israel were also high on the list, reflecting the intense attention the Reagan White House was now giving to Islamic militancy.

The sum of Reagan's policy was on display in its attitude toward Turkey. Within 16 months of assuming office, the president sent his secretary of defense and his secretary of state to Ankara to embrace the military dictatorship. Weinberger, meeting with the coup leaders in December 1981, declared that the United States would "be of as much assistance as we can with both military and economic aid." Alleged human-rights violations were brushed aside: "The admiration I expressed," Weinberger told reporters in a joint appearance with General Evren, "was for the ability of the Turkish government to do so much to eliminate what was virtually a state of anarchy and . . . terrorism." The day that Weinberger arrived, Bülent Ecevit was imprisoned for questioning the dissolution of political parties. The following spring, Haig's "personal friendship" with General Evren, with whom he conducted "warm and cordial" talks, was hailed throughout the Turkish press as another sign of America's unblinking support for the junta. Haig "repeatedly defended the military crackdown," went one news report. Later that summer, Haig's department vigorously objected to a European Commission criticism of Turkey's use of torture, saying that the junta "is the first Turkish government to move vigorously against this problem." Large amounts of aid were soon in the pipeline.

The Reagan rearmament was not just the procurement and export of massive and additional quantities of military hardware, with all the expectations for workers and communities—and recipient regimes—which that would inevitably stir up. Beyond that, it was the spirit of the endeavor: security would be gained not by the weak and appeasing gestures of diplomacy, but through military superiority, technological dazzlement, belligerent speech, covert intimidation. Rights were meaningless without freedom. Marxian terrorists should be defeated by any means available. Muslim radicals would be rooted out and destroyed. The preeminence of such a philosophy, popularly endorsed by the American people and seconded by European governments, conveyed to all the unmistakable message that the challenges to Western "interests" should and could be defeated by the ruthless application of military power. The United States of America, moreover, would be the first in line to supply it.

9

A LOVE AFFAIR WITH THE
BLACK HAWK

Advocates of the Reagan rearmament demanded one capability above all, one they believed was not conspicuous in the U.S. military: a lethal quick strike. That meant more high-tech machines, and among the premier technologies available was the helicopter. The paladins of ferocious tactical warfare during the Reagan years would transform the helicopter as much as the Vietnam war had; to those strategists, of course, the United States *was* at war again, and it desperately needed the tools to win.

War always accelerates the evolution of military technology, and the helicopter was no exception. For the visionaries of vertical flight, however, it was a painfully slow evolution. Back in the mid-1950s, when the battle lines of the U.S.-Soviet rivalry were cementing into place, the helicopter's role looked rather small. The Air Force was the big new force, uniquely able to deliver nuclear bombs, and the Navy was growing as well: with America's new global reach and superpower status, the "force projection" offered by Navy and Air Force were unmatchable. The Army was shaped by its duty to wage a ground war in Central Europe, and that meant tanks above all, tanks to counter the Soviets' ample inventory of armor and men. In those days the helicopter was stuck in a stage of arrested development, having not progressed much from its Korean War role as scout and rescuer.

However, the underappreciated chopper was gaining some fresh attention inside the military from a small group at the Army Aviation School in Alabama. Led by Colonel Jay Vanderpool, this first "Sky Cav" platoon in

1956 mounted weapons designed for other uses in the side hatch, creating for the first time an attack helicopter. This showed not only that the chopper could be a platform of considerable firepower, but that troops ferried by helicopters could be protected from the air as well.

The fireworks displays of "Vanderpool's Fools" did not quickly alter Army thinking—most of the brass thought them too fragile—even though copters had some strong advocates, including Generals Matthew Ridgway and Maxwell Taylor. Instead it was the French who demonstrated how flexible and durable helicopters could be in battle—first in Vietnam, then in Algeria (France's two colonial wars, both lost in the 1950s). Using Sikorsky S-55s with machine guns, rocket pods, and wire-guided missiles, the French showed decisively in Algeria how a helicopter could outperform fixed-wing aircraft or tanks in certain situations—in mountainous areas in particular, fighting an adversary without aircraft and organized in small bands.

By the early 1960s, the U.S. Army was becoming convinced. Believers in the helicopter had a strong ally in the Oval Office: President John F. Kennedy was emphasizing new techniques of warfare, hoping to engage communist insurgencies and do battle with Soviet surrogates "below the nuclear threshold," in the parlance of the day. A review board created by Defense Secretary Robert McNamara concluded that the Army needed more battlefield mobility. The new doctrine called for transport helicopters and attack helicopters to work in tandem, and for five brigades of air-assault helicopters (transport for five divisions) and three of air cavalry or attack helicopters. Perhaps not so coincidentally, these new ideas for mobility in combat would be tested very soon, in that "nursery of the combat helicopter"—Vietnam. In fact, the first U.S. air-assault mission using helicopters took place two days before Christmas 1961, just west of Saigon.

The star of Vietnam was the workhorse of the jungle, the Bell Huey. From humble beginnings at its manufacturing facility in Fort Worth, Texas, the Huey evolved from a four-passenger utility craft into a highly flexible and trustworthy fighting machine. Eventually, in its various incarnations, it could carry 16 soldiers and eight tons of payload, fly 300 miles per hour, and perform combat missions. The Huey Cobra, introduced in 1967, was the first dedicated attack helicopter. Some 12,000 Hueys were produced in Fort Worth, the largest number of helicopters ever made, and in Vietnam about 2,000 of the machines were engaged on any given day.

Other choppers were strong players in Southeast Asia, including the pis-

ton-engine Sikorsky S-58, used reliably by the Marines as an assault helicopter, and the "Jolly Green Giant," the Sikorsky HH-53, which rescued
hundreds of downed pilots for the Air Force. The Sikorsky craft were popular, widely used machines, but they were deployed in much smaller numbers than the ubiquitous Huey.

The unprecedented breadth and depth of helicopter use in Vietnam cut
two ways: it proved helicopters to be a remarkable technology, far beyond
the expectations of only a few years before, but the type of warfare it supported fared poorly in Southeast Asia. In the end, the missions accomplished overcame the doubts planted by the failed policy. The U.S.
experiment with counterinsurgency, however dismal the outcome, was
now clearly on the map of Army strategy, requiring different equipment
from the central European standoff, equipment that would include helicopters. At the same time, the Air Force withdrew its long-standing opposition to a larger helicopter force for the Army in exchange for a reduction
in the Army's fixed-wing fleet. So Vietnam was not only the "helicopter
war," it was the opening of an enduring helicopter era for the Army.

Just as the American military was quitting Vietnam, another new mission
was being created for attack helicopters. In the logic of the armed services, the greater the number of plausible missions found for each technology, the more of the budget pie that technology would earn. Advocates of
vertical flight were urged "to find new ways that aviation can contribute to
the Army's mission," in the words of one general. Choppers were still not
totally accepted in the grunt culture of the Army: one story tells of a division commander who would not allow his aviation chief to report to him in
his flying togs, making him change first into standard battle dress. But the
new mission was sure to win converts to the helicopter, returning as it did
to the central purpose of the U.S. Army in the "twilight struggle" with Soviet communism: the anticipated battle of armored divisions along the Iron
Curtain in Central Europe. The helicopter could become a tank killer, utilizing a new armor-piercing missile, the Hellfire, made by Rockwell International. In tests conducted at bases in West Germany in 1972, such lethally
equipped helicopters destroyed 12 to 17 tanks for every chopper gunned
down in return, a ratio highly acceptable to the Army. In that same year, the
Army declined the attack choppers proposed by Bell (a "King Cobra") and
Sikorsky (a prototype called the Black Hawk) to adopt an advanced design

stressing antitank lethality. They chose the Apache, now made by McDonnell-Douglas in Mesa, Arizona, a helicopter that has remained in service ever since. The Apache, with its tremendous firepower, seemed ideally suited to the high-density battles envisioned in Central Europe.

Military doctrine embraced the technology: in the 1976 Field Manual 100-5, *Operations,* the warfighting "Bible" of the army, the tank killers were clearly the darlings of the armed forces. And when a new Field Manual was issued in 1982, it gave air assault a more prominent role than ever. The Army may have been responding to the vogue for "military reform" then sweeping Washington (the ideas associated with Senator Gary Hart, among others), which urged a fresh assessment of actual threats rather than tying procurement and doctrine solely to the trench-warfare-in-Europe mentality that the reformers ascribed to the Army brass. One influential Army colonel put it bluntly: "Given the proposition that low-intensity conflict is our most likely form of involvement in the Third World, it appears that the Army is still preparing for the wrong war by emphasizing the Soviet threat on the plains of Europe." Whatever the influences, mobility and "active defense" were the watchwords in the evolving theory of warfare. "The reason there's a doctrine in the U.S. army," a high-ranking officer in the doctrine command said some years later, "is so the vision of how you fight a war precedes decisions on hardware you have to live with for ten or fifteen or twenty years." The decisions made about helicopters in the wake of Vietnam emphasized large purchases of agile, survivable, and lethal helicopters—namely, the Apache and a new assault copter then being designed in Stratford, Connecticut.

When Sikorsky Aircraft lost the attack helicopter fly-off to the Apache in 1972, it retained the name "Black Hawk" for later use, and that "later" came quickly. The army was opening a competition for a large new fleet of utility helicopters, the transport carriers of air assault that would also be a formidable platform for offensive weaponry.

The need for a new utility helicopter became evident in Vietnam. While the Huey performed nobly, it had limitations. It was vulnerable to being shot down by 7-mm gunfire. Nor did it fly well in hot or high conditions: both hot, muggy air and high altitude make lift and maneuver more difficult. So in 1972, the same year Igor Sikorsky died, the company he founded began to design a new craft that would not only become its biggest seller but would save the company from bankruptcy.

"We were about to go down the tubes," says a former Sikorsky engineer active in the firm at that time. "The Black Hawk contract had to be gotten to save the company. We'd built helicopters larger than what they wanted, and smaller than what they wanted, so we were well positioned. Bell had to scale up. One thing Sikorsky Aircraft learned in this is that the customer is always right; the Army does not always provide specifications for the best aircraft, but you have to meet their demands. They wanted reliability and maintainability, a result of what they'd learned in Vietnam, not necessarily the best aircraft aerodynamically."

The Army demanded that the new craft be able to fly at 4,000 feet at 95° F, achieve a vertical rate of climb of 450 feet per minute with a full payload, and fly at 145 knots minimum for at least two hours and twenty minutes. Maneuverability requirements included "nap of the earth" flying—the ability to fly at low altitudes to take advantage of natural camouflage like trees and hills—and it had to be able to withstand a crash. Its survivability also included taking a 7.62-mm slug, the first time the Army ever asked a helicopter to do so.

Sikorsky and Boeing Vertol were selected to build four prototypes. The engineers in Stratford had gained so much experience over the years that they felt confident they could meet the Army's flying requirements; the survivability dimension was newer and more perplexing. To tackle that, one Black Hawk engineer recalled, considerable "effort was expended in investigating configurations and selecting materials. Specimens were subjected to ballistics tests and development proceeded largely by trial and error." Redundancy was one key to the survivability puzzle: if the cable guiding the rear rotor blade was severed, for example, another cable was there to take over.

The Stratford engineers brought the first Black Hawk to the Army Proving Ground at Aberdeen, Maryland, six weeks ahead of schedule—a rare accomplishment in the dilatory world of military contracting that signaled Sikorsky's keenness in the competition. It flew on October 17, 1974, and while it was not perfect—several modifications were needed over the coming months—it was the leading design. More prototypes were delivered to bases in Alabama, Kentucky, and California for testing. Some 900 flight tests of the Black Hawk were conducted overall.

The competition was not finished for more than two years, until December 23, 1976. "The Army wanted the helicopter to fit into a C-130 transport," one of the engineers remembers as a deciding factor. "We had to put the rotor too close to the fuselage, but we figured out before Boeing Vertol how to do that and won a fly-off." That fly-off victory was enormous for Sikorsky Aircraft: the Stratford plant was operating at only 23 percent of capacity and had no government contracts at all. When the Army announced the decision, company president Gerald Tobias "was cheered loudly by many of the plant's 6,000 employees," said one account at the time, "as he drove through the factory in a golf cart equipped with loudspeakers and broke the news."

The new kid on the block was officially called the UH-60, the "UH" for "utility helicopter," the number designating a sequence. All military helicopters have such alphanumeric designations, as well as "clear" names chosen by the makers to convey a sense of fierceness. (Often, ironically, these successors to cavalry forces carry Native American monikers: Chinook, Apache, Kiowa Warrior, Comanche.) It fulfilled the Army's basic need for transport of eleven soldiers and a three-member crew. Compared to the Huey, it was sleeker—65 feet long, 12 feet high—and faster, able to cruise at 160 miles per hour and fly at 19,000 feet. It could carry three to four tons of cargo and range as far as 300 miles. At $7 million per ship, it wasn't cheap—the Hueys could be had for less than half that amount—but its enhanced capability seemed to make the price tag worthwhile. Sikorsky delivered the first of the new UH-60s in October 1978, and within six years had shipped 500 Black Hawks to the U.S. Army. Lagging by just a few years was the Navy version of the chopper, the Seahawk, which was procured mainly for transport, search, and anti-submarine warfare. From 1983, when the first Seahawks were delivered, until the Navy canceled procurement in 1994, some 246 served on such aircraft carriers as the USS *Ticonderoga* and on other ships. Two other versions of the UH-60 were also adapted for the Marines and the Air Force, with about a hundred manufactured by the mid-1990s.

The Army's original intention was to purchase 1,100 Black Hawks. As early as 1980, recalled General Charles Anderson, the Black Hawk program manager at the aviation command in St. Louis, the large inventory of Hueys was expected to be replaced by another new helicopter, then simply called the LHX—Light Helicopter Experimental. The "requirement" for Black Hawks was calculated by a complex formula that factored in the number of Army units that needed the chopper's capability for medium lift, the missions it would be called upon to perform, plus a set-aside for attrition and maintenance. (The requirement was also made, according to an industry analyst, "with quite a bit of interaction with Sikorsky officials.") But the utility version of the LHX was not to be—it would sorely stretch the modernization budget of the Army. So the Black Hawk requirement doubled "the night the LHX program was canceled" in 1987, Anderson said, and Black Hawks were then slated to replace virtually all the Hueys in the Army's inventory. A scout-attack version of the LHX stayed on the Army's wish list, however, and would later affect the Black Hawk's fortunes, because Sikorsky wanted to build that helicopter, too.

Through the years, Sikorsky engineers improved the Black Hawk to meet the escalating needs of the armed forces—high-tech avionics for navigation and communications, in particular, were installed—and the technology involved dozens of other corporations: GTE Sylvania, Magnavox, Emerson, Honeywell, and Hamilton Standard among them. The birds were powered by General Electric engines made in Lynn, Massachusetts. (For some reason, a local Sikorsky veteran noted, the Army didn't use the Lycoming plant to build engines for the Black Hawk.) Hundreds of subcontractors were drawn into the production scheme. It was an enormous enterprise; the bill for the Army in 1992, for example, totalled $400 million.

Without question, the Army was pleased with the performance of the Sikorsky star. Its real test came in the midst of the Reagan rearmament, during the invasion of Grenada in October 1983. "When they came back from the invasion of Grenada, the Army couldn't believe the bullet holes the Black Hawks took," said one Sikorsky worker. "They were just so durable and reliable." In the predawn hours before the American intervention on the Caribbean island, nine Black Hawks were disassembled and flown from their base at Fort Campbell, Kentucky, to Barbados in C-5A transports on the night of October 24. Within hours they were ready to go, loaded with the elite counterinsurgency unit Delta Force. Their mission was to capture the capitol in St. George's. The assault force encountered very heavy resistance, however, and the lightly armed Black Hawks, with only hatch-mounted machine guns, moved on to the second phase of the mission, the rescue of the former Grenadan government, now captive in Richmond Hill prison. Here, too, the Black Hawks took unexpectedly fierce gunfire from the Grenadans. In all, the Black Hawks performed well, especially given how much ordnance they absorbed; one chopper went down, and there were as many as thirty casualties with perhaps four dead (accounts differ). More Black Hawks were transported to Barbados the next day to support the Army Rangers of the 82nd Airborne Division, and again they had to fly into heavy gunfire when attacking Grenada's main military base, Camp Calivigny. Here the Black Hawk was less impressive: six of the eight UH-60s went down, some due to flying errors, and three Rangers were killed when a Black Hawk, its tail rotor disabled by Grenadan gunfire, tried to lift and instead flipped over onto the American soldiers. In all, thirty-two Black Hawks were used in its fighting baptism, with three destroyed and several others taking serious damage. Yet military analysts agreed that the helicopter did well. Said one, "The Black Hawks have a tremendous capacity for absorbing hostile fire and surviving."

The Grenadan experience not only burnished the Black Hawk's reputation for survivability; the military intervention, the first offensive action by the Army since Vietnam, lent a new sense of mission to air assault, which had just earned its own command structure the previous spring. Reagan's emphasis on low-intensity conflict was gaining adherents in the armed services, and Grenada was its laboratory. A special unit of the 101st Army Air Assault Division was quietly created in the early 1980s to bring special commandoes like Delta Force into battle. Known as the Night Stalkers, with the ominous motto, "Death Waits in the Dark," the air-assault unit was the leading edge of the Army's new commitment to low-intensity warfare, and the Black Hawk was clearly the most sophisticated technology in the quiver: of the helicopters dedicated to "special ops," most were Black Hawks. In tandem with the special teams were enhanced light infantry units, also seen as central to low-intensity conflict, and these too were heavily dependent on the air mobility afforded by the Sikorsky choppers.

Among the enhancements available to all Black Hawks is a stunning panoply of firepower: two 50-calibre machine guns, sixteen Hellfire anti-armor missiles (with reloading storage for sixteen more), 20-millimeter cannon, 70-millimeter rockets, land-mine dispensing pods, Stinger air-to-air missiles, and electronic warfare technologies like jammers and chaff.

The firepower made the Black Hawk resemble an attack copter. The Army's dedicated attack helicopter, the Apache, has larger guns and sophisticated techniques to "acquire" targets and withstand enemy fire. But its weaponry is similar to the Black Hawk's: the Apache, for example, also carries 16 Hellfire missiles ("smart" weapons with their own homing ability, and thus called "fire-and-forget" missiles). So the line between an attack helicopter and a fully equipped Black Hawk is blurry. By the early 1990s, Sikorsky was viewing the Black Hawk as an aircraft that could perform in an attack role. Sikorsky's vice president for international markets, Mike Baxter, noted that the smaller military budgets of foreign countries would drive them to select just one type of helicopter to serve both attack and utility tasks. The Black Hawk, he asserted, was ideally suited for such countries.

By the end of the decade, the Army's conversion of heart and mind to embrace the helicopter was complete. "Army aviation stands at the threshold of a unique opportunity," General Rudolph Ostovich III, the commander of the U.S. Army Aviation Center at Fort Rucker, Alabama, wrote at the time of the Desert Storm operation against Iraq, "an opportunity to write a new chapter in the book of land warfare—one that capitalizes on its inherent versatility, lethality, and deployability. Aviation will play a more important role than ever before on the future battlefield." The helicopter is the new "master weapon," one which "offers the means to combine superior mobility with superior firepower," another military theorist concluded. "An army operating at the pace of the helicopter will overwhelm any army operating at the pace of the tank."

The Sikorsky machine delighted the American military more than any since the Huey, and the Army was ready to order more. The versatility of the machine, combined with the toughness it displayed in Grenada, stirred keen interest from foreign buyers, too. Among the first major overseas sales was 24 "civilian" Black Hawks delivered in 1985 to the People's Republic of China. The U.S. Army would remain the primary customer throughout the decade, however, with its soaring "requirement" for 2,262 helicopters. The requirement was a shifting number, however, buffeted by the availability of money and the Army's own internal dynamics. It wanted lots of Apaches, plus the new light helicopter, the LHX, that would be called the Comanche, *and* its full complement of Black Hawks. Even when the Cold War began to wind down and the Army downsized, the requirement stayed up near 2,000.

But the Army's desire for so many helicopters—light, medium, and heavy; scout, attack, and utility—would be frustrated time and again by a paucity of money. And to the manufacturers, that fact soon made rich suitors from abroad all the more attractive.

10

A MARKET TO DIE FOR

The First Persian Gulf War

About the time the Black Hawk was entering Army service, the complexion of the Middle East was rapidly shifting again, due to the enmity that had long festered in the Persian Gulf between its two twentieth-century giants—Iran and Iraq.

In Baghdad, the coming of the Islamic revolution in 1979 was most unwelcome. A traditional rival of Iran, predominantly Sunnī, and with ambitions to dominate the Persian Gulf, Iraq saw both danger and opportunity in Khomeini's ascendancy. The danger was the large Shī'ī minority in southern Iraq. The opportunity was the military weakness of the new regime.

Iraq had followed the secularist path pioneered by Kemal Atatürk a generation earlier in Turkey and the Arab nationalist path blazed by Nasser in Egypt. The latter was more alluring, as it fulfilled the heroic self-image of Iraq's leader, Saddam Hussein. The anti-Western, vaguely socialist message of Nasser, while of doubtful viability by the late 1960s, resonated in Iraq and among Arabs generally, and Saddam was drawn by the wild popularity Nasser enjoyed across North Africa and Western Asia. Nasser's appeal to Arab outrage and the sense of loss born of hundreds of years of foreign domination was like a symphony composed for Iraqi ears.

Foreign influence in Iraq began long ago. Mesopotomia—the area drained by the Tigris and Euphrates Rivers—came to the West's active attention in the sixteenth century as the easternmost outpost of the Ottoman Empire, confronting the Persian Empire of the Safavids to the northeast. This confrontation, which lasted more than two centuries, sparked any number of border disputes, raids, and subterfuges. At stake was the Persian Shī'ī access to the many holy sites then in Ottoman territory, and Turkish fears of insurrection among its many Shī'ī minorities. A treaty was forged that covered, among other subjects, the nettlesome Kurdish peoples who would not respect the rules of either empire. By the early nineteenth century, two empires newly competing in the region, the British and the Russian, attempted to regulate the frontier to their respective advantages. Gradually, the outside powers did defuse open hostilities, though a sort of guerrilla warfare—such as the Persians encouraging the Kurds to rebel against the Ottomans in the 1830s—kept the region tense.

The discovery of oil, followed soon by the Great War of 1914–18 and the dissolution of the Ottoman Empire, combined to alter the political landscape of Iraq dramatically. Following its decisive victories over the Turks in the Arabian Peninsula and the Levant (aided by the Arab uprisings orchestrated in part by T. E. Lawrence), Britain took control of this area they called Iraq, drawing its borders and those of its twin creation, Kuwait, both separated by an indistinct frontier from the independent kingdom of the House of Saud to the south. Among the intended consequences of this British border-drawing exercise, which bore in part the hand of Winston Churchill, was to deny Iraq a Gulf port and thereby make it even more dependent. Britain installed a son of the sharif of Mecca, Faisal, as Iraq's king. (Another son of the sharif, Hussein, was installed as king of Jordan, which is still ruled by that family.) And the British maintained an ostentatious role of political management and oil extraction in Iraq for nearly four decades. The country became nominally independent in 1932, but no one doubted Whitehall's supremacy in Baghdad.

By the late 1950s, anti-British feeling was coursing through the Arab world. The Arab-Israeli wars of 1948 and 1956, the rise of Nasser in 1952, and his successful confrontation with Britain over the Suez Canal in 1956 all stirred Arab nationalism. In Iraq, the anticolonial sentiments were further roused by Britain's and America's strong-arm tactics in the Gulf region: the deposing of Mossadegh and the forging of the Baghdad Pact were particularly incendiary. Both events illustrated how the Western powers were using the region to serve their own interests, as they had during World War II when it was their supply platform for the Soviet Union. Mossadegh was turned out of office to preserve the West's control of

Iranian oil. The Baghdad Pact was an "alliance" of Iraq, Iran, Turkey, and Pakistan along with the old Western power, Britain, and the emerging Western power, the United States, to contain communism along the USSR's southern flank. To the growing numbers of Arab nationalists in Iraq, the repeated and blatant using of their country by the West was becoming intolerable. At the very least, they argued, Iraq needed to recreate itself as a truly independent state.

In July 1958, the pro-Western Iraqi monarchy was overthrown by a band of military officers in the name of nationalism and republicanism. The result was nationalistic, in the sense of asserting independence from Britain and the United States, but Iraq stumbled through a decade of coups and turbulence (including a Kurdish rebellion in 1961) until the Ba'th Party took power in July 1968. The Ba'thists, who derived their pan-Arab ideology from the Arab unity movements in Syria and Egypt (but who had split from the Syrian Ba'th Party in 1966), consolidated their power ruthlessly with the deft use of terror under their new internal-security chief, Saddam Hussein.

This "new" Iraq, following the Nasser path, was suddenly enriched by the oil revolution of 1973–74; Iraq possesses petroleum reserves second in OPEC only to Saudi Arabia. The oil wealth was devoted in part to infrastructure and social-welfare projects, and to a formidable military acquired with the eager assistance of the Soviet Union—the superpower aligned with Iraq since Baghdad broke off relations with Washington over the Arab-Israeli war of 1967. The march toward modernization and regional power was not smooth for the Ba'th regime, however, and most prominent among its problems was the large and restive Kurdish population in the north, in the old Ottoman province of Mosul, Iraq's richest oil-producing region.

Saddam Hussein was dispatched to forge an understanding with Mullah Barzani, the Kurdish leader, and an agreement was signed in 1970 granting autonomy to the Kurds. (Along the way, goes one story, Saddam tried to assassinate Barzani by sending him a delegation of clerics, one of whom was unwittingly carrying a tape recorder rigged as a bomb; Barzani survived only because a servant shielded him from the blast.) But the Ba'th government in Baghdad never intended to grant the Kurds true autonomy, and denied them control over the oil fields at Kirkuk, which was clearly part of the Kurdish bailiwick.

The Kurds' growing sense of despair over their status in Iraq led to an astonishing ploy from Washington. In 1974, Secretary of State Henry Kissinger prompted the Shah of Iran to foment a rebellion by the Iraqi Kurds. It was a classic surrogate power play: Iraq was a friend of Moscow, and an attempt to destabilize Baghdad was simply another gambit in the long history of vicarious confrontation between the United States and the Soviet Union. Iran supplied arms and money to Barzani, enabling the Kurds to pose a serious threat to the Ba'thist regime. Barzani's 90,000-strong guerrilla force, long a thorn in the side of the Baghdad government, became truly menacing: roughly three-quarters of all Iraqi troops and half its armored divisions were deployed to quell the uprising. The conflict sapped Iraq, which received no support from Moscow, and resulted in 30,000 or more casualties. Facing an all-out war with Iran, Baghdad opted for a settlement—the 1975 Algiers Agreement. The Shah abruptly ended his support for the Kurds and their rebellion imploded; Barzani was forced to flee the country. (It also precipitated a split among the Iraqi Kurds between their leaders Barzani and Jalal Talabani, an enduring enmity that roiled Kurdish politics in Iraq for more than two decades.) The rebellion in Iraq, however, spurred the imaginations of other Kurds in other places—they now saw that armed rebellion to achieve autonomy had a chance of succeeding.

The Kurdish rebellion, and Kissinger's singular role in stimulating it, were not forgotten by Saddam Hussein. He saw it, correctly, as part of the U.S. strategy to recast Britain's role in the Persian Gulf—that of guarantor of Western interests—with the Shah. That perceived change in 1971 caused Baghdad to reach for closer ties to Moscow—which, in turn, marked Iraq as a potential threat to the West. Weakened by the Kurdish rebellion, Iraq needed time to recover and to build its military, and the 1975 accord with Iran produced some breathing room. The lull in tensions with Iran also afforded Saddam an opportunity to repay the Kurds, and in 1978 he attacked Iraq's Kurdish areas ruthlessly.

The other "ethnic" problem Iraq faced was its large Shī'ī population: two out of every three ethnic Arabs in Iraq were members of the Shī'ī sect that dominated Iran. The holiest site in Shī'īsm, Karbala, is located in southern Iraq. The Shī'ī were disenfranchised—their rulers were Sunnī—and opposed to the secular nature of Ba'thism. The "underground" of Shī'ī militancy was unintentionally expanded by the Ba'thists' murderous suppression of communism in Iraq, since both the poor and the social activists turned to the Shī'ī once the communist opposition had been eliminated. Groups like the Islamic Cell and the Muslim Warriors *(mujāhedīn)* were constant irritants to the Ba'thist rulers, and Saddam Hussein harassed them relentlessly throughout the 1970s, culminating in a massacre and mass arrest of Shī'ī pilgrims and rioters in the holy city of Najaf in 1977. Some attempts were made to cool Shī'ī unrest, but these were mainly cosmetic and unable to dampen Shī'ī rage at such actions as the expulsion of the Ayatollah Khomeini, who had resided in exile in Najaf for more than a decade.

The ongoing Shī'ī problem was brought into sharp focus by Khomeini's triumphant return to Teheran and accession to power in early 1979. Now the Ba'thists were facing a traditional rival with a freshly minted revolutionary ideology that could instantly enlist millions of Iraqis. A full-fledged Shī'ī revolt aided by Teheran, moreover, might encourage the Kurds to rebel again, and a two-front civil war was a harrowing prospect for Saddam Hussein. At the same time, Saddam perceived political flux in Iran—a tussle over civil authority—and he sensed that the ardor of the revolution had sapped the strength of the Shah's extravagant military: Iran would be unable, for example, to procure spare parts for its fighter jets from an America indignant over the 444-day hostage crisis. He could, he reasoned, solve all his problems at once by cutting off the fount of Koranic zeal flowing from the mullahs. He could also grab the oil-rich province of Khuzestan under the pretext of freeing Arab minorities. After trading insults and charges of violating the Algiers Agreement, Iraq invaded Iran in September 1980. An eight-year war had begun.

Saddam Hussein's perception of military weakness and civil discord in Iran was not guesswork. His calculations were shaped by U.S. intelligence reports conveyed to Baghdad through Riyadh. It was an election year in America, an unusual campaign in which the sitting president, Jimmy Carter, was bedeviled by the Teheran hostage crisis and was careening toward defeat if he could not find a way to win the release of the embassy prisoners. A dreadfully botched U.S. rescue operation had failed even to get near Teheran. Back-channel threats and promises were leading nowhere; the new Khomeini regime was determined to punish Carter for supporting and sheltering the Shah. In the White House, a desire for sweet revenge against the Islamic revolution began to take shape: the one thing that conceivably could force Khomeini to release the hostages before the November election would be a mortal attack on Iran. Iraq was just the right choice for the job.

The stage was set for U.S. involvement several months before the intelligence estimates were sent to Baghdad. Four months earlier Zbigniew Brzezinski, Carter's national security advisor, spoke approvingly of Saddam's regime on television. His thinking stimulated "the emergence in Washington of a notion that the United States should tilt toward Iraq to counterbalance America's lost influence in Iran," recalled an observer inside the administration. "As early as January 1979, Brzezinski was discreetly floating the idea that perhaps Washington should reconsider its 'nonrelationship' with Iraq." Saddam saw the winks and nods along with the CIA forecast that Iran's military would stall out in three weeks without spare parts, and his conclusion was easy to arrive at: the United States would support his invasion. So too, he reasoned, would Moscow—had it not occupied Afghanistan to protect its interests from the same sort of religious fanatics?

The tacit approval of Washington for Saddam's invasion masked a desperate attempt by Carter to provide spare parts to Khomeini in return for the hostages' release. It included statements by U.S. diplomats that Iraq had "gone too far" in its actions, as well as explicit promises to airlift $500 million worth of spare parts to Iran just days before the election. But Carter's gambit was blocked by two cleverer moves. The first was Ronald Reagan's alleged deal with Iran to delay the hostage release until he was president, after which the U.S. embargo on Iran would be lifted. The second was Iran reaching out to procure, in an especially ironic twist on the Nixon Doctrine, their needed spare parts from another source: Vietnam.

U.S. meddling in the early weeks of the Iran-Iraq war was a precursor to a continuous, often shadowy involvement in a conflict that ultimately claimed more than a million casualties. The frequently heard refrain of "a plague on both your houses" only partially described the reality of U.S. policy considerations. Strategists both in and out of government did see the war as a peculiar blessing, engaging two noxious ideologies in a death grip. More formally, such strategists framed the Iran-Iraq war as symptomatic of a balance of power in the Gulf that would benefit America's friends and allies—Israel and major OPEC sheikhdoms led by Saudi Arabia—and American interests. The balance-of-power idea grew to official prominence later in the decade, but throughout the 1980s it tended to mask U.S. actions in the Gulf and provide an intellectual rationale for the public stance of U.S. neutrality.

For the United States was not neutral. Apart from the hostage machinations of 1980–81 and the tawdry Iran-contra affair five years later, the
Reagan administration clearly favored Iraq. The support was rarely public.
It was politically tricky to embrace the ruthless Saddam Hussein, a scourge
of Israel and friend of Moscow. But the policymakers in Washington saw
two distinct advantages in quietly backing Baghdad.

The first drew on Cold War reasoning. Iraq was part of the radical Arab
camp that included Qaddafi and Assad and aligned itself with the Soviet
Union. The Islamic revolution in Iran and the Soviet invasion of
Afghanistan were all the more alarming if one also saw the other major
power in the Gulf—Iraq—as a Soviet ally. Moscow was not pleased by
Iraq's invasion of Iran; it signaled more of the instability that drove it to
"help" Kabul in the first place. In the Reagan White House, thinking
drifted toward a gradual warming of relations with Saddam Hussein, including military support, which might pry him loose from the Soviet circle
of friends.

Far more central to U.S. actions were abiding fears of Islamic fundamentalism. Stopping the spread of militant Islam was the key goal of policy, and there could be no greater incentive than to imagine Iraq—with its
large and angry Shī'ī population, its enormous oil reserves, and its growing
military power—as a brother-in-arms of the Iranian mullahs. Hard on the
heels of the embassy hostage crisis, with militants bombing U.S. Marines
in Beirut and airplanes hijacked before worldwide television audiences, the
terror of Islamic militancy grew in the public mind as *the* problem of
American foreign policy.

The U.S. "tilt" toward Iraq came early and often, continuing with more
above-board visibility as the war dragged on through the decade. Support
came in several forms. Most prominent was financial aid in credits for
commodities—farm products—which were first conveyed in 1983 with
the subsidized sale of $460 million worth of rice. This visible gesture of
support bolstered the confidence of other countries that doing business
with economically shaky Iraq was an acceptable risk. As became clear in
the Banca Nazionale del Lavoro (BNL) scandal—in which managers of an
Atlanta branch of an Italian bank were illegally providing credit to Iraq,
possibly at the bidding of the U.S. government—the creditworthiness of
Iraq was a pivotal asset with which it could purchase weapons. The BNL
alone provided $4 billion in loans, one-quarter of which was enabled by

the U.S. commodity credits, and was used for weapons purchases; nearly 10 percent of Iraq's weapons imports during the war were underwritten by this one source. The commodity credits granted during the Reagan administration, seen in this light, had a profound effect in favor of Iraq's military and the flow of arms from Western sources into Iraq. By 1989, Iraq had received $5.5 billion, or one-fifth of the total program, of these U.S. food credits. The commodities dealings not only brought desperately needed food to Iraq, itself essential to the war effort, but also an assortment of trucks, cranes, and military spare parts as "after-sales services" from the American corporations bidding for the enormous grain contracts. The Reagan administration also pressed the Export-Import Bank to loan Iraq $485 million for an oil pipeline to be built to Aqaba by the Bechtel Corporation in 1984, and later another $200 million loan, which was never repaid. The signaling of support for Iraq was crucial to each case.

A second key component of the U.S. tilt was political recognition. In 1983 the State Department, which was a leading proponent of the tilt, took Iraq off its list of states supporting terrorism. This act was coupled with several high-level delegations to the Gulf monarchies declaring U.S. interests— that is, a defeat of Iraq by Iran was unacceptable. That same year, the administration began Operation Staunch, a diplomatic game of hardball in which the United States pressured all its allies to stop any weapons flows into Iran. Just weeks after removing Iraq from the terrorism list, the State Department placed Iran on it. Formal diplomatic recognition between Washington and Baghdad followed in early 1985. This unambiguous tilt provided Iraq with international standing, which could be converted to money and arms.

Actual military support from the United States was notably less than what Iraq received from others in the West. But covert and illegal arms shipments from the United States, including components for large-scale weapons systems and armament manufacturing, could never be adequately counted. The BNL conspirators funneled an enormous quantity of weaponry to Iraq, as their scheme was to finance and procure the flow. Dozens of U.S. firms shipped military equipment to Jordan as a convenient cover for its actual end destination in Iraq. Some American allies and recipients of arms transfers were generous with Baghdad. The Saudis, in particular, seeing the Iranian mullahs as a threat, sided with their Arab brothers and sent large quantities of aid. The European suppliers—France,

Britain, and Germany were particularly active—kept up a heavy export agenda with the private encouragement of the Reagan administration. Overall, in excess of $100 billion worth of war supply was delivered to Iraq and Iran during the eight-year period, including roughly half of all arms shipped to the Third World during that time.

Once formal relations had warmed between Washington and Baghdad, the transfer of militarily useful technologies picked up. Of particular value were dual-use items such as computers, which would be used to design weapons. Above-board trade included more than a hundred helicopters, 60 from Hughes, 45 from Bell; an $8-million deal to supply two Black Hawks from Sikorsky for the Iraqi dictator was permitted to bypass the normal review procedure. All the choppers—$102 million worth—were described as commercial but were easily adapted to military use, and were seen by reporters to be deployed as such. California congressman Howard Berman asked the State Department about the helicopters and was curtly told by Secretary of State George Schultz that the sale was good for the commercial market and boosted employment in the American aircraft industry.

Other military advantages were accorded to Saddam Hussein's warmaking, including a steady flow of intelligence from the Saudi AWACS and U.S. satellites. The information may well have saved Iraq from defeat; several large-scale Iranian offensives that threatened the very existence of the Iraqi state may have been blunted by the rapid alert provided to Baghdad by U.S. intelligence. Within moments of the takeoff of squadrons of Iranian warplanes, for example, news of the event would be transmitted from U.S. sensors to the Iraqi military. Satellites could sense in detail the movement of Iranian ground forces, and the data would be instantly sent to Baghdad through Riyadh or the U.S. embassy. The daily provision of such information, unreplicable from any other source, was more valuable than any weapon or financial credit.

The most controversial aspect of Reagan's support for Saddam, the "reflagging" of Kuwaiti oil tankers in 1987 and his unambiguous siding with Iraq during the so-called tanker war, was less decisive than the other, quieter activities. Iraq actually initiated the attacks on the oil tankers, but the White House depicted this escalation—an especially symbolic escalation, given the central meaning of oil to the Gulf—as a deadly threat from Iran.

President Reagan's decision to protect Kuwait's oil tankers caused a stir in Washington. The predictable concern was that the United States would get drawn into the conflict, a fear made credible by the U.S. shootdown of an Iranian commercial airliner filled with civilians and the Iraqi attack (with French-made Exocet missiles) on the USS *Stark,* both of which were attributed to human error. The tanker war did draw the United States more visibly into the war—one assistant secretary of state said bluntly that we would not let Iraq lose—but the die had been cast years before. The tanker war was more a gesture of assurance to the oil monarchies and an ostentatious display of American naval power than the most important element of U.S. intervention.

While creating a fuss among opinion leaders, President Reagan's support of Iraq in the tanker war was widely seen as preferable to evenhandedness toward Iran. (The policy was significantly political: the president needed to renew his anti-Khomeini *bona fides* after the embarrassing revelations, in late 1986, of the covert arms shipments to Iran.) Favoring Iraq was clearly interpreted as a blow to the Islamic militancy that Iran represented. "There will need to be a totally different kind of government in Iran," Defense Secretary Weinberger said in 1987, "because no one can deal with an irrational, fanatical government of the kind that they have now." The tilt toward Iraq was already seven years in the making, but it had been largely done underground. Its new naval presence in the Persian Gulf affirmed America's determination to contain and turn back the Islamic revolution. As it had been throughout the 1980s, the containment of Iran was a more significant objective in the Gulf than the containment of Soviet influence.

The results of the first Persian Gulf war were not altogether apparent when Iran suddenly accepted a UN cease-fire resolution in the summer of 1988. The human costs and the loss of oil were enormous, but the common view in the West was that the two ancient antagonists had simply brought this disaster upon themselves. U.S. interests—the protection of its oil and its key allies in Israel, Saudi Arabia, Kuwait, and the United Arab Emirates—had been preserved. Iran's economy was in shambles. With few exceptions, the Arab states had backed the secular Arab Saddam Hussein. Ostensible American involvement, measured by casualties and dollars, seemed minor. All in all, it looked like a foreign-policy triumph, though one garnering small public attention. In 1988, the Reagan era was drawing to a close, a presidential campaign was in full swing, and the Gorbachev revolution was afoot in the Soviet Union and Eastern Europe. The nasty Gulf war seemed remote.

The apparent success of U.S. assistance to Iraq strengthened the idea that Iran could be handled—contained, turned back, maybe even destroyed—by arming its neighbors. The Khomeini revolution seemed to be in retreat. Into the bargain, the American tilt brought with it, as some argued, a more moderate and accommodating Iraq. The war "changed Iraq's view of its Arab neighbors, the United States, and even Israel," two prominent analysts wrote in *The New Republic* in April 1987. "These allies have forced a degree of moderation on Iraq. . . . Iraq is now the *de facto* protector of the regional status quo." Saddam Hussein became the favored object of a new balance-of-power equation in the Gulf. Reconstruction funds for Baghdad were made available by the new president, George Bush, who pursued Reagan's policy with little restraint.

The Gulf monarchies were more circumspect about the achievement. The royal families of Saudi Arabia, Kuwait, and the UAE liked neither of their powerful neighbors, but they reasoned that Iraq was the safer bet—it was Arab and Sunnī—and they backed that wager with enormous amounts of money, military assistance, and political capital. Saddam was a rogue, but Khomeini was a genuine revolutionary, and they feared the potentially disruptive force of his rhetoric. They were corrupt, in the imam's view, and the incredibly lavish royal privileges they enjoyed were vulnerable only to Islamic ferment. This outlook was carefully and repeatedly conveyed to Washington.

The one clear beneficiary of the Iran-Iraq bloodbath was Turkey. Like Iraq and Saudi Arabia, it won fresh support from Washington as a new bulwark against Khomeini. Saddam's attack on Iran occurred ten days after the Turkish military's seizure of power in 1980, so the junta's attention was otherwise engaged in the opening stages of the war far to its south. But new relationships with Iran—which was ideologically menacing to Turkey's secularism—and Iraq were forged in short order, driven by the generals' need to turn their lackluster economy around. Trade with both combatants skyrocketed. From 1978 to 1987, Turkey's exports to Iraq increased by a factor of thirteen, and imports increased four times; to Iran, Turkish exports ballooned by 2,400 percent from 1978—the final year of the Shah's reign—to 1985, and imports rose four fold. Overall, in that period (1978–87) Turkish exports worldwide climbed by 400 percent. Turkey exported a variety of goods, including steel and iron (it then had no arms industry to speak of), and imported mainly oil. Moreover, Turkey provided Iraq with its sole avenue of petroleum export, a pipeline from Kirkuk to a port on Turkey's Mediterranean coast, and thus enabled Iraq's war effort in a fundamental way.

But while the war profited Turkey, it also had a price: the Kurdish rebellion that had been brewing before the military coup resumed in 1984, not least because the border with Turkey could no longer be controlled by the Iraqi military. The Iraqi Kurds sided with Iran during the war, mounting insurrections and fighting alongside Iranian soldiers, and the PKK used northern Iraq as a sanctuary with impunity until 1988. The junta's foreign minister flew to Baghdad in 1983 to threaten to close the oil pipeline if Saddam did not end a cease-fire with the Iraqi Kurds—which Iraq needed to shore up the southern front with Iran. Saddam complied. The Turks worried incessantly about the possible unification of the typically fratricidal Kurds, and they wanted to keep military pressure on them nonstop. In 1984, Turkey and Iraq renewed an agreement first forged and utilized in 1978 to allow Ankara "hot pursuit" of the guerrillas into Iraqi territory; the Turkish military carried out such pursuits in 1986 and 1987. But the air strikes hardly damaged the PKK. The Kurdish insurgency was growing, and the Iran-Iraq war was one of the reasons why.

The postwar outlook was tempered by other troubling signs. Iraq, which claimed victory, emerged from the conflict desperately poor—the cost of the war, including lost oil revenues and sheer physical damage to the nation, was some $500 billion. Iraq's foreign debts were huge: it owed $70 billion, mostly to the Saudis and Kuwaitis, and $26 billion to Western banks. Remarkably, its oil-exporting capacity had actually increased during the war with the construction of the oil pipeline through Turkey, and by August 1988 it was pumping in excess of its OPEC allotment. Apart from the staggering losses, however, the most salient impact of the war was to vastly expand the size and sophistication of the Iraqi military and the military's hegemony over Iraqi political life. The domestic arms industry grew to produce all of its own light weapons as well as substantial manufacture of artillery, rockets, and armored vehicles. Its enhancement of the Soviet design of the Scud missile, worked out in cooperation with Egypt, further extended its military capability. Its military and political relations with the United States and Europe had improved vastly. The war changed Iraq from a mildly irksome, Nasseresque friend of Moscow into an independent, militaristic regional power.

Iran was also battered by the war; the financial price reached $620 billion, far more than its annual gross national product, by the end of the decade. Its war dead totaled more than twice those of Iraq—some 262,000, including 11,000 civilians. Its oil industry was severely damaged, but at war's end it was producing close to its OPEC quota. Its military, with fewer options to import weapons, became impressively self-sufficient. Iran displayed an uncanny ability to acquire weapons from abroad (at times, capturing Iraqi hardware) and to copy them. It manufactured aircraft, missiles, artillery, and light weapons; tanks and antitank weapons were created from U.S. designs. By 1987, its domestic military output equaled $2 billion.

As in most nations under siege, war nourished patriotic fervor in both nations, and led to more political repression in each. In Iran, the fervor was that of Shī'ism, and it empowered Iran's leaders. Anticlerical feeling was running high in Iran at the beginning of the war, and uncertainty about the revolution's fate was pervasive. At the same time, the desire of the more militant mullahs to export their revolution, beginning in Iraq, was resisted by Khomeini. But the combining of military and religious energy became inevitable with Iraq's attack. The war then became a device to consolidate the power of the most radical elements in the Islamic revolution and to envision an armed extension of the faith: "The road to Jerusalem goes through Karbala," said a popular slogan. As long as the war served the goals of the radicals, Iran resisted all attempts to forge a cease-fire. Khomeini finally accepted the UN resolution only because his lieutenants sensed that the people had had enough. The politics of Iran then reverted to a struggle between the moderates and the radicals, with confusing indications of who was winning. Some high-level attempts at reconciliation with the United States were made, while the Revolutionary Guard was unleashed against moderates. Public hangings of dissidents were a common sight.

Repression in Iraq after the war followed familiar contours. Saddam was creating a personality cult, and any challenges to his authority earned harsh punishment. The most notorious of his domestic campaigns was that against the Kurds. Saddam could not abide their open rebellion and alliances with Iran, and from 1987 on a mounting campaign of attacks on Kurdish villages became a standard feature of Iraq's northern landscape. Near the war's end, Saddam wreaked a terrible vengeance on the city of Halabja, which the rebels and Iranians had captured. The Iraqis bombed

Halabja with nerve gas, an outlawed chemical weapon, killing 5,000 people. It was nearly unprecedented, this attack by a government on its own people, and it caused a momentary stir of moral conscience from Iraq's allies, though no change in policy. Saddam's vengeance did not end there. After the war, thousands of Kurds were executed; in one instance, an estimated 8,000 followers of Barzani disappeared. Four thousand Kurdish villages were razed. Objections were registered, mainly by American and British human-rights groups, but they were essentially ignored. Official policy toward Iraq remained cordial and supportive. Others with Kurdish problems took note.

A final, troublesome result of the Iran-Iraq war was the growth of the arms industries that supplied the antagonists. Because of the various arms embargoes that applied to both countries during the eight years, the black market for arms enjoyed an unprecedented boom. The effect on the legal market was more profound, however. New exporting countries gained a foothold in the world market—South Africa, Brazil, Greece; Israel substantially supplied Iran. Thousands of new business and political contacts were nurtured. In all, Iran and Iraq together imported $53 billion worth of arms during the war, with Iraq outpacing its rival by a margin of four to one. Not only did the warring nations acquire weapons at this astonishing rate, but nearby states steadily built their own arsenals.

The intrigue of black marketeers, of corporations and banks and shady individuals running the embargoes, of double-talking presidents and prime ministers gained much attention in the aftermath of the Iran-contra scandal and the Iran-Iraq war. The black market delivered no more than 10 percent of the weapons, however, and the rogue banks and colorful arms dealers rarely had significant access to policymakers (though some, particularly BCCI and BNL, may have been instruments of officials). Most important were the legal ties and cultivated relationships that became, far from the public's view, a nexus of influence over policy. Here the Iraqis excelled. From possessing virtually no useful links to the U.S. government in 1980, to becoming a favored anchor of regional stability in 1988, Saddam Hussein managed his Washington connections deftly. The official rationale for such a turnaround in the Reagan and Bush administrations, and for strengthening ties to the Saudis and the Turks, was to protect our oil and to hem in the Islamic revolution of Iran. The currency of the new friendship was militarism.

11

RIDING THE PROCUREMENT WAVE

The reelection of Ronald Reagan in 1984 by an astonishing margin delighted the defense industry, which, from corporate suite to union hall, had supported the president. The campaign against Walter Mondale revolved around issues like military spending, the nuclear-arms race, and the support of counterinsurgency, among other domestic matters, and the results apparently confirmed the nation's backing of the buying spree of high-tech military hardware. The now-legendary Russian bear advertisement that the Reagan campaign ran on television, intended to capture the all-important swing voter, conveyed the national mood: we're not certain how dangerous the Soviet threat is, but there *is* such a menace ("There's a bear in the woods"), and we'd better be on the safe side. And the safe side of the street was the one with lots of weapons.

In Connecticut, which voted 61 to 39 percent for Reagan, the results of the election simply bolstered the conventional wisdom that the good times of military spending were here to stay. The numbers did not lie: in 1984, Connecticut received $5.5 billion in defense contracts, more than 8 percent of the total economic activity in the state, which, with the "multiplier effect" of the contracts, was equal to about one in every three or four jobs. The new contracts were especially welcomed because the Northeast had for a decade been losing manufacturing jobs. The contagion of "deindustrialization" had infected Connecticut with a vengeance, becoming more virulent in the 1980s as smokestack industries fled to the nonunion South or across borders. The erosion of blue-collar employment made the defense dollars all the more welcome, and illusory.

The Pentagon numbers, moreover, had been climbing since the late 1970s. After the steady growth of procurement that marked Reagan's first term, there was little reason to believe it wouldn't continue in the wake of his smashing second victory. The emphases of his presidency, after all, were the backbone of the state's production lines: nuclear subs for deterrence, fighter jets and tanks for Europe's Iron Curtain front, and helicopters for both Europe and counterinsurgency elsewhere. Connecticut's military industry and Ronald Reagan's ideology were a match made in heaven.

The former United Aircraft, now United Technologics Corporation, accounted for nearly half of the state's military prosperity. Like Connecticut itself, Sikorsky's parent company was virtually made for such a time, for Washington had long been UTC's principal means of support. UTC was a conglomerate before that word was commonly used, created as such in the late 1920s with government contracts for aviation as its main focus. By the early 1930s, United had acquired Sikorsky Aircraft, Pratt & Whitney, Boeing Airplane Company, Hamilton Standard Propeller, Northrop Aircraft, and numbers of smaller concerns. It made airplanes and operated them through transport companies, such as its own creation, United Airlines. It was unrivaled in the aviation business.

One of the lucrative markets in those early days of aviation was the mail. The new enthusiasm for air mail, the government's willingness to subsidize the enterprise, and United's dominant position in the industry combined to yield handsome profits for the company. The profits were so handsome that United came under tremendous pressure from Senator Hugo Black's investigative committee on Capitol Hill in the mid-1930s. Profiteers, especially those using public tools to turn a big profit, were subject to popular wrath in those years, and United became a pariah in the public eye. The episode signaled much of what UTC's history would be, however: very strong links to federal contracting, continuous expansion and contraction as a result of those contracts, and a certain public distaste for some of the practices of the company.

Another long-standing strategy of the company was exports. Early on, United's leaders, Fred Rentschler and Bill Boeing, aggressively marketed their aviation wares overseas. United products were particularly popular with the military in Latin America and Asia, and by 1930 half of all aviation exports from America were United's. Another scandal brewed as the company sold to Germany and Japan in the 1930s: Senator Gerald Nye's hearings on such exports again exposed United (among other firms) to public wrath. But the company's sure footing with the U.S. military—Pratt & Whitney supplied the Army Air Corps with more than half of its engines—would not be dislodged, and the onset of the Second World War averted any further damage.

World War II and its aftermath, the onset of the Cold War, benefited United much as they did Sikorsky: Pratt & Whitney dominated engine making, and Vought and Hamilton Standard were major contractors as well. Most of the production took place in Connecticut, Pratt being the largest division and being long established in the Hartford area. In the mid-1950s, United was still beholden to the federal procurement business: the company had nearly $1 billion in sales in 1956, making it one of the very largest industrial concerns in the United States, but 86 percent of its sales were to the U.S. government. The military-spending slowdown after the Vietnam War increased the drive to nurture nondefense business, and United did so by purchasing other companies, such as Otis Elevator. By 1980, its dependence on the U.S. military was down to 22 percent, but nearly all its military work was done in Connecticut. And the lure of the Reagan rearmament was irresistible: the total share of UTC's sales to the Pentagon rose again—to 35 percent by the mid-1980s.

Dependency was not limited to U.S. purchases; United's aggressive exporting spurted again in the 1970s, much of it at the behest, and with the money, of the U.S. government. The Shah of Iran eagerly bought more than 240 fighter jets and 200 Bell Cobra helicopters, all powered by Pratt & Whitney engines. The Shah also bought some 30 Sikorsky helicopters. Israel was a steady buyer of the same or similar items. Saudi Arabia started a buying spree that included over 200 fighter jets and 400 Cobras powered by Pratt. Many of these exports were financed by the Foreign Military Sales program of the U.S. Defense Department.

The most controversial of these, and a telling example of UTC's assertiveness, involved the AWACS—the highly sophisticated Airborne Warning and Control System manufactured by Boeing and flown with Pratt & Whitney engines. Ten of the flying radar craft were to be sold to the Shah during the Carter administration, and five were slated for Saudi Arabia in 1980–81. The lobbying for the AWACS was fierce. In the

Saudis' $8-billion purchase, Boeing and UTC had to overcome the formidable alliance of Israel's friends in Congress, so UTC chairman Harry Gray mounted one of the most aggressive lobbying campaigns Capitol Hill has ever witnessed. With Boeing, he pried lobbying support out of the thousands of subcontractors involved in AWACS production—"raw economic blackmail," as one of them put it—by appealing to "lost U.S. exports and jobs" if Congress voted down the sale. At stake was not only the AWACS sale but the entire Saudi arms market. The Senate approved the sale by a margin of four votes. Among the nay-sayers was Connecticut freshman senator Christopher Dodd.

When the procurement dollars began to flow, when the foreign sales programs of the Pentagon were ready to export, United Technologies was well positioned through years of lobbying experience and an entrenched product line. This seemed to be good news for Connecticut, which weathered the recession of the early 1980s and its eroding manufacturing base mainly on the strength of the defense contracts of Pratt & Whitney and Sikorsky Aircraft.

The optimism attending this windfall lasted throughout the decade. "Five years into the most durable economic boom since World War II, nobody in Connecticut seems too worried about the military hardware pipeline drying up," wrote business columnist Robert Wiesman in the *Hartford Courant* in 1987. Even though Democrats had taken back the Senate in 1986 elections, and even though the appearance of Mikhail Gorbachev on the world stage had signaled the demise of the Cold War, optimism about military acquisition remained giddy. "Defense spending is not forecasted to diminish between now and the early 1990s," said one top private economist. "You cannot compare this to Vietnam," said another, alluding to the sharp drop in defense spending in 1970. "Today we're involved in defense preparedness and refurbishing the defense infrastructure, and that could go on for years."

The warning signs of a fall were just becoming apparent. Connecticut defense contracts actually took a dip of about 10 percent from fiscal year 1986 to 1988, but because appropriations, contracts, and delivery dates all stretch out over so many years, the actual trend line was not so easy to pinpoint at the time. "Saying the defense budget has stopped growing is like saying your six-foot-six son has stopped growing," said another newspaper in early 1987. "It may be true, but you've still got one big boy on your hands." "DEFENSE SEES GOOD PROSPECTS," ran a headline in the *Boston Globe* in January 1989.

The peak year for Connecticut was 1990, "after the Wall," as defense-industry honchos are prone to say, after the Berlin Wall came down and the Cold War was clearly a thing of the past. So even that signal event did not convince state officials and economists that they were riding the down side of the procurement wave. "The impact of the Cold War's end on the Connecticut economy will be low for several reasons, the experts agree," went one report in early 1990. Over at Electric Boat, general manager James Turner said that "we're in the best niche in the defense industry." And the president of the American Helicopter Society contended that choppers were so much a mainstay of the Army now that "I've never seen a brighter picture." UTC had a backlog of $17 billion in military orders.

Jobs in Connecticut defense firms were slipping slightly in the late 1980s: from 116,000 in 1988 to 110,700 in 1990. But even measuring employment impacts is guesswork. The number of jobs related to even a single major contract is difficult to gauge, since hundreds of small machine shops or electronics firms may be subcontractors supplying the "prime," the major contract holder like UTC or Electric Boat, and many of those small suppliers are likely to be doing other, nondefense work at the same time. Sikorsky may win a $400-million contract one year for Black Hawks, but some components, even parts of the airframe, will be made outside Connecticut. In the late 1980s, moreover, UTC in particular was tightening operations, shedding employees for efficiency, increasing overtime, and sending some jobs to cheaper plants out of state. So the slippage of 5,300 jobs in the last years of the Reagan decade could have been due to many factors and scarcely ruffled the experts.

By the mid- to late 1980s, the Black Hawk seemed an indispensable part of the Army's arsenal and was Sikorsky Aircraft's most profitable endeavor. It was earning the company more than $100 million annually. With Boeing, Sikorsky was also developing the new light helicopter called the Comanche, and it lobbied hard through years of ups and downs. The Comanche, exceptionally advanced in its avionics and in its use of composite materials, was considered by many defense analysts (and many in Congress) to be too costly, however, and its fate was iffy at best. It would not help the Stratford workers in any case, since the six prototypes the army envisioned would be built at a Sikorsky plant in Florida. The Black

Hawk would clearly be the breadwinner and job fount for the company throughout the 1990s.

Still, the Pentagon and Congress put Sikorsky through several hoops. In January 1988 the Army announced that it ultimately intended to buy more than 2,250 Black Hawks, and that month awarded the company nearly one billion dollars—the largest contract in Sikorsky's history—to build 252 Black Hawks to add to the Army's inventory of 900. Just a few months later, chastened by the tightening budgets for its modernization program, the Army said it would buy just over one thousand Black Hawks—meaning the total buy was nearly complete—but yet another estimate early the next year raised the figure to 1,600 ships. It was still a healthy number, but the heady predictions of just months before, followed by sharp adjustments down and then up, were sobering. Clearly, the production line could not rely entirely on the U.S. Army: exports would have to become more prominent for a company that to date had not paid much attention to the overseas market.

While the "experts" continued to gush optimism about U.S. procurement, the industry's leaders knew better. The redoubtable Harry Gray, who was ushered out of the UTC chairmanship in 1986 but remained a major force in the industry, made the export case before Congress in 1987. "International sales are an essential revenue source for funding defense-related R&D," he argued to a House panel contemplating sharper scrutiny of military exports. "Overseas sales allow the defense industry to maintain a larger production base . . . [which] provides the U.S. with a comforting surge capacity. We are aware of cases in which an entire production line would have been shut down had it not been for the foreign sales." Gray's emphasis on maintaining the "defense industrial base" through exports was an indication that he saw the writing on the wall for U.S. orders. He was, after all, on several advisory panels at the Defense Department and the White House. He knew how crucial exports were becoming to United Technologies. "Defense-related sales represent five percent of U.S. export revenue," he told the committee, "and, I submit to you, that is a big number."

The keen interest in exports by Harry Gray and his confederates in early 1987 signaled their awareness of the coming decline of the Reagan boom. But that view was hardly unique. For many in Connecticut, the Pentagon's spending surge was like fool's gold. It looked like the real thing but it wouldn't last, just as previous military binges had merely left nasty hang-overs soon afterwards. The defense spending slowdown of the early 1970s was a wake-up call to many in the state. They reasoned that the Carter/Reagan buildup could not be sustained—nor could the exports fu-eled by petrodollars—and that a crash would be especially unpleasant for Connecticut, the Pentagon's favorite state.

So a few social activists and academic economists, and fewer still politi-cians and unionists, began a modest but determined effort at what was popularly called economic conversion—the intention to "convert" mili-tary bases and production to civilian use. The best organized and most ar-ticulate activists were those in the southwestern part of the state, where Bridgeport's decline and the heavy presence of military contractors were ready targets for conversion rhetoric. But the entire state was vulnerable, and little pockets of activism could be found in nearly every town and city.

One of the first salvos of the campaign to pacify the economy nation-wide was a well-argued book, *Jobs, Security, and Arms in Connecticut,* pub-lished in 1980 by the American Friends Service Committee, a Quaker organization. The author of the book was Marta Daniels, a soft-spoken woman in her early thirties who lived in New London and was active on a number of peace issues, including the Trident Conversion Campaign.

Much of the activists' concern stemmed from a belief that the American military-industrial complex was the engine driving the new arms race. "The defense industry and the Pentagon have used the threat of commu-nism and the Soviet Union to justify the need for new weapons," Daniels wrote in her book. The chief architects of this fear, she said, were the Com-mittee for the Present Danger, a group of neoconservative intellectuals, and the Coalition for Peace Through Strength, a collection of retired military officers. "With corporate resources at their disposal, groups such as these have created a belief that only increased arms spending, more nuclear bombs and a confrontational foreign policy will 'stop the Soviets' and pro-vide security." Against this she offered arms control and cuts in military spending as surer routes to security, preaching both economic security—steady, civilian jobs that would make products and provide services that so-ciety actually needed—and the "real security" of lower levels of armaments and confrontation.

This theme, common to all conversion activism in the 1980s, was not new. Since World War II, when the economy was lifted out of the Depression by war production, and recession followed the end of the war and demobilization, analysts on the political left had asserted the strong connection between the economy and the military. Paul Baran and Paul Sweezy had first popularized this connection in their 1966 tract, *Monopoly Capital,* which argued that capitalism now *required* large-scale military production to remain viable. The theme was reasserted by the more mainstream John Kenneth Galbraith in *The New Industrial State* (1967) and other works. And they were forcefully detailed and argued some years later by Columbia University economics professor Seymour Melman in his influential 1974 book *The Permanent War Economy,* appearing as it did in the economic doldrums of the post-Vietnam defense drawdown. Among Melman's conclusions were that defense contractors become so accustomed to Pentagon ways—gold-plated technology, endless paperwork, a single buyer, and so on—that they cannot readjust to purely commercial work; that their market power is derived not from efficiency so much as from lobbying muscle; and that the political power of the aerospace firms was complemented by the "revolving door" whereby Pentagon officials go to work for the military contractors, and those in industry go into positions of influence in the government. In Connecticut, the phenomenon was neatly illustrated just at the time of Marta Daniels' book when General Alexander Haig, recently the supreme allied commander of NATO, became UTC's president, soon served a brief tenure as Reagan's secretary of state, then returned to UTC's board.

The vogue for industrial policy came to the fore just as the Connecticut conversion advocates were making their case. Comparisons with the booming economies of Japan and Germany underlined those governments' intensive involvement with economic planning and their relatively small budgets for defense. The contrast with America was sharp: Washington's economic policy was limp and desultory, and our military spending was enormous. The most powerful economic player in the United States was in fact the Pentagon: its research and development money was far greater than private R&D, its procurement policies affected everything from missiles to socks, and its employment was vast. This "back-door" industrial policy was widely lamented by liberal economists like Galbraith and Robert Reich as well as by conversion advocates. Using the Pentagon as the Keynesian stimulus for economic growth was perverse, they argued, because its "products" were essentially unusable in the civilian economy and its putative spinoffs exaggerated. At the same time, the Pentagon was a superb political planner, strategically placing contracts for major weapons systems in every congressional district. Politicians could vote against such projects only at their peril. A genuine industrial policy, stressing commercial products, was put forward as the solution to two dangers: defense dependency and the arms race. Conversion had to play a central role in such a solution.

These ideas looked good on paper, but the political and economic realities were inhospitable. All the reasons that brought Ronald Reagan to power were at work, and the labor unions, seemingly natural allies of conversion, were almost uniformly hostile to its logic. With few exceptions, American labor did no more than pay occasional lip service to conversion. The AFL-CIO's long-standing anticommunism was in play: the leadership, by 1980 in the hands of Lane Kirkland, supported the rearmament under way both as a foreign-policy imperative and as a source of high-paying jobs; the defense industry, after all, was largely unionized.

The defense industry was also private. However beholden they were to public monies, the individual contractors were private corporations, and their deliberations about what they would produce were nearly impervious to democratic influence. Attempts to convert these enterprises constantly ran up against this immovable brick wall. The manufacturers' decisions were made in concert with the Defense Department, but the procurement system hardly bent to the popular will—particularly as long as Congress was rubber-stamping the Pentagon's plans. And exports of military technology were even more remote from public view.

The culture of conversion activism was an additional burden. The advocates for a peace economy came largely from the antiwar movement of the 1960s and '70s and were linked with the growing antinuclear activism that was the main contentious voice against Reagan's rearmament. But the peaceniks needed the support of the unions to have any hope of changing the military procurement system or the decisions of individual corporations. American labor was transforming itself into "Reagan Democrats," rejecting the social agenda of the left and its fervent critique of U.S. foreign policy, while heartily embracing the jobs that rearmament brought. Union leadership rejected the seeming anti-Americanism of the peace movement, and the rank and file were offended by the moral denunciations of their

work. Each caricatured the other broadly enough to create an unbridge-
able chasm between them. Disarmament organizers did attempt to appeal
to workers and hold them blameless for the sins of the system, but in the
feverish climate of the early 1980s, when the specter of nuclear war
seemed more threatening than any time since the Cuban missile crisis,
these fine distinctions were drowned out by the noisy and bitter national
debate.

However long the odds, the peace activists felt they had no choice but
to spread the gospel of military conversion. Leading the mission was a
young Episcopal priest, Kevin Bean, who quickly captured a following
with his mix of idealism and pragmatic ideas for converting the industries
in the defense corridor along the Connecticut coast.

Tactics were often confrontational. "UTC cedes to the government . . .
any of its moral responsibility regarding the type of economic activity in
which it will engage," Bean wrote in the *Hartford Courant* in 1986. "This is
the very heart of the issue behind the arms race—namely the need for an
exercise of moral responsibility at the individual, corporate, and national
level." The Freeze and other antinuclear groups would sometimes stage
protests outside the Electric Boat facility in Groton, comparing the manufacturer's activities with Auschwitz.

The activists seized the moral high ground because the blind optimism
of the state and industry officials did not permit a rational dialogue about
the boom-and-bust cycle of defense procurement. Only later in the decade
would the conversion advocates become less accusatory. Conversion's "first
obstacle has been the peace activists themselves," Reverend Bean noted in
1988. While the tactics of nonviolent civil disobedience are "faithful and
right," given the dangers of a nuclear war, he said, the "military-dependent
workforce, as well as the management of these firms, see little concern by
peace activists about the local economy." Not until it was possible to see
the end of the Reagan rearmament—i.e., the end of the Cold War—
would workers listen to conversion ideas or activists mute their moral outrage and speak to workers' real worries about jobs. Until then, politicians,
unions, and managers were only too happy to ride the procurement wave.

12

THE FALCON GOES TO TURKEY

Fort Worth was also enjoying boom times in the early to mid-1980s. Once the cattle capital on the northern prairie of Texas, and the unglamorous twin city to nearby Dallas, Fort Worth bootstrapped itself from its cowtown past when the War Department located the nation's largest aircraft manufacturing facility on the west side of town just before the outbreak of World War II. There, in a mile-long, six-stories-tall building were made the versatile B-24s, used for bombing, transport, and reconnaissance. The plant had more than 30,000 assembly line workers (including 11,000 women) in a Fort Worth population of just over 200,000. After the "good war" was over, about two-thirds of those lost their jobs, but the plant stayed on to produce a succession of bombers and then in 1973 to begin work on the fighters, first the F-111 and in 1976 its most remarkable invention, the F-16 "Fighting Falcon." It was that last product of General Dynamics, the St. Louis defense firm encompassing Electric Boat and the Abrams tank, which was the source of such good times in north Texas during the Reagan rearmament.

Actually, the plant had been humming since the first F-16 orders came through in the mid-1970s, and it hadn't stopped since. Early on, the fighter was considered to be a marvel of speed, agility, and versatility. It was both an air-to-air dogfighter and a quick-strike bomber. Congress provided unusual multiyear funding to procure 650 planes, and within a few months allies in Western Europe announced they would purchase more than 300 F-16s. By 1983, a thousand of the Falcons had rolled off the Fort Worth line. In East Hartford, that also meant 1,000 of the F-16's enormous engines, for the powerful aircraft was powered by Pratt & Whitney technology.

When the Turkish military began to show interest in the F-16 as a major military modernization program, the possible sale was not a do-or-die proposition for General Dynamics. The plant's employment was ramping up—it would again reach more than 30,000 in 1990—and the company was already exporting F-16s around the world, well beyond the NATO partners. Through upgrades in avionics, the F-16 kept renewing itself and selling to ever-eager buyers. The enthusiasm of the U.S. Air Force—which would still be procuring the aircraft in the 1990s, twenty years after its first order—was the best sales pitch, since the foreign purchasers always want what's in the superpower's inventory. Turkey was no different.

While the war of the two Gulf giants raged to its south in the early 1980s, Turkey was gradually going through a transformation. The slow withdrawal from military rule did not diminish the military's influence, of course, and in fact the restoration of "order" allowed Turkish leaders to turn their attention to modernizing their arsenal of weaponry. Beleaguered by internal strife in the 1970s, hindered in arms purchases by the American arms embargo of the late 1970s, seen as the poor cousins of the NATO family, the Turks felt it was their right and duty to dramatically upgrade their firepower. They had F-4s and F-5s in their air force, they had Hueys and armored personnel carriers and tanks in the army, but somehow these weapons and the largest army in NATO—apart from America's, of course—were not enough to satisfy the self-image of the Turkish generals fresh from their three years of supreme political and military power.

The Soviets were becoming bogged down in Afghanistan, the Syrians remained fixed on Israel, Iran and Iraq were otherwise engaged, and even the Greeks were reasonably quiet, so it was difficult to discern what military threat would so obsess Turkey that it would seek to build hundreds of fighter-bombers, more hundreds of helicopters, plus a thousand armored vehicles and tanks. Turkey not only wanted to *possess* the top-of-the-line military hardware, but was determined to *make* it, too, *and* export it, to become an independent arms merchant. No doubt the U.S. embargo—a traumatic, pride-piercing blow to Turkey—was at the root of this desire to make weapons. The only catch was that some other country would have to supply Turkey with the manufacturing know-how and equipment. Fighter jets and assault helicopters are not simple machines: what took the likes of Igor Sikorsky and Arthur Young many years to create in the most sophisticated industrial environment in human history could not simply be copied.

The export of an entire industry was not by 1983 a commonplace. The Carter administration had put a hold on the burgeoning practice, which had spread to Taiwan, Korea, and even Iran. Major weapons were still largely the manufacturing province of America, Europe, or the Soviets only. The Turks were seeking something that had largely been forbidden to outback countries—the ability to make and even sell high-quality weapons. And that is what they negotiated with the United States, first for fighter-bombers, then for armored vehicles, and finally for helicopters.

In America, in the industrial hubs of the military, the "coproduction" of weapons was greeted ambivalently, at first with a detachment born of prosperous times, and later with a wariness grown from the defense drawdown. In neither mood did anything other than the impact of jobs and revenues enter the equation of the managers and workers at the factories, the chambers of commerce or the newspaper editors, the mayors or the local members of Congress. It was always about jobs and nothing else. In Turkey, of course, it was about much more.

Turkey in the mid-1980s was *the* arms market. The Middle Eastern states had exhausted themselves during the 1970s and were no longer prime customers; Iran and Iraq needed arms badly, but for the major companies there were high hurdles in selling to either. On the other hand, Turkey had announced plans for a $10-billion military modernization, a project large enough to lure every arms manufacturer in the world. The Iran-Iraq war was bringing Turkey unexpected riches. The modernization, Turkish officials openly hoped, would enable them to build total, major weapons systems by the late 1990s and export weapons across the region from Pakistan to Algeria. The purchases of coproduction would include, Ankara promised, a total of 720 helicopters, more than a thousand armored combat vehicles, naval frigates, tank upgrades, and a broad array of electronics and communications hardware. It was an astonishing display of chutzpah, since no other country had accomplished such a complete makeover, going at one bound from importing Korean War–vintage equipment to exporting space-age technology. Some of the oil-rich Arab states had tried to do that and failed. Unlike the Saudi AWACS purchase or this or that tilt to the Persian Gulf autocracies, the creation of an entire arms industry in Turkey went virtually unnoticed in the West. The mid-1980s were heady days for the Turkish generals, days in which they could envision Turkey as a pivotal player in the region, a natural replacement for the Shah. And the first and most important step in their enormously ambitious plan would be the acquisition of the F-16 fighter and a factory like the one in Fort Worth to make them in.

A coproduction deal, in which a new facility would be built in Turkey to assemble the plane, was announced in early September 1983, while the military junta was still in power in Ankara. The sealing offer in the deal was the offsets, the mixture of inducements that enhanced the main deal. General Dynamics gave Turkey $1.3 billion in the offset grab-bag (out of a total deal worth $4.5 billion), including "direct" offsets—the coproduction of the aircraft—and "indirect" offsets, which meant investments in Turkey's hotel industry and purchases of Turkish marble, tires, and boric acid. "We were encouraged to take vacations in Turkey," said one executive at the Fort Worth plant. The oddball aspects of the offsets—the marble exports from Turkey, for example—were handled by a broker outside the corporation. "We used to view these as a necessary evil," said a vice president in Fort Worth, "but now we just see it as part of our global business." The offsets probably made the difference in Turkey's decision to choose the F-16 over McDonnell-Douglas's F-18, as it was the first time the F-16 had outfoxed the F-18 for a foreign sale. A couple of years later a former General Dynamics executive charged that kickbacks to the Turkish military had added persuasion, but the company denied the charges. The Turkish generals had granted themselves total immunity to prosecution under the constitution they wrote in 1983, so no proper investigation could be mounted.

The core of the coproduction deal, which would be financed by the Pentagon's Foreign Military Sales program, was the new plant to be built in a wheatfield 20 miles south of Ankara, next to Turkey's Mürted air force base. "This will not create any new jobs in Fort Worth," said a company spokesman on the day the deal was announced, "but it will provide a large number of jobs for Turkish workers and export sales for many Turkish companies in a variety of fields for years to come." The deal would "aid the country's fledgling military aircraft industry." And indeed it would: a state-of-the-art facility that would produce 240 of the very best military aircraft in the world, plus the export of more to friendly countries like Egypt. "We're not here just to build airplanes and go home," said Joe Jones, the General Dynamics vice president who got the Turkish plant built and running. "In the final analysis, the Turks expect this to be an operating aircraft-production facility, and it is General Dynamics' responsibility to see that that happens." The Turks created a new company, Tusas Aerospace Industries (TAI), to operate the plant, in which the government retained a 51 percent share.

The entire plane would not be built in Turkey. The United States kept control over vital technology by building in Fort Worth the forward fuselage and cockpit, including all the avionics, and shipping those to the Mürted site in Turkey. This partial work satisfied the unions in Fort Worth in the mid-1980s, when there was plenty of other work, and it also passed muster with the export-control bureaucrats in the State Department, although if the deal had been with the Japanese, everyone would assume they could "reverse engineer" the cockpit and be building a better one in two years—a worry that did attend the FSX deal with Tokyo a few years later. But no one voiced such a concern about the Turks.

Indeed, there was no concern of any kind expressed in official circles. "Turkey shares borders with Iran, Iraq, and Syria and is exploring a new, more active role in Islamic affairs," said Richard Burt, an assistant secretary of state, before a House subcommittee in February 1984. "Given the impact of all three countries on current unrest in the Middle East, Turkey's potential role takes on added significance." The Reagan administration viewed Turkey not only as a hindrance to supposed Soviet designs in the region but as a unique strategic platform for U.S. operations, as it was during the Lebanon deployment in 1983. The seriousness of this purpose was signaled by Reagan's boosting of foreign aid to Turkey from $465 million in fiscal 1983, approved more than a year before the military dictatorship relinquished power, to $755 million, sums making it the third-largest recipient of U.S. aid in the world. Fully one-fifth of Turkey's defense budget came from the American outlays.

"It was done, the coproduction, to hold down costs and help make Turkey self-sufficient," recalls Glen Rudd, the Pentagon's chief of military exports at the time. "Özal made a big pitch for the F-16, then it took them a year to sign up after we went through so much to get it for them. There was a major improvement in Turkish armed forces as a result of U.S. assistance." It may have taken so long because Özal's top advisers were skeptical about the deal, which they saw as both "very expensive" and aggressively pushed on them by the United States.

Still the mammoth deal went ahead. The first few F-16s to go into the Turkish air force's inventory were assembled in Fort Worth, and were delivered with the kind of ceremony that is a ritual of martial societies, where the world-class hardware is displayed as evidence of the military's grand importance. The rite was played out solemnly in July 1987, wherein "acceptance papers" were signed by the Turkish chief of staff and several U.S. officials before a select audience of four hundred, including sixty members of the Turkish air force brass. The crowd was then treated to a show of the F-16's remarkable agility, a thrilling aerial performance by Kevin Dwyer, the company's chief test pilot, who had similarly wowed the Paris Air Show just a month before.

The Turks' own production line in the former wheatfield near Ankara would yield F-16s just a few months later. But by 1992, when the war against the Kurds was really heating up, they wanted forty more—above and beyond the 160 of the original deal. They were also keeping the line humming by exporting some 46 planes to Egypt, a deal that raised the hackles of union president Pat Lane, who called for a protest rally at the Fort Worth plant to register members' displeasure at the foreign production, which was also occurring in South Korea. Things had changed since the mid-1980s. Fort Worth employment was in a free fall from a peak of 30,000 in 1990, and dropping fast. It was 20,000 in 1992, and would dive another 50 percent in the coming three years. General Dynamics, Lane sarcastically told a reporter, "is being real generous. Our employees are going to be getting their layoff notices and at the same time they're going to be training Koreans on how to do their jobs." The same was true, he complained, for the Turkey deal.

The export of defense jobs was gaining notoriety, but virtually unnoticed was the impact of state-of-the-art military exports on America's perception of its own defense needs. (By 1996, two years after Lockheed bought the F-16 line, more than 1,300 F-16s were serving in thirteen countries outside the United States, including Thailand, Indonesia, Pakistan, Israel, Egypt, Bahrain, Greece, and Turkey—earning the F-16 the top spot as the most significant military export in U.S. history.) "We've sold the F-16 fighter all over the world," one Lockheed official mused.

"What if one of those countries turns against us?" An Air Force officer concurred: "I cannot determine the intent of any of these countries 15 to 20 years from now." Those nervous comments were meant to underscore the need for the next-generation aircraft, the F-22, which Lockheed will also build. So the export of 1,300 F-16s, and the export of the production line itself, was used officially as a *threat,* which could only be countered by an even more advanced fighter, slated to cost $72 billion, nearly $200 million per airplane, ten times the cost of the F-16.

Oddly, the F-16 coproduction may have been the high-water mark of Turkey's ambitions to be a major producer and supplier of weaponry, for the deal had the effect of souring many companies on Turkey. The vast modernization program was moving along in fits and starts, with the Turks reversing decisions after making awards or drastically scaling down orders. Some in the Turkish press had criticized the government for not getting a good deal from General Dynamics, and that prompted the issuance of off-set guidelines that established a *minimum* of 30 percent in offsets for all military purchases. That would turn off many bidders for Turkey's contracts. Other factors—not least the continuing instability that constantly roiled Turkish politics—slowed the modernization program.

But the felt need for military hardware and the long-standing desire to become a big player in armsmaking spurred Ankara on. One other major deal was negotiated in the 1980s, the coproduction of armed, and armored, fighting vehicles from the FMC Corporation of Chicago, a billion-dollar transaction eventually enabling Turkey to export the useful army weapon to countries like Algeria, which had its own rebellion to set right. The FMC deal in 1987 came right after Ankara withdrew from another contract with a French firm because the Turks were offended by the French foreign ministry's criticism. "The Turkish government has sent a message to international bidders," said an industry newsletter of the incident, "that technology, capital, and financing packages are not sufficient to win the contract; these must be supplemented by political support for Turkey's international interests." The French and Americans racing for the helicopter bonanza took the lesson to heart, as did FMC. It was responding, the report continued, "to Turkey's message: they have recently begun to portray themselves as lobbyists on behalf of Turkey with their respective governments."

In 1994, Turkey ordered up another forty F-16s from its partnership with the Fort Worth plant, by then owned by Lockheed, and in 1996 the Mürted facility began to make another twenty fighters for Egypt. By this time, Mürted was making 95 percent of the aircraft, rather than just the original 75 percent. ("They have the capability to do more, certainly," said a Lockheed manager.) Meanwhile, Spain asked the Turks to build them fifty-two light-transport aircraft. And the managers at TAI were also working on an unmanned reconnaissance aircraft. Turkey wanted to keep the Mürted line "warm" until the facility could be converted to make military helicopters.

"The variety of production at the Mürted plant," said Ilnur Çevik, an aide to Turkey's president, "is a great asset for manufacturing new aircraft types in the future." The factory, Çevik said in 1993, would eventually build not only combat helicopters but multirole military jets from nose to tail, plans going well beyond the deal to assemble the F-16s. By the time Çevik made that prediction, the significance of the fighter-bomber was tragically apparent to all in the Turkish military.

13

TURKEY'S WAR WITH ITSELF

The "need" for F-16s and assault helicopters, in the minds of the Turkish generals, was provoked by the likes of Ramazan Ülek. The small, intense man with thick glasses could speak with remarkable good humor about his life, his people, his incarceration. Ramazan Ülek, one of the most prominent Kurdish activists in Turkey, was sitting at his desk at the offices of a newspaper in Istanbul. Or, more accurately, what had been a newspaper, three successive newspapers in fact, before the Turkish authorities shut them down for "separatist propaganda." The spare cement-block office building, in a poor section of Istanbul not far from the massive Byzantine walls, was the second home to the nettlesome Kurdish periodicals; the first, about a mile away, had been blown up one night in 1994, some believe at the behest of the Turkish prime minister.

"Many here in Turkey are still living under the Ottoman idea of empire," Ramazan explained. "There are thirty-five million Kurds in the Middle East today. The Kurds are different now from the time they were divided between feudal lords. They are aware of their history." It was not always so. While the growth of Kurdish populations has been rapid (probably totaling twenty-five million, not Ramazan's thirty-five million), the growth of self-knowledge has been slow. Even bright young Ramazan Ülek was awakened only gradually.

"I was a law student at the University of Istanbul in 1980. I was influenced by Marxist writings, the '68 revolutions, and literature on self-determination," he recalled. "We were trying to grasp Kurdish identity within these ideologies. I was also getting informed about Kurdish history and culture. When I went back to my province in Kurdistan, I would talk to my villagers about what a 'people' is, a people whose history had been made to be forgotten by the Turkish government. It was taboo in the 1960s and '70s to even say there were Kurdish people."

It was precisely this burgeoning self-awareness of the Kurds that so worried the Turkish military that they would undertake their harshest coup d'état yet.

The thirty-eight months of military rule in Turkey from September 1980 to November 1983 gradually restored a sense of peace and security to the streets of Istanbul, Izmir, Ankara, and other cities in the western provinces of Turkey. General Evren and his cohorts in Ankara's vast military headquarters along Ismet İnönü Boulevard, just a stone's throw from the ineffectual legislature, the Grand National Assembly, upheld the military's invasive attitude toward Turkish political life. Even at the conclusion of their rule, the generals could scarcely let go: they hand-picked the candidates for the first post-coup election; the military's candidate was crushed by the electorate, receiving just 25 percent of the vote despite veiled threats of another coup. This result clearly belied the widely touted assertion that the coup and the junta were overwhelmingly popular.

Still, the Turkish public probably welcomed the renewed sense of security that martial law afforded them. Arrests, particularly the arrests of leftist politicians, journalists, trade unionists, and students, were the price of such security. But the junta's rule in the Kurdish Southeast was an altogether harsher affair: like the military's rule in Turkish Kurdistan for nearly sixty years, it was brutal, racist, and hidden from the view of the Turkish as well as the Western public. In addition to an enormous human toll, it provoked a new Kurdish nationalism that flourished even as the military crackdown grew more ferocious.

None of the reports from Turkey in September 1980 mentioned the "Kurdish problem," the long-festering discontent of a people whose nationality was illegal to acknowledge but who also were never accepted as Turks. Only late in 1980, when 1,400 Kurdish activists were prosecuted for "separatism," did the military indicate that the "Eastern question" was a significant factor in their overthrow of the democratic government. They would break the back of this Kurdish movement, they vowed, and that would be the end of it. The rest of the world, blinded by a news blackout of the Southeast imposed by the junta, scarcely took note of the military's campaign there. But then that, too, had been the history of the Kurds.

The Kurdish people—nomadic, tribal, Muslim, and independent—are of mysterious origin. Occupying the unforgiving mountainous terrain of the Zagros and Taurus ranges, which run along the present-day borders of Armenia, Iran, Iraq, Syria, and Turkey, the Kurds have a known history that stretches back to the second century B.C. An amalgam of Indo-European and Semitic tribes, they speak a tongue linked to Iranian languages. The first distinctively Kurdish literature was a brief description of the Arab invasion of the seventh century, which resulted in the widespread conversion of Kurds to Islam. Their conversion from Persian forms of Zoroastrianism and other older religions allowed the Kurds to "enter history" as they had not before—an entrance marked mainly by their contribution of music to Islam. They also lent military acumen to the powerful expansion of the new faith. Salah ed-Din, or Saladin, the great conqueror of the Christian crusaders, was a Kurd; his exceptional leadership of Islam established a brief Kurdish dynasty in the Middle East. However lightly chronicled their early history, the Kurdish people were established in modern-day Turkey well before the Seljuq victory at Manzikert in 1071 that ushered Anatolia into the Turkish era.

The Kurds established a set of principalities throughout their area of kinship, ruled by sheikhs who at times were at odds with each other but more often with the Ottoman and Iranian dynasties that constantly rubbed up against what was generally known as Kurdistan. "The pattern of nominal submission to central government, be it Persian, Arab, or subsequently Turkic, alongside the assertion of as much local independence as possible, became an enduring theme in Kurdish political life," observes David McDowall in his history of the Kurds. A *modus vivendi* was established with the Ottoman sultans that was viable (despite the occasional uprising) largely because of the Kurds' submission to the caliphate—three out of every four Kurds were Sunnī—and religious fealty sufficed where political expediency or shared interests could not be sustained.

By the end of the Ottoman period, the growth of Turkish nationalism was being faintly echoed in a stirring of Kurdish nationalism: like the Ottoman Turks, the Kurds' first loyalties had been to the Prophet and to the tribe. Those Kurds who had migrated to the cities found assimilation rather easy, and the appearance of a few Kurdish-language journals in Istanbul created a sense of identity among the small intelligentsia of the diasporan Kurds. This incipient self-awareness as a separate nation became a pivot point during the upheaval wrought by World War I, the rise of Atatürk, and the collapse of the Ottoman Empire.

During the Great War, Kurds and Armenians were pitted against each other by the Turkish authorities in the eastern provinces: pogroms resulted in one million Armenian dead, and as many as 700,000 Kurds, in 1915 through 1917. The Kurds remained loyal to the Ottoman generals even though their territory was terribly ravaged by the war. By 1918, mass starvation and rampant disease had so crippled Kurdistan that only the wealthiest were secure.

The victorious Allies then began their postwar attempt to humiliate the Turks and divide the Ottoman lands. For the Kurds, the prospect of statehood was a startling new reality. The British were to become the dominant power in the region, and they had appropriated the provinces of Mosul and Baghdad for themselves via the creation of Iraq. But the British also wanted a buffer state between their Persian Gulf acquisitions and the Turks, and an independent Kurdistan seemed to fill that bill. The British could not agree amongst themselves precisely what "Kurdistan" was to be—an autonomous province of Iraq, a string of states protected by Britain and France, or an independent country? The Treaty of Sèvres granted the Kurds the right to form their own state, *if* the League of Nations "considers that these peoples are capable of such independence and recommends that it should be granted to them." The accord also provided for unification with the province of Mosul, should the Kurds there desire it. Exact borders were indistinct—for example, those of the newly independent Armenia were to be drawn, oddly enough, by President Woodrow Wilson, whose enthusiasm for self-determination did not seem to extend to the Kurds.

Sèvres became a rallying cry for subsequent Kurdish nationalists, but at the time it was far from a popular cause in Kurdistan. Nor was the treaty ever viable: Atatürk was already on the march; the treaty itself had been signed by a Sultan who would soon be in flight. Far more significant for the Kurdish sheikhs in the postwar tumult was the problem of whether to align with the occupying British forces in Iraq or cast their lot with Atatürk. The Turkish leader was urging the Kurdish sheikhs to revolt against the British in northern Iraq, to join him in his war of independence against the Christian interlopers. Although there were anti-Atatürk outbursts by the Kurds, and Turkish officers quashed Kurdish nationalist organizations, the tribal chieftains, like many others in Anatolia, joined with Atatürk in the name of defending the caliphate. Until 1922, when Atatürk told the Grand National Assembly that "the state we have created is a Turkish state," the Kurds could believe that a multiethnic Islamic nation was being preserved, and that some measure of Kurdish self-rule, reflecting centuries of practice, was to be preserved as well.

Atatürk wasted no time in turning on his "Kurdish brothers." From 1923 on, his repression of Kurdish nationalism and even Kurdish identity was savage and predatory. In the new Turkish Republic, Kemal filled the Kurdish Southeast with Turkish administrators and gave land to Turkish war veterans, forbade the use of the Kurdish language in court, and, most important, banned the native tongue in schools.

The measures quickly spurred a new Kurdish uprising, led by Sheikh Saïd, which erupted throughout the Southeast in 1925. It was only fitfully nationalist, more reactionary, in fact, seeking a return to the days of the caliphate. But it was fired by the inchoate discontent that Atatürk's rule engendered. It was rebuked by overwhelming Turkish force: Atatürk, using the ragtag revolt as a pretext for assuming dictatorial powers which he never completely relinquished, put down the Kurdish insurgents quickly. Sheikh Saïd and 660 of his compatriots were executed, most by public hanging, and another 7,500 were arrested. "Whole villages were burnt or razed to the ground, and men, women, and children killed," a British foreign-service officer observed. Massacres were reported. The response was well in excess of the challenge, particularly since Saïd's rebellion was far from uniformly popular among the Kurds. But the army's terrorism actually bred more resistance, and individual towns and villages rose up through the ensuing years. The army's reply was equally harsh: hundreds of villages were razed, thousands of Kurds killed, and perhaps a half-million were deported. Turkish Kurdistan was placed under a nearly permanent state of martial law and a news blackout.

The root and branch of the confrontation was the fanatical Turkish nationalism bred by Atatürk. The Turkish state from 1923 onward simply refused to acknowledge that the Kurds even existed—they were known until the 1990s as "Mountain Turks." The new mythology of the Turks as founders of the great Asian civilizations neatly folded the Kurds into that conceit. Scholarly work on Kurdish history was outlawed. A "Turkification" program was instituted in the Southeast, raising the visibility of Turkish culture, moving Turks into the area, and earnestly promoting the cult of Atatürk. At the same time, the area, so long a pastoral and agrarian economy, was steadily impoverished by the pogroms (in which treasured livestock were victims en masse alongside their human shepherds), deportations of Kurdish elites, and the disappearance of the Christian entrepreneurial class.

Chief among the cultural insults was the persistent attack on the Kurdish language. The state's insistence on using Turkish penetrated deeper than the formal venues of court or schoolroom. The Ankara regime replaced Kurdish village names with Turkish equivalents, forbade the naming of children with Kurdish names, and outlawed the singing of Kurdish folksongs. Since only one in twenty Kurds could speak Turkish in the first years of the Republic, the silencing of their own language was economically devastating. Peasants bringing their crops or flocks to market in the larger towns were subject to arrest if they spoke Kurdish. As one observer notes, "The ban on speaking Kurdish turned the Kurdish peasants into a race of outlaws permanently at odds with the officials."

Language is the sturdiest feature of nationalism. Atatürk instinctively grasped this early in his dictatorship, and he saw, too, that sanctifying Turkish also meant degrading Kurdish. If Atatürk's Turkish-language reforms were among his most profound contributions to "Turkishness," his attempt to obliterate Kurdish eventually became the foundation of Kurdish nationalism—transforming Sheikh Saïd's reactionary revolt to regain the caliphate into a modern movement to reassert the basis of a distinctly *national*—and secular—identity.

The tribal rebellions persisted through the 1930s, in the bloodiest of which, in Dersim province, which the Kemalist regime renamed Tunceli, the army's reprisals may have taken 40,000 lives. A period of quiescence ensued, but began to fade in the late 1950s. Poverty in the Southeast was growing worse; successive governments in Ankara ignored the economic needs of the area, and the unhappy results were increasingly evident as the rest of the country modernized and prospered. Agriculture was becoming more mechanized and traditional ways of life were gradually disintegrating, and this led to a steady migration of Kurds to cities, with few prospects for ready employment. A revolution in Iraq in 1958 returned

Mullah Barzani to the Kurdish northern area, an event that stirred Kurdish nationalism in Turkey as well. Some bloody incidents in Mosul between Kurds and Turkomen in 1960 and a scattering of protests against economic conditions in Sivas, in Turkey, suddenly raised the temperature of the latent conflict. The leader of the military junta, General Gürsel, declared that the "army will not hesitate to bombard towns and villages; there will be such a bloodbath" that the "rebellion" would disappear. Although far from public view, the Kurdish problem, in the mind of the Turkish military, had scarcely gone away. The generals would react to any sign of independence with overwhelming force and new restrictions on traditional Kurdish life. A series of laws were decreed by the military to advance assimilation, which again stirred Kurdish nationalism. At peaceful demonstrations against the laws in 1961, some 300 Kurds were killed by the military in the streets of Kurdish cities like Diyarbakir, Mardin, and Van.

The new constitution of 1961 opened political activity wider than ever in Turkey, and this miscalculation by the military rulers enabled a fresh Kurdish nationalism to flourish. Newspapers and journals in Kurdish appeared regularly (and were regularly banned and confiscated), and a Kurdish political party took form. Predictably, the fresh evidence of Kurdish assertiveness provoked a reaction on the Turkish right—a series of articles and books dehumanizing the Kurds, linking them to Armenians, and calling for "a solution as sharp as the sword."

The attack from the right may have spurred a Kurdish turn to the left. Through the 1960s, Kurdish nationalists were drawn to the Turkish Workers Party and other, less significant leftists for the simple reason that only the left recognized and validated their struggle. While most Kurds, and many even among those with a strong nationalist bent, were socially conservative—upholding the ways of traditional village and Islamic life—the embrace of the left was irresistible. A non-Soviet labor party, the Turkish Workers Party, actually declared openly in 1971 that there was a Kurdish people who were being repressed in Turkey, a stance which led to the disbanding of the party and the jailing of its leaders. But its impact on Kurdish activists was lasting. Nationalism can take many political forms, from extreme right to extreme left. Marxism was originally devoid of any nationalist tinge; the whole thrust of the ideology was to see conflict and "consciousness" through a class or economic lens. Later, Lenin and Mao used peasant nationalism as a substitute for the proletarian solidarity their preindustrial countries lacked, and, indeed, most "communist" uprisings in the twentieth century, from Vietnam to Cuba to Angola, were more nationalist outbursts against colonialism than they were proletarian movements beholden to Marx. But nationalism as a fulcrum of political organizing is hardly the property of the left, as Atatürk demonstrated with such clarity. The choice the Kurds made to align their nationalist struggle with the weak Turkish left was more than gratitude toward the parties that acknowledged their cause. It was a natural reaction to the overbearing rightist dogma that guided official Turkey—Kurdish nationalism as a reaction to Turkish nationalism—and to their desperate circumstances of abuse by large landowners, economic backwardness, and malign neglect. However they arrived at this choice, it was enormously fateful.

Throughout the late 1960s and 1970s, as political turmoil escalated throughout Turkey, the Kurdish situation became more desperate: impoverished, polarized, and unstable. Poverty intensified. Unemployment rose by 150 percent between 1967 and 1977. By the early 1990s, after repeated promises from Ankara of economic development, less than 10 percent of adults in the Kurdish Southeast had industrial jobs, and those tended to be in low-skilled industries like brickworks or mining; six out of eighteen Kurdish provinces had no industrial output to speak of; the rest contributed only 3 percent of Turkey's total industrial output. On the large landowners' estates, the peasants would work eleven hours a day for the equivalent of $2.00. Children would work alongside their parents if they survived the 30 percent infant mortality rate. Less than a third received a formal education; of women, less than one in five attended school.

The demise of viable agrarian life and the growth of the urban poor and unskilled youth radicalized large segments of the Kurdish people, who by the 1980s were at least 20 percent of the population of Turkey. However varied in social outlook and separated by tribes, dialects, and rates of assimilation, they were a people ripe for rebellious nationalism. Until the early 1970s, however, the outburst were peaceful protest, intellectual ferment, and dependence on a few Turkish intellectuals and unionists to express the Kurds' discontent. The Turkish government, as always alert to any signs of unrest, retaliated harshly after the military again seized power in 1971; the interior minister cited Kurdish militancy as one of three reasons for the coup.

Tepid Kurdish leadership and the repressive measures the State enacted in response drove a number of Kurds to more extreme forms of dissent. The signal event was the creation of the Kurdistan Workers Party, or PKK, in 1974 on the campus of Ankara University. The founder, a former student of the social sciences named Abdullah Öcalan, came from the revolutionary left and thought himself a Marxist. From the start, Öcalan modelled the PKK after other liberation movements that had earned the romantic devotion of young leftists the world over. Öcalan would not be shy about employing revolutionary violence: the "bourgeois" and their path, the Kurdish landowners and assimilated parliamentarians, the pleading for recognition—all had failed so miserably as to earn only contempt. "Its program was simple and radical," writes one observer. It is "the independence of Kurdistan as the prerequisite for the construction of an authentically communist society through the elimination of the middle class and the taking of power by an alliance of workers and peasants." Through the 1970s, the PKK seemed just one more radical group on the margins of Turkish politics. It was insular and nearly consumed with splintering and internecine conflict. By 1980, however, it was poised to respond to the pivotal event of the Turkish-Kurdish conflict: the coup on September 12 of that year.

For the outside world, the coup that was engineered by a reluctant military was bloodless, temporary, and necessary to restore order in a country riven by terrorists of all stripes. To the Kurdish people of southeastern Turkey, the generals' reign was a new wave of terror and repression that rivaled the sanguinary pogroms of the 1930s. While many Turkish militants of left and right were prosecuted, vast numbers of Kurdish nationalists were targeted. The new constitution promulgated by the junta and remaining in force today was skewed sharply to deter and punish Kurdish nationalism: the mere recognition of a distinct Kurdish identity was made a crime, and the Kurdish language was in effect outlawed. General Evren's statements at the time of the coup, which focused on keeping Turkey undivided, and the arrests and trials of so many prominent Kurds immediately after the military seized power clearly exposed the junta's primary, obsessive fear of Kurdish separatism.

The fear was made manifest by an astounding number of arrests. Overall, some 15,000 militants and activists—branded terrorists—were imprisoned during the junta. By the end of 1980, more than 32,000 suspected terrorists had been detained; by 1983, the official number reached 60,000. Unofficial estimates of arrested and detained were as high as 175,000.

Under the new powers the junta gave to itself, the detained could be held incommunicado for months (technically, up to ninety days, a limit honored often in the breach), and by the spring of 1981 there were 6,000 such detainees. It was stressed in the international press that the junta was pursuing left and right terrorists with equal vigor, but this assertion was superficial to the point of distortion. Not only were ten leftists and Kurdish militants prosecuted for every ultranationalist, but the growth of the latter faction was fostered by the military as an extralegal antidote to the leftist and Kurdish agitation.

For the Gray Wolves, as the Turkish ultranationalist groups were known, were not intent so much on changing their own government as on attacking non-Turks—much as fascist gangs have operated in Europe throughout the twentieth century, carrying out a program of violence against the ethnically impure or communistic. The Gray Wolves, who were linked to if not directed by Colonel Alparslan Türkeş and his National Action Party, were quietly sanctioned by the military as useful tools to attack the militants of the left. The center-right parties and the military might blanch at the Gray Wolves' depiction of their enemies as "people who are racially degenerate, villains, whose origins are not known and who are not Turkish." But they agreed, in effect, with the goal to eliminate these "enemies from within."

So this useful mythology of the coup—that left and right were being equally prosecuted by the junta—masked the terrorism of the Gray Wolves *before* the coup—which, in turn, had created a climate of insecurity leading to the military's seizure of power. It was that violence *between* left and right that was used to justify the generals' overthrow of the democratic government. The daily killings appeared to be the result of an "anarchy" that the civilian leaders simply could not contain.

The junta, by its own reckoning, arrested some 1,800 members of the PKK. By some estimates, the junta jailed as many as 80,000 Kurds. Although they were the main target of the military, the PKK had begun to go underground before the coup—Öcalan himself had gone to Syria—and were less easily apprehended once the coup was in full fury. But the Turkish army was nonetheless dedicated to crushing Kurdish separatism: despite the "threats" from Greece, the Soviet Union, and revolutionary Iran, and the occupation of northern Cyprus, fully two-thirds of Turkish land forces were deployed in the Southeast during the junta.

The brutality of the military regime toward the Kurdish activists was not unprecedented—the retaliations of the 1930s were as harsh—but its ferocity was new to the generation of Kurds who had developed a sense of Kurdish secular nationalism and entitlement. Ramazan Ülek, the Kurdish activist, was both typical and atypical of this new generation. He was typical in his search for an identity beyond that of a "Mountain Turk." He was unusual in his intelligence and drive; he went on years later to found the dissident newspapers *Özgür Gündem* ("Free Agenda") and *Özgür Ülke* ("Free Country"). In 1980, as he remembered it, he was under the influence of the quasi-socialist ideas that somehow provided the theoretical framework for his restless yearning. Ramazan's taste for Marxism, his proselytizing among his village people, his youthful idealism—these were all typical of the Kurdish nationalism of the time. It was vaguely pink—"I went to the Southeast in 1979," recalled a scholar, Doghu Ergil, "and when I heard the *Internationale,* I knew something was afoot"—but mostly it was a search for identity. For the vast majority of these young Kurds, that search was nonviolent. But violence suddenly entered their lives.

A couple of months after the September 12 coup, I was detained in my home town and kept incommunicado for fifty-seven days," Ramazan remembers. "I was electrocuted in my genitals and hung on 'Palestinian hangers,' naked and blindfolded, and beaten on the soles of my feet. My jailers said, 'You are defending the PKK.' I told them I was not associated with PKK, but they forced me to sign a statement that linked me with eight murders. They never produced any proof of my guilt. It was nonsensical.

"I was very open with them in court about my being a Kurd and believing in freedom of speech for Kurds. They said, 'This is what the PKK believes!' They got a former PKK member to accuse me. I got a sentence of twenty-four years. In Diyarbakir Prison."

The prison, in the main city of the Southeast, had been notorious for some years as a place where the principal Kurdish militants were incarcerated. "The prison situation was worse in the military regime," said Mahmut Tali Öngören, a prominent human-rights activist in Ankara. "There were 640 prisons, and none obeyed UN standards. Torture was implemented mainly in prisons. (Now it's more in police headquarters.) Diyarbakir prison was notorious for torture—doctors, lawyers, many non-PKK." Anyone who sympathized with Kurdish identity was suspect, and many were sent to the prison.

Ramazan Ülek was one such activist, professing innocence of the crime but serving his sentence all the same. "We were placed in tiny cells, sometimes twenty people. The guards would ask us, 'Are you a Turk or a Kurd?' I always said 'Kurd,' and that would provoke a violent beating. They gave us no food and no beds when we were put into solitary confinement; they barely gave us enough food to keep alive—a very small portion of bread and rice, maybe a palmful, each day. I was all skeleton then. The guards would pour water on the floor at night in the cold winter where we were sleeping. They would hit us with sticks. We'd ask them, 'How can you do this? Where is your humanity?' And they would say, 'If you were a Turk we'd let you go.' We had to recite Atatürk's oath, 'How happy it is to be a Turk,' and sing the Turkish military songs and learn Atatürk's testament, line by line: it was a form of brainwashing. They'd want you to repent and confess on television, to say we were fooled by the Soviets to believe there was a Kurdish people, and say 'I am a Turk.' They wanted to conquer our soul."

The Kurds of Diyarbakir Prison had virtually no links to the outside world. To protest their treatment, they would stage hunger strikes, taking no food at all, and "death strikes," taking nothing at all; in 1984, a death strike resulted in a dozen fatalities. In 1982, a group of four prisoners burned themselves to death, declaring their loyalty to the Kurdish people, huddled together, shouting slogans as they died.

"Diyarbakir was a laboratory for torture all over the world," Ramazan explained. "I never imagined I would get out alive. There were many times I wanted to die. I witnessed such atrocities. I saw a lot of courageous acts in court and in prison. The reason I survived [was] because I never regretted what I had said or done. Perhaps this was a phase of history, a sacrifice that had to be made. As a member of the Kurdish people, this was my mission."

His eyesight failing from the hunger strikes, his body scarred by beatings, Ramazan Ülek was released after ten years in Diyarbakir Prison. As he discovered upon his return to Istanbul, the cause of Kurdish nationalism had been transformed during the long night of his incarceration. The "rebellion" in 1980 and during the remainder of the junta's rule amounted to no more than scattered outbursts of violence against landlords, tribal chieftains, and the Turkish police and military. But the PKK was successfully awakening much of the rural Kurdish people to see their oppression in a new way, the way of Marx, which reoriented all the explanatory signposts of their world. The abusive landlord—sometimes Turkish, sometimes Kurdish—was part of a larger system buttressed by state military power. The old social organization of tribe and village, the local authority of tribal chief and Muslim 'ulama,' had done nothing to relieve the intensifying misery of the Kurdish provinces. The military junta banned all use of the Kurdish language, Kurdish songs, Kurdish names. To this insult was added the injury of worsening poverty.

The PKK addressed the deepening despair in the Southeast on new grounds, and was slowly taking hold. Starting in 1984, the rebels punctuated their propaganda with selective acts of violence—attacking in small bands at isolated targets—and while the ruthlessness of the attacks frightened and alienated many Kurds, others were drawn to the sense of power the PKK conveyed.

The guerrillas mainly turned their wrath on the "village guard" system, instituted by the military in 1985. This system, modeled on counterinsurgency tactics employed in other countries like Guatemala, rests on a simple logic: recruit locals into an armed constabulary to protect their villages against the insurgents; this invests the villagers in the system while protecting the regular army from the rebels. The money offered to those who joined was very generous. Still, recruitment was often forced and harsh. Kurdish men in the villages, when confronted by the army, had no choice but to join or be vulnerable to reprisals. "I lived in a village of sixty houses," a thirty-three-year-old Kurdish woman from near Mardin recalled, "and of these, six families were targeted by the government because everyone else was a village guard. The others were forced to become village guards about two years earlier, and some were tortured to take up arms. We refused to do so. One morning at five o'clock the special teams of military came and seized my husband. They beat him and took him to Mardin, where they kept him for twenty days. I went to find him and the prosecutor said they had released him, but he was never found. When I persisted they jailed me and beat me for the next several days. I was eight months pregnant. I lost the baby. I went back to my village, and a soldier came to my house the second day. He said, 'Don't worry that you lost your child, we'll make you another one.' That night, I gathered up my children and left the village." She ended up in Istanbul, supported by her ten-year-old son.

The village guard system bolstered the PKK, because many young men joined the rebels both to avoid joining the village guards and to protest the policy itself. The system turned Kurd against Kurd, which was one of its objectives. The PKK's assaults from 1987 to 1991 were vicious, going well beyond the strategic goals of intimidation and redress, and the extent of the terror and counterterror had a corrosive effect on the region. Victims of PKK killings included families of village guards and went beyond even those, to teachers of Turkish and other such innocents. The village guard system was weakened by the attacks, which brought in more military, raising the number of clashes between the guerrillas and the army as well.

Terrorism serves many purposes. Violence inflicted on civilian populations, a tactic going back at least to Oliver Cromwell's seventeenth-century savaging of the Irish, is a form of social control, more often practiced by whoever runs the military or police. But guerrillas employ it as one of the few tools available to them in the face of overwhelming state power, to convince the populace of their revolutionary daring. It provokes the military into ever harsher reprisals. It polarizes the villagers, forcing them to take sides. In this the PKK partially succeeded. Each year through the 1980s the civil war escalated. What was considered in the mid-1980s to be just another leftist group making trouble grew to be viewed by Turkish elites and public alike as a major insurrection. And it was. By 1991, the war's fatalities since the end of the junta totaled 3,300, with roughly equal shares attributed to PKK, Turkish security forces, and civilians.

Having achieved a measure of success—bringing Kurdish grievances to the fore of Turkey's politics—the PKK shifted tactics at the end of the 1980s to repair their relations with the Kurdish people and to explore the political options ever so slightly opened by a handful of Turkish politicians. The "Kurdish reality"—the fact of a distinct, oppressed people living in its midst—had just dawned on Turkey's conscience. But the military would brook no compromise or "political solutions." Reared on its overpowering dominance in the Southeast, the generals would attempt to quash the insurrection by armed force, and they were avidly seeking new arms to finish the job.

PART THREE

14

THE REAGAN LEGACY

Although few in Connecticut and the other epicenters of U.S. military production fully appreciated it, the end of the Reagan rearmament began long before the conservative icon retired to his ranch near Santa Barbara. Spending for the military started to slide in 1986, and only the lag in making contracts and delivering weapons kept the military economy buoyant through the remainder of the decade. Then, in October 1989, the Berlin Wall was torn down by thousands of Germans on both sides of the Iron Curtain, and with it fell the military contractors' hopes for the future.

With the winding down of the Cold War, which the disassembling of the Wall most clearly symbolized, a debate arose over the impact of the rearmament, the Reagan Doctrine, and military exports. The right wing, naturally enough, claimed victory and drew the lesson of military strength. But the examined results were not so kind. The Cold War was like a heavyweight championship fight in which two boxers slugged it out for many rounds before one of them dropped dead of a heart attack. It could be said, and most conventional wisdom had it, that the expired boxer was exhausted and thereby defeated by the survivor. But the autopsy showed systemic illness that would have felled the deceased rather soon anyway. Chortling over the dead body, in this light, seemed foolishly misguided.

It was especially misguided when we examine what the impact was on the other body—or on bodies politic around the world. The Reagan Doctrine was especially destructive. By the late 1990s, Central America was still reeling from the impoverishing consequences of the wholesale militarization of El Salvador, Guatemala, Honduras, and Nicaragua. Southern Africa, with Reagan shipments of arms to the violent insurgents in Angola and Mozambique, was ravaged by civil war and crime-ridden poverty, which endured for years afterward. Some six million AK-47's were floating around the region in the 1990s, easily purchased from the demobilized rebels the White House had created and supplied. The civil wars themselves had claimed more than a million lives. Places like Somalia, Ethiopia, and Cambodia were similarly afflicted.

The shining case, however, was Afghanistan. Billions of dollars were supplied to Pakistan to funnel into the Afghan mountains, where Islamic radicals were fighting the Soviet army's occupation. The strategy of bogging down Moscow worked to some degree, but the price was extraordinary. Afghanistan immediately descended into a decade of chaos, with tens of thousands more killed in the factional strife that followed the Soviet pullout. The country has since become the principal source of heroin in the world. Pakistan became infested by the worst sorts of fanatics from the *mujāhedīn* factions, and is still constantly besieged by those forces. Karachi's corruption was furthered by CIA tools like the infamous Bank of Credit & Commerce International (BCCI), which became a money conduit for drug and gun trafficking, bribe-giving and -taking, and other nefarious activities.

The training and supplying of the *"muj"* is the legacy that has had the most powerful impact on the region. The U.S.-supplied weapons—a thousand Stinger anti-aircraft missiles and three million Kalashnikov automatic rifles—are now for sale around the region, from Kashmir to Turkey and beyond. The AK-47 copies were purchased by the CIA from China, Egypt, and other places so as to be untraceable to the United States. Now, from the arms bazaars of frontier towns in Pakistan to the supply stores of Iran, these Soviet-style assault weapons are finding their way to Kashmir, Kurdistan, even Mozambique. The Stingers, which the CIA has tried to buy back, to no avail, are also rumored to be proliferating widely. The CIA's guns now stock the arsenals of Hezbollah, Algerian insurgents, and the PKK.

The "blowback" phenomenon was not limited to the spread of weapons, however, as the bombing of U.S. military facilities in Saudi Arabia proved. Islamic fighters all over the region, trained by the CIA in Pakistan, are now turned against the pillars of U.S. interests in the Middle East. Said one Reagan Doctrine enthusiast: "I don't think the United States realized what the consequences might be," that is, the consequences of providing millions of weapons to the most ferocious, most anti-Western Muslim fighters in the world.

More routine exports of weaponry reverberated powerfully, too, though they lacked the éclat of a John Le Carré novel. The F-16 deal to Turkey was the largest export of any weapon worldwide, and by 1989 the Fighting Falcons were in the skies over the Kurdish precincts of Turkey and Iraq. Supplies to Egypt, Jordan, Saudi Arabia, and Israel kept the arms race started during the Nixon years going at full steam. By 1988, exports to the Third World had risen to $12 billion. Secretary of State George Shultz was urging more exports, prompting one Florida congressman to ask on the floor of the House, "Don't we have any policy other than arms sales and Stingers?" One answer was the balance-of-power "diplomacy" in the gulf: covertly supply Iraq with weapons and military intelligence, while overtly giving it financial credits and political credibility.

The Reagan rearmament was most closely identified with the buildup of American forces, and here, too, the results of the 1980s were dreadful.

All the spending did not increase America's readiness as promised. Some knowledgeable analysts show that the amount of weaponry in the U.S. arsenal, the capability of that weaponry, and the training of our forces scarcely increased at all. Said one analyst: "The Reagan Pentagon has spent 150 percent more for armored vehicles than Carter did, but gotten only 30 percent more of them. Reagan has spent 90 percent more for missiles, but gotten only 6 percent more missiles; spent 75 percent more for aircraft, but gotten only 9 percent more." If readiness and technology were not obviously improving, the dollars flowing into the defense industry were obviously increasing. Among the biggest winners were the aerospace companies, which realized a 27 percent profit in 1984, to cite one typical year, considerably higher than the 11 percent earned by all manufacturing. Most of that money, moreover, went to products that were not consumable, but did pump wages into the economy at a record rate, going from 4.9 percent of the gross national product in 1979 to 6.6 percent in the late 1980s. Such spending exerted a strong inflationary pressure (more wages without more products to buy bids up prices), keeping interest rates artificially high and retarding nondefense economic activity by about one percentage point each year. The enormous budget deficits incurred for the rearmament also jacked up interest rates and swallowed capital that might have been used for civilian economic growth.

When the drawdown began shortly after Reagan rode off into the California sunset, the impact on the workers who had been drawn into the defense industry was stunning. More than a million jobs would disappear over the next several years. Thousands of subcontractors would be particularly hard hit, but the "primes" would also be rocked. One could regard this as a "normal" economic cycle, and note that the million disappearing jobs represented just one percentage point of total employment in the country. It was occurring just as the phenomenon of wage stagnation was discovered, and is one of that problem's main contributors.

Blue-collar workers at places like Sikorsky, Pratt, Lockheed, and the Stratford Army Engine Plant were paid a higher hourly wage than virtually anyone else in manufacturing. With the rest of the smokestack industries declining, military factories offered the last good assembly-line jobs left in America, especially in the Northeast. The laid-off sheet-metal workers, welders, machinists, engineers, and other skilled men and women would not easily find jobs elsewhere. They were the industrial backbone of the Cold War effort, and all the mythology of the "twilight struggle" accrued to them as well as the uniformed services. And they were unionized, with powerful representation in the Democratic Party to complement the natural sympathy for them found among more conservative politicians.

So the defense drawdown created unique pressures on politicians. Sudden large-scale job losses in a district are the most devastating possible political blow to a member of Congress, and such catastrophes are all the more shattering when the loss comes from a federal contractor. Representatives are expected to do something about such losses, and they are held accountable in ways that a large layoff from a private concern like IBM or AT&T would not stimulate.

The Reagan rearmament created these pressures and expectations. The endless speculation about how to soften the fall in military spending, how to maintain the "defense industrial base," how to retrain workers for manufacturing jobs that did not exist—all of this was the consequence of an unnecessary and costly buildup to defeat a foe who was tottering anyway.

By 1989, when the Wall came down and the Bush administration, no enemy of a strong military, was forced to cut procurement sharply, the politicians knew what lay ahead. Since few in Washington had the vision or courage to plan for an industrial transition to other kinds of manufacturing, the alternatives were only too apparent: layoffs or exports. To just about any politician, the choice was easy.

15

THE DEAL OF THE DECADE, PART ONE

One politician above all recognized the painful choices of the defense drawdown, and he did something about it. Connecticut's Democratic senator Christopher J. Dodd was, by 1989, one of the surviving liberal beacons in the long night of the Reagan presidency. He had returned to Washington fifteen years earlier with the Watergate class of 1974, a beneficiary of Richard Nixon's humiliation and his own family pedigree in Connecticut politics. The son of Senator Thomas Dodd, Chris was imbued with the reformist zeal of the New Frontier of Jack Kennedy and the liberal Catholic movements of the 1960s and '70s. After graduating from Providence College, he joined the Peace Corps and served in the Dominican Republic from 1966 through 1968. The Peace Corps was the type of formative experience that shapes a person's life: it crystalized his social concerns and committed him to an enduring involvement with foreign affairs. The law school at the University of Louisville, from which he graduated, appears to have been an afterthought: Chris Dodd was going into politics and would make a Kennedyesque mark on the world.

A less confident or engaged person might have walked away from politics. His father, a Nuremberg prosecutor who lost his first Senate bid to Prescott Bush, went to the Senate in 1959. A crusading anti-Communist but a friend of the working man, Tom Dodd was censured by the Senate for a minor financial scandal in 1967 and lost his bid for reelection in 1970.

The Senate censure was both unusual and embittering. But the younger Dodd's appetite for congressional life was whetted, and his opportunity came quickly: a Republican congressman in Connecticut's second district left to run for governor, and Dodd jumped into the race and won. Six years later, he stepped up to the Senate when Abraham Ribicoff retired, bucking both the Reagan victory and a conservative opponent, James Buckley.

In the ensuing eight years, Chris Dodd forged a political profile on an eclectic range of issues—children and families, banking regulation, and Central America among them. Behind him were a divorce, years of night-life escapades with Senate pal Ted Kennedy (he was once described as "part of this city's carousing political royalty"), and any plausible worries about the safety of his Senate seat. With his shock of prematurely gray but still stylishly long hair and his short but energetic figure, Dodd easily conveyed an image of feistiness, intelligence, and principle—not unlike the Kennedy brothers. He was devoted to the Senate—a devotion that perhaps stemmed from his father's disgrace—and harbored no apparent ambition for the White House or cabinet posts.

When Prescott Bush's son George became president in 1989, Dodd sensed some new opportunities, and new dangers as well. The opportunities arose from the perception that the harsh ideological bent of the Reagan White House was over, and more modulated policies on social programs and foreign affairs were in the offing. Chris Dodd was one of the few Senate Democrats to support John Tower, Bush's tattered nominee for secretary of defense, a vote widely believed to have been given not just in a spirit of cooperation but because Tower, a longtime senator from Texas, had backed his father Tom in his censure imbroglio. That summer, Chris Dodd gained more attention by another magnanimous gesture toward the new president—a willingness to give Bush's policy in Central America a chance to succeed.

Throughout the 1980s, Dodd was a trenchant critic of Reagan's anti-Communist crusade in Central America—the *contra* war in Nicaragua, the virtual occupation of Honduras as a military staging ground, and support for military heavies in Guatemala, Panama, and El Salvador. By 1987, when he gained the chair of the subcommittee on Latin America in the Foreign Relations Committee, Dodd had easily established his *bona fides:* he was a Peace Corps veteran of the region, was fluent in Spanish, and had mastered the complex issues of aid, intervention, covert action, fitful negotiations, and the nature of rebellion and repression. He cut a path through the thicket of diplomatic politics, conducting his own policy heedless of the State Department; Oscar Arías once teased Dodd as "the president of Central America." In 1989, however, El Salvador became an ice-breaker for Dodd. Bush and his assistant secretary of state for Latin America, Bernard Aronson—a former Democratic Senate staffer and an apostate on the *contra* war—had cooled the vituperative rhetoric of the Reagan years and seemed to offer an olive branch, not just to the Senate Democrats but to those seeking an authentic peace process in the region. Dodd was willing, at the risk of his liberal credentials, to go along with unconditional U.S. aid to a new government in El Salvador, a position at odds with the almost routine practice of demanding compliance with certain human-rights provisions in exchange for aid. Dodd was apparently willing to give Aronson a freer hand if it meant that genuine peace negotiations would be the result.

That summer and fall, the hope for progress in El Salvador was overshadowed by the great swirl of events in Eastern Europe. The ungluing of Soviet hegemony over Poland, Hungary, Czechoslovakia, and East Germany rewarded the cautious faith that congressional Democrats had invested in Mikhail Gorbachev's reforms. Since Gorbachev's ascent to the post of General Secretary in 1985, conservatives had insisted he was a wolf in sheep's clothing. But now, with Stalinist diehards watching helplessly as their masses challenged the forty-year-old police states, Gorbachev's sermons about ending the Cold War became remarkably literal. Restraint was the watchword in both Moscow and Washington as the velvet revolution of the streets ran its astonishing course.

But the liberation of Eastern Europe had a dark side for Connecticut's economy, and Chris Dodd knew well what it would be. Popular demands for an end to the Cold War also animated American politics, demands for sharply reduced expenditures on the U.S. military and a transfer of Pentagon wealth to the kinds of social programs Dodd had long championed. The defense drawdown was already in train by 1989, and the core of the U.S.-Soviet rivalry—the military standoff in Central Europe—was quickly vanishing. The defense industry of Connecticut, United Technologies and Electric Boat in particular, was sure to be ravaged. And Chris Dodd's constituents expected him to do something to soften the blows.

Not many options were available. The procurement budget for U.S. weapons would soon come under new pressure. Already, the ballooning federal deficits of the Reagan years were rebounding against the Pentagon. UTC and other contractors could trim their sails, cut costs, and promote efficiency, but that invariably meant layoffs. Only one other tactic was conceivable: boost exports of weaponry. And to that end, Chris Dodd assembled his considerable parliamentary skills and went to work.

The main opportunity for Connecticut exports came from Ankara two years earlier. Turkish coproduction of the F-16 was finally in full swing, with the factory at Mürted geared to assemble the original lot of 160 fighter-bombers, and the FMC deal for armored combat vehicles had just been penned. So the Turks began to look ahead to their next major priority: military helicopters. They not only wanted to acquire a handsome fleet of choppers for their air force, but to make them as well, to wangle another coproduction partnership that would be based at Mürted after the F-16 bonanza had run its course. With the F-16s, the armored vehicles, an M-48 tank upgrade, and the new helicopter deal, Turkey would achieve much of the modernization it desired to complement its enormous armed forces.

On September 2, 1987, the major acquisition office of the Turkish government, the Defense Industries Development Administration (DIDA), issued a "Request for Proposal" for a buy of 335 helicopters. It was, DIDA officials said quietly, the first phase of an ambitious plan to coproduce 720 choppers. With its F-16s and other aircraft, such a fleet would give it unrivaled air power in the region, power greater than most of its NATO partners. It was a terrifically bold move, costing in excess of $3 billion, and instantly became, in the words of one American aerospace executive, "the deal of the decade." There had been little action in the late 1980s as many of the oil sheikhdoms in particular pulled back from their profligate buying spree of a few years before; oil prices had slumped, after all, and only the Al Yamāma aircraft deal being cooked up in Saudi Arabia (later hailed as "the deal of the century") would overshadow the Turks. But this would be, without a doubt, the largest international sale of helicopters in history.

Ankara's "requirement" resulted from DIDA's calculations, completed the month before, which envisioned 252 light reconnaissance helicopters (like Bell's Kiowa Warrior), 73 attack helicopters (like the Apache or Cobra), 41 cargo helicopters, and 6 antisubmarine helicopters plus 23 more for training; the largest element were the 325 multipurpose choppers, which would be for transport of troops and would have attack and reconnaissance capability. All but a few would go to the military and its national police force, the Jandarma. The Request for Proposal, or RFP, called for the delivery of ten multipurpose helicopters "as soon as possible" for the Jandarma, with a large share of the remaining 315 choppers to be assembled in Turkey. The multipurpose aircraft were front and center in the 1987 RFP, as those were seen as the most versatile and the best candidate for co-production.

As expected, this RFP was a strong magnet for every major helicopter maker in the Western world. Sikorsky and Bell would bid for the contract, as would four European makers: the French firm Aérospatiale; Messerschmitt-Boelkow-Blohm of Germany; Italy's Agusta; and the Westland Group in Britain. Only Bell had much experience in Turkey; it was its Model 205, a version of the Huey built for the U.S. army between 1963 and 1967, which was to be replaced in the Turkish arsenal, and Bell would again offer its newest Huey this time. But by 1987 the Huey had been surpassed in the American air-assault world by the Black Hawk. Given the Turks' propensity for American weapons, the Black Hawk was the early favorite to win the contract.

One key to the RFP was the way local production would be set up. How many of the multipurpose helicopters could be assembled in Turkey? How much "local involvement" with Turkish subcontractors would be offered? The contract would also demand an offset agreement, "any sort of involvement of Turkish companies," said a top DIDA official. Given their experience with the F-16, the Turks were determined to gain an enormous offset, possibly as much as 100 percent of the helicopter price, an expectation which one European dealer called "a little excessive." But offsets were becoming a standard practice of the international arms trade, and the Turks were riding the wave of a buyer's market.

The other pivotal aspect of the deal would be financing. The Turks needed the whole package to be underwritten by private Western banks or the government of the winning entry. Conceivably, the offset, if indeed as large as 100 percent, could comprise part of the financing package, but other schemes would suffice. Altogether, it was a cheeky plan, but given the sour market and the gradual demise of the Cold War—Reagan and Gorbachev were then negotiating a treaty to reduce conventional forces in Europe—the Turks were holding all the aces.

But they weren't holding enough cash, and the deal had to be delayed and reconfigured. As one American defense official put it, "They had

10,000 priorities and no money." Some fourteen months after the original RFP was due, the Turkish defense minister was in London telling the Britons that Turkey was keen to diversify its defense dependency—heretofore a dependency on the United States—and hoped to go forward with the helicopter sale in that very year, 1989. He said Turkey hoped to be building whole weapons systems by the late 1990s, and to be exporting them throughout the region. The F-16s and assault helicopters, plus some Stinger short-range missiles and the armored vehicles, were all part of that vision of Turkey as a major arms merchant.

The next phase of the deal came down in 1989. At an early May arms bazaar in a dusty field west of Ankara, Vahit Erdem, DIDA's president and the chief architect of Turkey's rotorcraft dreams, told a small gathering that a new RFP would be issued in June, reflecting a more modest idea—the coproduction of 200 multipurpose choppers. The big scheme, the 720-copter buy, was on hold, he said, which was not a revelation to the frustrated industry that had once again been jerked around by DIDA's fits and starts. (Hints of the larger plan, however, would still resurface periodically over the next few years.) "It's a long and discouraging process," one industry chieftain at the arms fair lamented, "and if you aren't willing to make a long-term commitment, you might as well pull out immediately." Another delay followed, with the RFPs set back to December and a decision from the Turks not due until mid-1990.

The downsized helicopter deal looked rather certain, however, and it had the industry salivating. "The figure of 200 is a guarantee we are giving to the industry for the initial contract," Erdem said in July. It remained the largest deal in the world for helicopters. Sikorsky was still the leading candidate, but the defense minister's words about diversifying Turkey's military imports was worrisome. So, too, was the financing dimension, because with the multibillion-dollar F-16 and FMC deals already under way, the cash in the Pentagon's kitty for financing new projects for Turkey was scant. As a result, the copter deal was a commercial rather than a government-to-government transaction. Turkey was earmarking only $400 million for the purchase, a woefully small figure. Clearly, other financing mechanisms would have to be found—or created.

That was the task for Chris Dodd in the summer of 1989. His clout in the Democratic-controlled Senate was considerable, but the climb was uphill: not only was there precious little will to increase the budget for military exports, and not only were the Greek and Armenian lobbies certain to protest any favors for Turkey, but the financing scheme Dodd put on the legislative table was a brash gambit likely to earn the opposition of many Democrats and possibly the Bush administration as well.

Dodd proposed to open the coffers of the Export-Import Bank to "guarantee" a private bank loan for the helicopter purchase. A guarantee is, as it sounds, a backstop for a bank loan should the borrower default. Eximbank, as it is known, provides many such guarantees as part of its normal business. It was created in the 1930s to help find financing for American exports, particularly to countries that seemed dicey to the risk-averse banking community. The Soviet Union was one of the main targets of Eximbank activity following World War II, but the program grew to include dozens of countries around the world. It was always a bit controversial; free-marketeers saw it as an unnecessary artifact of the New Deal and tried repeatedly to kill it off. But Congress, mindful of the small-business constituency that was always powerful in home states, kept it alive.

It was precisely that set-to between the administration and Congress that arose again in 1989. President Bush proposed to "zero out" the budget for Eximbank, but Congress was determined to keep it afloat. There was some mild concern that the Bank was undercapitalized at the time, with too much credit extended, thus the possibility of mounting costs to the taxpayer for bad loans. But defaults in fact were few, and Congress was not about to let one of its few tools for economic growth die on the vine.

Dodd tried in several ways to attach riders to bills to open the Eximbank to the Turkey deal, with, of course, Sikorsky in mind as the contractor likely to gain Ankara's favor. His seats on the Foreign Relations Committee, the Budget Committee, and the Banking Committee provided access, but his efforts could get no traction and the bills failed. Finally, nearing the end of the session, he hit on a winning strategy: quietly amend the bill for Foreign Operations and Export Financing, which appropriates funds for Eximbank.

Much of the power in Congress is held by the appropriations committees; it's "where the rubber hits the road" in fully exploiting the legislative prerogative. Congress holds the purse strings, and while other committees can demand policy changes and enact regulations, investigate and extol, it is the control of money that drives the government. By tinkering with that engine, Dodd could most effectively fuel Sikorsky's bid for the helicopter deal.

The foreign operations bill for fiscal year 1990 was passed by the responsible subcommittee on September 11. When the panel convened a few days earlier, chairman Patrick Leahy of Vermont described their task: "We have seven pounds of requests to put in a five-pound bag." Foreign aid was a way to burnish one's credentials with ethnic constituencies, and the events in Eastern Europe—that very week, thousands of East Germans were fleeing through Hungary to the West—meant that new demands for aid to those countries would soon be on the table. Leahy also anticipated a floor fight on the more controversial aspects of the legislation: aid to El Salvador and U.S. funding of the United Nations' vast work to stabilize the world's population growth.

The subcommittee reported its sharp disagreement with Bush's attempt to defund Eximbank, and actually raised the Bank's authority for loans and guarantees from $14.4 billion to $15.2 billion. They lamented the large outlays for military assistance, too, which totaled $4.7 billion, down from their peak of $7.7 billion in 1984. Much of the report commented on various human-rights concerns as well, though notably unmentioned were Turkey and Iraq.

The Senate was acting on the House bill, H.R. 2939, covering the same agencies, and as the committee's rewritten version came to the floor of the Senate some passages from H.R. 2939 were deleted and other provisions added, as is customary. Dodd's financing scheme was not discussed in the committee report, but when the bill came to the floor, introduced by Senate majority leader George Mitchell on September 19, the Dodd amendment had been inserted. It was surprising that it elicited so little attention, because the provision was virtually unprecedented.

Eximbank had long eschewed financing military exports. It prided itself on being a purely commercial enterprise helping small businesses, and the military hardware sold abroad was neither small nor commercial. Even though the State Department would retain the authority to license any export financed by any means, government or private, the involvement of Eximbank was widely seen as grossly inappropriate. The Pentagon had several mechanisms to underwrite weapons exports, including loans and outright giveaways. Eximbank was supposed to be nonmilitary, and opening it to the defense industry was asking for trouble, not least the howls of protest certain to emanate from commercial businesses. A purchase of 200 Black Hawks could cost Turkey $2 billion, and a loan guarantee of that size would soak up a large portion of the Bank's resources.

Dodd did not sit on the Appropriations Committee, and so he had to wrest cooperation from someone who did. And it had to be someone who could bring some votes with him, for there was sure to be skeptics, not least some key members of his own party. He found an ally in Senator Robert Kasten of Wisconsin, the ranking Republican on the subcommittee, who offered the amendment for Dodd in full committee. An aide to Kasten later said the senator "believed in the purpose of the legislation." Leahy and others reportedly opposed the amendment, but Dodd lobbied his colleagues assiduously, and it passed.

When the bill was read on the floor of the Senate, the simplicity of the wording of Dodd's addition belied its significance. Under Title IV, "Export Assistance," it provided Eximbank with loan-guarantee authority that "may be used by the Bank to participate in the financing of commercial sales of defense articles and services destined for NATO countries." It would have been too bold to write Turkey exclusively into the bill; the Greek lobby would have crushed such an attempt, and the broader reference to NATO was more palatable.

The next day, September 20, 1989, the Senate debated the foreign-operations funding after its traditional "morning business," the period when senators extol the virtues of home-state heroes and randomly offer comments on a wide range of topics. As he did every day, Daniel Patrick Moynihan of New York rose to note the continuing captivity of Terry Anderson, the American being held hostage in Beirut by Islamic militants; it was day 1,649. Patrick Leahy paid tribute to poet Robert Penn Warren, who had died in Vermont the previous Friday. And Chris Dodd likewise spoke of the passing of New England hotel magnate Walter Dunfey.

The foreign-ops bill was then opened for debate by its floor manager, Leahy, who directed attention to the controversial aspects of the legislation: a cut of $12 million from Bush's request of $97 million in aid to El Salvador (to which Dodd spoke at length); the U.S. contribution to the UN's population-control activities, particularly the hot-button issue of coerced abortions in China; and a new provision, to prohibit soliciting other governments to undertake activities that are against U.S. law, or, in Leahy's pointed words, to prevent "another rogue operation like the madcap Iran-

contra fiasco." Remarkably, the Dodd amendment stirred no comment on the floor at all, and the bill was passed as amended on September 26.

The easy ride of the amendment faltered later that autumn. As with most appropriations bills, the House and Senate versions differed and those differences had to be resolved by a conference committee, with members from each chamber appointed to hammer out a compromise. The Dodd amendment was decidedly unpopular with the House, and most unpopular of all with David Obey, the Wisconsin Democrat who chaired the foreign ops subcommittee. Obey, then fifty-one, was known as a fiercely principled congressman who openly disliked weapons exports and was ready to sink Dodd's plan. His 20 years in the House had given Obey stature and skills, and a conference committee, with an enormous workload and compromise an hour-by-hour necessity, was a perilous place for any amendment so disliked by one of the cochairs. Eximbank also registered its dismay. Bank president John D. Macomber wrote to Obey on October 10 urging the conference committee to reject the measure: "Bank financing of such sales would represent a major departure from U.S. government policies. As you may recall, a similar proposal was considered and rejected earlier this year by every relevant agency within the Administration."

The conference began on the first of November, and in the following days the 295 differences in the legislation were whittled away. The arduous work climaxed on a historic night: across the Atlantic, in the very crucible of the Cold War, Germans from both sides of Berlin had opened the Wall and were passing freely through the melting Iron Curtain. "But inside their closed room in the Capitol," said one report, "members of a House-Senate conference committee spent the evening of November 9th haggling over the U.S. foreign aid program." The late-night session lasted six hours, but agreement was finally reached.

One of the sticking points was Dodd's amendment. Obey strongly objected, saying that such a major change in Eximbank practice should be handled by the authorization committees, not appropriations. Representative Dean Gallo, a New Jersey Republican, also worried aloud about the possibility of defense contractors muscling out small businesses for the Bank's limited resources. But the amendment survived. "After several hours of work by Dodd and others," reported *Congressional Quarterly*, "Obey relented on Nov. 9 and agreed to what he insisted was a 'one-time' exemption" for the loan guarantees.

The wrangling was heated. On another measure prompted by Louisiana Democrat Bennett Johnston, who wanted money for a "leadership center" for Louisiana State University, Obey challenged the pork-barrel move. Johnston derided Obey for being "pure" and quipped: "I'm not for good government. I'm for pretty good government." Dodd employed a similar tactic. "He made it into a jobs issue," said one Senate staffer close to the debate. "Dodd took it very personally as a jobs and constituency issue. Typically, Senate protocol demands that such a request be approved."

Obey was incensed, however, and he vented his anger over another provision, a Bush ploy to convert all military aid from loans to grants. Of two likely beneficiaries, he cried, "Why do we want Greece and Turkey to get more weapons? They're blackmailers. They're ripping us off."

Dodd was not alone in his efforts. "It was done totally at the behest of United Technologies," said an aide to one of the measure's opponents. Lobbying was exerted with the usual logic—promote jobs, help our friends around the Aegean—and the Administration, while wary, voiced no opposition. But the surface calm hid a swirl of controversy behind closed doors. "It was an extremely emotional fight," said a Senate aide.

When the conference committee finished its work, the public stance of the legislators remained muted; the House conference report noted the change in their bill and declared that "the conferees have agreed to allow, on a one-time basis only" the loan guarantees for weapons sold to Turkey or Greece, and that "in the future such proposals shall be resolved through the appropriate authorizations bill"—meaning, that is, that such a policy change needed to be debated in the House Foreign Affairs Committee, or its counterpart in the Senate, rather than in the appropriations committees. When the foreign-ops bill came to the House floor on November 14, Obey dutifully moved "to recede from disagreement" with the Dodd amendment. Oklahoman Mickey Edwards, the GOP's ranking member on the committee, asked for unanimous consent. The presiding officer asked, "Is there objection to the request from the gentleman from Oklahoma?" And, with all present maintaining the decorum of the chamber, there was none. It passed the Senate the next day.

Later, Dodd was accused of trading his vote on El Salvador policy to Kasten in exchange for Kasten's insertion of the Eximbank amendment. Dodd angrily rejected the charge of log-rolling, but the perception stuck. His support of Administration policy became decidedly more uncomfortable when six Jesuit priests in San Salvador were murdered by the military on the night after the Senate approved the bill. His reversal of his El Salvador position, back to outright opposition the next year, made his vote on September 20 look a lot like a "one-time exemption."

Dodd was pressuring the Eximbank as soon as his amendment was passed. Eximbank chief John Macomber reacted in an unusually strong note to President Bush: "You are likely to hear from Chris Dodd about his unhappiness with the Eximbank policy not to finance the sales of military equipment to Turkey," he warned on December 11. The Dodd amendment, he told the president, "is purely budget gimmickery as a way to circumvent reductions" in the Pentagon's export financing program. "The UTC transaction," he concluded, "will set a bad precedent."

The Dodd amendment was one of thousands of laws made that and every year which virtually escape notice of any kind, even though they can have powerful impacts. Another such provision in the same foreign-ops bill allowed "excess defense articles," those being removed from Central Europe in compliance with a new arms-control treaty with the Soviets, to be given away to "southern flank" NATO countries; these were articles like the tanks and attack helicopters that found their way to Turkey and Greece. This, too, earned little attention. Apart from the *Congressional Quarterly,* which covers legislation week by week, the dramatic change in Eximbank policy wrought by Dodd's gambit went unreported in the news media in 1989.

That media silence changed the following year. The first sign of trouble rose in April 1990, when the Turks purchased five utility helicopters from the French firm Aérospatiale. The French chopper, called the Super Puma, was chosen over the Black Hawk. And while it was a small sale, it sent a signal to Stratford and Washington. "According to an industry executive here," explained a report from Ankara, "the Super Puma's selection over the Black Hawk for this off-the-shelf purchase is an indication that the future utility helicopter procurement project will be much more competitive." Aérospatiale was also merging with the top German maker of rotorcraft, making it a more formidable foe: French and German politicians would be pressuring Ankara together, and they held a very high trump card in Turkey's hope to join the European Union.

One way to keep Sikorsky competitive was to ensure that the U.S.

Army kept buying the Black Hawk. For the first time, the entire Connecticut delegation—six representatives and two senators—began to meet weekly that June to assess the defense drawdown and how to protect their state's industry. Their first act was a letter to Defense Secretary Richard Cheney pleading the Black Hawk procurement. "We're talking about the universe in Connecticut here," Dodd told a reporter. "It's a whole new world we're dealing with." But the delegation had an uphill climb. A former congressman from Sikorsky's district, Robert Giaimo, underscored the trap Connecticut's lawmakers were entangled in. "It's a liberal delegation," said Giaimo, who was lobbying his former colleagues for United Technologies. "It hasn't been overwhelmingly pro-defense, and other people who are pro-defense know that. If you vote No, No, No on a lot of defense things and then turn around and want help on a project that's built in your state, you don't get a hell of a lot of sympathy." The Black Hawk buy was saved, but the state's arms industry needed more.

Although the Dodd amendment of 1989 provided the financing Sikorsky needed to seal the deal with Turkey, the actual sale was slow in coming, and the provisions for loan guarantees could expire before Ankara made up its mind. So Dodd wanted to create a permanent mechanism in Eximbank to finance military exports. This time he offered an amendment to the Export Administration Act, which he did through his membership of the Senate Committee on Banking, Housing and Urban Affairs. In mid-July 1990 the committee was rewriting the Act to loosen restrictions on high-tech goods going to the old Warsaw Pact countries, and it was in this reformist atmosphere that Dodd pressed the measure on his twenty Senate colleagues.

The House banking committee had already acted, and its bill explicitly rejected military exports. The committee, stated its report, "is adamantly against involving Eximbank in financing defense articles." Such mechanisms, they insisted, should rest with the Department of Defense so as to draw on its expertise and not erode banking resources from commercial exports. It went further: a prohibition on manipulating Eximbank in this matter should be written into law to "prevent future exceptions." Another House bill from Obey's foreign-ops subcommittee also declared war on such exemptions. The Dodd gambit had slipped through the net of congressional scrutiny in 1989, but would not be so lucky in 1990. Attention would be paid.

When Dodd made his move in the banking committee on July 17, 1990, he immediately ran into opposition. He had a cosponsor this time, Missouri Republican Kit Bond. Propitiously for the duo, McDonnell-Douglas in St. Louis had announced a massive layoff the day before the committee vote—17,000 workers would lose their jobs. The two could argue forcefully that their amendment was about jobs and the need to match Europe's subsidized arms makers. "I would prefer, quite frankly, that all countries stop this process," Dodd told the panel, "but the hard facts and realities of life are that they're not about to do it in the short run."

The amendment had detractors. Paul Sarbanes, the veteran Democrat from Maryland, took the point for the opposition. A Greek-American widely expected to become secretary of state had Michael Dukakis been elected in 1988, Sabarnes was naturally a skeptic about Turkey. But he stood on other grounds. He contended that the Bank would be skewed away from commercial activities as a result of the Dodd scheme. "We will rue the day if we permit this policy to take effect," he told the committee. "We will rue the day if we continue to place American industry on an uneven playing field," Dodd retorted. And later he said that failure to pass his plan could "mean that a lot of these industries would end up going out of business."

The possible misuse of the arms sent to the allies was scarcely mentioned. "The Senator from Connecticut is worried about military sales to less-developed countries," John Heinz, a Republican from Pennsylvania, interjected. "Does that make the technology that some of our NATO allies from time to time use against uprisings any less awful?" His question was never answered.

The Bank itself was opposed. One of their officers explained that "we do not have the strategic and political type expertise to assess the implications of a military sale." When pressed by Heinz on the Administration's position, she said, "We do not have a consensus. This has been an issue of great debate over many months." Eximbank president John Macomber again complained in a letter to the committee that the provision would be a "fundamental reorientation of the Bank" and would "divert personnel from commercial export financing."

But the Senate committee did act. On July 17, the amendment was passed by a lopsided 16–5 vote. When it went to the Senate floor on September 13, 1990, it passed again, but it was headed for another conference committee showdown with the House.

Over the Columbus Day weekend, the conference committee on banking and housing began to merge the legislation. In order to rustle up votes for his amendment, Dodd was hoping to find House Republican support. He apparently decided to trade his vote on a key controversy: Representative Charles Schumer, a New York Democrat, was fighting a rearguard action by Secretary of Housing and Urban Development Jack Kemp to cut the appropriation for rental-housing construction by $500 million. Dodd sided with the Republicans, and Kemp's position prevailed. "Public housing advocates were puzzled by Dodd's refusal to discuss his reasons for opposing this program," said one report. A few days later, Dodd tried to convince Henry Gonzales, the House Banking Committee chairman, to support his amendment for Eximbank military exports. But Gonzales refused, telling Dodd in a note, "I think issues should stand on their own."

Dodd was beaten. The conference committee rejected his amendment, saying that the next Congress should examine the issue. The liberal senator from Connecticut had given away his vote to support housing for the poor and had gotten nothing in return.

"We had problems with the amendment because we were trying to adjust the imbalance between military and economic aid, and this was a new form of military assistance that would be made for economic reasons," a Senate staffer bitterly recalled. "There was a huge fight in committee, a huge fight on the floor, and a huge fight in conference over this. People didn't know how they were going to vote right up to the last minute. We saw it as a new way to export arms to the Third World. It became a jobs-versus-principles issue. Staff people stopped talking to each other for years over this."

Sikorsky still had its financing for the Black Hawk deal. But Chris Dodd's efforts did more than give Sikorsky a leg up to the Turkish contract. He opened the gate to other multibillion-dollar schemes to promote arms exports. He also revealed the lengths to which a senator respected for his principled stands on a range of foreign-policy issues might go to secure defense jobs in his home state. In the long run, the cost to rental housing subsidies or Salvadoran dissidents was probably greater than the gain for Sikorsky's workers. Those were the trade-offs forced on decision makers, then and now.

16

THE SECOND PERSIAN GULF WAR

With the Dodd amendment in his pocket, Jim Baker flew to Ankara on August 9, 1990, to recruit Turkey for a coalition to defeat Saddam Hussein. Dodd's scheme was one of several carrots the secretary of state offered Turgut Özal. In what became an arms-trade revel, Baker was meeting with all potential allies for a military confrontation to punish the erstwhile pillar of U.S. interests for his invasion of Kuwait one week earlier. Given its geography and NATO membership, Turkey was essential. Baker bargained with the Turks, including an offer of six Black Hawks, and the former Ottoman overlords of Mesopotamia eagerly joined up. Baker went on to other capitals with other offers in this extraordinary action to retrieve a small Arab monarchy.

The sharp contrast to America's response to Iraq's invasion of Iran ten years earlier was instructive. Kuwait and Iran shared some important similarities—they were both Islamic and held large reserves of oil. They were both regarded as undemocratic. The pivotal difference was their relations to the major Western powers. Kuwait, like Iraq, was "created" by the British after World War I. The dominant sheikhs of the area, the al-Sabah family, were anointed monarchs and ruled much as the House of Saud reigned over the larger nation to the south. Kuwait depended on Britain to conduct much of its business and diplomacy, and while it lent support to the Palestinian cause and was an eager participant in the OPEC price hikes, its geostrategic outlook was pro-Western. This central fact guaranteed that a far different set of responses would be set in motion.

As rash and horrifying as Saddam Hussein's invasion was, and however important Kuwait was as an oil exporter, the West's reaction hinged on two other considerations: Saudi Arabia and Israel. The possibility that Iraqi forces might push down the Gulf coast to the Saudi oil fields became a ringing alarm that moved the major Western powers to their first military response—fortifying the Saudi-Kuwaiti border. (President Bush's initial reaction was, indeed, extremely mild—"We contemplate no military intervention," he said—until Margaret Thatcher bucked him up.) Saddam Hussein in control of 60 percent of the world's oil was not a tolerable prospect. The danger to Israel was an unexpressed but highly motivating factor. Saddam had shown a vehemence toward the Jewish state that was truly scary—he had vowed just a few months earlier to "burn half of Israel" with chemical weapons. The Israelis had long identified Saddam as one of their mortal enemies: they had bombed Iraq's Osirak nuclear reactor complex in 1981 and had unblushingly aided the Ayatollah Khomeini in the Iran-Iraq war. A war that involved Israel and Iraq could alter the dynamics of the fragile peace existing between Israel and its Arab neighbors and ignite the entire region.

The United States, Britain, and France gradually deployed a sizable military force in Saudi Arabia while demanding Iraq's withdrawal from Kuwait, and through the late summer and early autumn the standoff hardened. Saddam dismissed UN resolutions and pleas from Arab leaders. As his recalcitrance became more apparent, the position of Egypt's President Hosni Mubarak, Jordan's King Hussein, and other friendly heads of state became agonizing. (Syrian president Hafez al-Assad was a longtime adversary of Saddam's and found the entire situation exceptionally convenient.) Could they side with the West against the self-styled inheritor of Nasser's mantle? The Saudis, in accepting the swift deployment of 100,000 U.S. troops, were in the most awkward position of all, allowing "infidels" into their country to protect the holy cities of Mecca and Medina.

Among the embarrassments was the impotence of the Gulf Cooperation Council, the alliance formed after the Islamic revolution in Iran to protect the littoral states of the Gulf—Saudi Arabia, Kuwait, the United Arab Emirates, Oman, Qatar, and Bahrain. The oil-producing Arab states had been exceptionally active buyers of U.S. military technology in the previous decade. But the acquisition of such firepower had done nothing to dissuade Iraq from invading one of their number and in effect threatening the remainder.

More significant in that autumn of 1990 was the splintering of Arab opinion about the confrontation in the Gulf. Saddam Hussein's action against an Arab brother, an unprecedented event, was an unvarnished affront to Arab sensibilities, but the amassing of an American and European military force against him turned the issue back to one of East versus West. Mubarak's position was particularly difficult. As the leader of the one country with a peace treaty with Israel and as a recipient of enormous amounts of U.S. aid and arms, he had to prove his Muslim *bona fides*. Egypt was chairing the Arab League, so Mubarak had an opportunity to find an "Arab solution" to the crisis, a diplomatic errand that none of the other principal players—notably the United States—wanted him to run. The chance for a mediated Iraqi withdrawal from Kuwait was scuttled early in the crisis: an Arab League meeting in August in Cairo passed a resolution, sponsored by Mubarak, to remove Iraq from Kuwait by force, if necessary—an unusually hasty and split decision. Mubarak explained that someone "was holding a gun to his head." The United States did not want a muddled game of negotiation that would open the door to division in what became the anti-Iraq coalition. Sharply defined lines of loyalty and position were preferable, in Washington's view, so the potential of Arab diplomacy was never tapped. Mubarak was the vehicle for the U.S. tactic.

As positions hardened during the autumn of 1990, Saddam articulated a powerful appeal to Arabs and taunted Mubarak. The confrontation, Saddam was saying, was about four things: the control of oil pricing and the redistribution of oil wealth from the sheikhs to the Arab people; the unity of the Arab world; the insult of Western, and especially American, imperialism in the region; and the liberation of Palestine. However disingenuous on the part of Saddam, each point undermined Mubarak: he too championed the sharing of oil wealth and, wearing the mantle of Nasser, what remained of pan-Arabism. The Camp David Accords with Israel rendered Egypt suspect on the Palestinian issue. And the thorny matter of U.S. imperialism ensnared Mubarak from the start; his regime was significantly reliant on U.S. support. His servitude to U.S. interests seemed to be confirmed when Bush canceled an outstanding $7 billion debt and Egyptian troops were deployed to the Gulf to defend the Saudis.

The U.S.-Egypt debt relief lent an air of the bazaar to the war's prelude. The Syrians were rewarded with the ceding of Lebanon and some $1 billion in oil revenues, financial aid previously held up by the fear of sponsoring terrorism, and direct compensation for dispatching troops to the Gulf. (The courting of Syria was an oddity, given its long hostility to Iraq.) Even the United States was to be compensated by the Saudis and Kuwaitis for its intervention. And everywhere in the region, the sale of weapons was proceeding furiously.

The centrality of oil created this mercantile climate. There were larger principles at stake, as President Bush constantly said, including the specter of an Iraq armed with nuclear weapons. But the assertion of values like nonaggression and sovereignty were thin veils for the powerful logic of oil, typified by James Baker's pithy response to the question of why the United States was deploying such a large force in Saudi Arabia. "Jobs," he said, meaning that the price and the supply of Gulf oil was a pillar of the American economy. By August 1990, world oil supplies were even more concentrated in the Persian Gulf than they were in 1973, and there were fewer new finds—like those in the North Sea and Alaska—coming on line. Despite the deregulation of petroleum prices in the United States, domestic oil production had plummeted in the late 1980s, and America was importing just as much oil as it was in the dark days of the first energy crisis. So when American lives were risked to guarantee a petroleum supply to the West, the peace movement's cry of "No blood for oil" resonated with surprising force. Their persuasive case nearly subverted Bush's plan to drive Iraq from Kuwait: in the weeks leading up to the beginning of the war on January 15, 1991, American public opinion was evenly divided on the wisdom of the war, and a Senate resolution to support the war passed by just five votes.

Operation Desert Storm proved beyond a doubt that the politics of oil and international security were closely intertwined, and that economic interests—however they were characterized—were driving foreign and military policy. The links between economic growth, profits, and jobs on the one hand, and the projection of U.S. military power on the other had long been a central tenet of both *Realpolitik* and its left-wing critique. But other rationales had frequently obscured this most salient feature of American globalism. The second Persian Gulf war revealed this feature more vividly than any major event in memory, in part because the Cold War had muddled America's motives for forty years. The threat of Soviet-style communism was not merely an affront to U.S. economic interests but a genuine scourge of political freedoms. Desert Storm instead demonstrated with total clarity that the imperatives of economic growth at home would necessitate military activism abroad, even if the two were not coordinated as such. Ordinarily the link was mainly visible in the arms trade; in the Gulf in the winter of 1991, it was visible as war.

The swiftness and lethality of Desert Storm briefly masked the chronic weakness of American policy in the Gulf. The tilt toward Iraq in the 1980s was widely and rightly cited as an embarrassing blunder, one that had continued without alteration into the Bush administration. Most egregious was the infamous meeting between Saddam Hussein and U.S. ambassador April Glaspie one week before the invasion of Kuwait, when she told the dictator that "we have no opinion on the Arab-Arab conflicts," and that Kuwait's oil pricing policy "is, in the final analysis, parallel to military aggression against Iraq." But the U.S. support and encouragement of Saddam had been in train long before Glaspie conveyed the good wishes of the president. Within a few months of taking office in 1989, staff of the National Security Council and State Department had drafted National Security Directive (NSD) 26, approved by President Bush, which set a policy remaining in force until August 2, 1990: "Access to Persian Gulf oil and the security of key friendly states in the area" were the two rationales of an outlook that would "pursue, and seek to facilitate, opportunities for U.S. firms to participate in the reconstruction of the Iraqi economy. . . . Also, as a means of developing access and influence with the Iraqi defense establishment, the United States should consider sales of nonlethal forms of military assistance." Said a senior official of NSD 26: "The concern over Iranian fundamentalism was a given." Over the course of ten years, Iraq had replaced Iran as one of the twin pillars of U.S. strategy in the Gulf, despite the clear nature of Saddam Hussein's reign of terror and his known ambitions to create a military hegemony in the area. An astonishing example of an absence of realism in a White House priding itself on just that quality, NSD 26 would have opened the door to a larger flow of financial and military support had not two events intervened: the discovery of the scandal centered in the Banca Nazionale del Lavoro (BNL) in August 1989, and Saddam's horrifying threat to Israel the following April.

Despite the uproar over Hussein's "burn half of Israel" speech and the media coverage of the BNL affair (or "Iraqgate," as columnist William Safire, linking it to Bush, insisted it should be called), the administration held fast to NSD 26 and the balance-of-power tilt toward Iraq until it collapsed with the invasion of Kuwait. "It pursued this policy in the face of overwhelming evidence," writes a historian of the policy, "that Iraq was violating human rights, using and producing chemical weapons, producing biological weapons, violating nuclear non-proliferation agreements, evading U.S. export controls. . . , utilizing illegal BNL loans for weapons procurement, and mismanaging and misusing" U.S. agricultural and financial credits.

The tactic of bolstering a tyrant to counterbalance or contain the supposed expansionism of a noxious ideology had a dismal record during the Cold War, and it failed U.S. policymakers again in the Gulf. The war was not just "politics by other means," but the abject failure of U.S. political leadership. The human costs of the war for Americans was low—a few dozen fatalities, with the mysterious "Gulf War Syndrome" causing by far the highest number of casualties—and the nation rejoiced in this rather shamelessly. The cost to Iraq should have been more sobering. Between 50,000 and 100,000 soldiers died, many of them in the infamous "turkey shoot" of retreating troops in the war's last days. More lasting damage was caused by the combination of the war and the decision to leave Saddam in power while imposing economic sanctions—that is, deprivation—on the Iraqi people. "The real victims of America's technical ingenuity were the children of Iraq," concludes Kanan Makiya, the dissident Iraqi author of *Republic of Fear.* Some 50,000 deaths and many more permanent psychological and physical traumas were visited upon Iraqi children. "More Kurdish and Shī'ī children died as a direct consequence of the American decision to target power stations and then wash its hands of Iraq, leaving them unrepaired," reports Makiya. "For the Middle East as a whole, UN officials estimate that nearly 5 million children risk spending their formative years in deprived circumstances as a result of the Gulf crisis." But these were "the other," a lesser race whose misfortunes were easily ignored.

The casualties of the enemy were of no consequence to the architects of the anti-Iran tilt, either; the war and its endgame was stirring other problems. It could not, and did not, address what American political elites saw as the key security challenge to Western interests in the region: the specter of Islamic fundamentalism. Many would argue in the aftermath of Desert Storm that precisely such a specter had actually grown up.

The first and clearest indication that war would exacerbate tensions between Islamic militants and the Western-oriented regimes of the Muslim world was visible well before the anti-Iraq coalition fired a shot. The splintering of pan-Arabism was one manifestation. The opposition to "Western imperialism" significantly took the form of an Islamist outburst, all the more remarkable in light of Saddam Hussein's own secularism and repression of Muslim activism. Large demonstrations in support of Iraq—some of them massive and frequent—broke out in Algeria, Tunisia, Yemen, Pakistan, Lebanon, the Palestinian West Bank, Jordan, Morocco, Egypt, Syria, and the Sudan. In several of these countries, official government policy on the war was altered to reflect the public's apparent revulsion at any pro-Western stance. In each place, local politics and previous alignments were at work, but the prevalence and breadth of "Muslim rage" was unmistakable. Years later it could not definitively be said that Islamic militancy gained appreciably as a consequence of the war, but there were plentiful signs that it had done so in Algeria, Egypt, Jordan, Pakistan, and Turkey, and among many Palestinians.

The conclusion of the war in Iraq further revealed the weakness of the U.S. strategy toward Iran. The rout of Iraqi forces was suspended as it became apparent that the collapse of Saddam Hussein's regime could usher in an Islamist alternative, possibly even a pro-Iranian Shī'ī government. An advisor to Bush explained to Congress that "Our goal is to get rid of Saddam Hussein, not his regime." Bush's infamous "call to arms" for rebellious Iraqis was disavowed when his advisers realized that U.S. support was expected for a revolt that was unpredictable in outcome. Although the coalition forces did provide a no-fly zone for the Shī'ī in southern Iraq after the war, this thin cover never approached the scale of protection afforded the Kurds in the north. (Even there, 25,000 Kurds died as refugees in the mountains and while resisting Iraqi forces.) Saddam's repression of the Shī'ī—who were seen, rightly or wrongly, as tools of Teheran—was largely unopposed by the coalition forces. Thousands of Shī'ī died in the *intifāda* against Saddam. Repression of Shī'ī in Saudi Arabia after the war also went forward without objection from Washington. In the end, the maintenance of governments hostile to Iran was the sum of U.S. policy, even though the cost—the continued presence of Saddam Hussein, most obviously—was exceptionally high.

From the vantage point of Washington, the inflaming of Muslim rage could be absorbed as a temporary phenomenon; the most important regional allies, Israel, Turkey, Saudi Arabia, and Egypt, would manage it and remain true to Western objectives. The shattering of Arab unity, in contrast, was a welcomed side effect. Along with the decline of Soviet influence, the disarray caused by Saddam and the war elevated American influence even higher than its awesome display of military prowess could have done alone. Among the beneficial results was a new momentum to resolve the Palestinian claims in the territories occupied by Israel. The Jewish state had acted with admirable restraint in the face of Iraq's wicked provocations, which included the infamous Scud missile attacks and the wildly pro-Saddam sentiment in the West Bank and Gaza. Israel emerged from the war with unprecedented strength. The Gulf monarchies, which had financially backed various factions of Palestinian militants, including Islamist insurgent groups like Hamas, were newly restrained. Syria was placated by its reward of Lebanon and chastened by the retreat of Soviet support. Jordan, squeezed by its untenable geography, had meekly sided with Saddam and was weaker than ever.

If the war's blow to pan-Arabism had its benefits, it was also likely to raise the prominence of other, non-Arab states in the region: Iran and Turkey.

Iran's benefit from the war derived from a studied passivity. The death of the Ayatollah Khomeini in June 1989 presented the possibility that Teheran would now transform itself from a revolutionary vessel into a more conventional ship of state. The strengthening of the radical mullahs and their "Trotskyist" urge to permanent revolution, stirred up by the war with Iraq, had waned. The toll of that war and the need to rebuild the country with bricks and mortar cooled Islamist fervor, and the political leader to emerge from the 1980s, Hashemi Rafsanjani, was reconstructing Teheran's ties to the outside world to end Iran's isolation. Some small conciliatory gestures toward the West were made in the short interval between the wars, but the barriers were high: Iranian anger over the U.S. siding with Iraq—and over the downing of an Iranian civilian airliner in July 1988—and the belief that the United States was planning a more aggressive attack on Iran, were not easily soothed; and Iranian-sponsored terrorism, including the recent murder of the Shah's last prime minister, kept U.S. policy leaders wary. The Americans had formed a strong friendship with Iraq in any case, and saw no need for rapprochement with Iran.

Iran's relations with the other Arab Gulf states were more complex. Saudi Arabia was particularly leery, fearing Shī'ī rebellion. Riyadh and Teheran traded vitriolic denunciations during the Iran-Iraq war, with each calling for the overthrow of the other's regime. The Saudis had, along with Kuwait, supported Iraq to the tune of $30 billion during the war. The enmity was not easily overcome, though some efforts to do so were delicately begun in the interwar period.

Iran found itself in unfamiliar geostrategic terrain when Saddam Hussein occupied Kuwait scarcely two years after the Iran-Iraq war ended. The suddenly altered position of Iraq presented both opportunity and danger for Iran. The Iranians played a remarkably cool game throughout the eight-month crisis. Rafsanjani was able to improve relations with Saudi Arabia, and his ties to the other Arab Gulf regimes also strengthened. Not least significant was Saddam's instant elevation to world's number one villain, replacing the ghost of Khomeini. His untenable isolation drove him to court Rafsanjani; he immediately revived the Algiers Agreement and made other overtures. Rafsanjani neither accepted Iraq's pleas nor joined the anti-Saddam alliance; he excoriated the presence of Western imperialists in the Gulf and at the same time offered to mediate. That offer was summarily rejected by President Bush.

The near-destruction of its ancient rival by Desert Storm instantly raised Iran's fortunes. Its trade relations with the West improved. Rafsanjani began a series of diplomatic overtures intended to demonstrate a more moderate course for the Islamic Republic. There were some minor, mainly rhetorical, gestures from the Bush administration as well, and for a brief moment it appeared that some reconciliation might be in the cards. But the radical mullahs still had a few trumps to play: continuing incidents of terrorism, mainly against Israel, sustained Iran's status as a "backlash state" unworthy of entry into the community of civilized nations. The triumph of the *mujāhedīn* in Afghanistan, growing Islamic militancy in Algeria, Egypt, the West Bank, and Pakistan (all, it was alleged, backed by Iran), and fears of an Islamist resurgence in the former Soviet republics all combined to stamp Iran with the stigma of "exporting revolution." When Rafsanjani quickened the pace of arms purchases to rebuild a military decimated by the war with Iraq, the alarms started ringing even louder in Washington. Iran was too menacing toward its Arab neighbors, said the conventional wisdom in Washington, too threatening to U.S. interests in the Persian Gulf. Despite the openings afforded by Khomeini's death and the Gulf war, Iran would officially remain a pariah state.

The outcome of the war for Turkey was also mixed. For seventy years, while yearning to be part of the West, Turkey maintained cordial, if fitful, relations with Iraq, Iran, and Syria, including neutrality during the Iran-Iraq conflict. Its links to Iraq were the strongest; the oil pipeline from Iraq to Turkish ports had been a lifeline for Iraq during the 1980–88 war, and Ankara remained one of Iraq's largest trading partners afterwards. Iraq and Turkey had cooperated in suppressing Kurdish separatism. And while there were festering disputes over the large dam projects in southeastern Turkey, which deprived Iraq of a reliable water flow from the Tigris and Euphrates—dams meant to bring badly needed irrigation to the Kurdish areas of Turkey—the disagreements seemed manageable. Iraq's militarism was worrisome to Ankara, but the leverage of Iraq's pipelines and water neatly counterbalanced such concern; there was little if any prospect of a military confrontation, given the historical absence of war between the two and the natural barrier of the rugged Taurus Mountains. Iran was somewhat more troubling: the Ayatollah Khomeini routinely criticized Turkey's secularism and supported Islamic groups in Turkey. But again the differences were not alarming, and a sizable military conflict—of which there had been none in the twentieth century—was nearly unimaginable.

When Iraq invaded Kuwait, Turkish president Turgut Özal recognized a unique opportunity. For forty years, Turkey's strategic role was scripted entirely around its proximity to the Soviet Union, and the decline of the Cold War promised the end of that drama. With his political position in Turkey shaky, Özal was ready to embrace Washington's vision of the anti-Saddam coalition. He masterfully pledged three key contributions to the American-led effort: he would close Iraq's oil pipeline, provide a platform for coalition attacks on Iraq, and deploy 100,000 Turkish troops on the Iraq border. In one stroke he confronted Iraq with a second front, deprived it of oil income, and endeared himself to the West.

Özal's actions stirred controversy in Turkey. The military's chief of staff resigned, worried about Turkey's capacity to go to war with Iraq. Some popular opposition also appeared, mainly from left-wing and Islamic elements, but as the coalition's case grew stronger, Özal grew politically stronger too. The war itself—with no Turkish casualties—seemed to reward his gamble handsomely. U.S. financial and military support rose. Turkey's case for entry into the European Union was enhanced. A new place in the geostrategic constellation seemed assured: with Iraq converted in one day from pillar of U.S. interests to outright enemy, Turkey's new stature in the region was apparent to all. Its prospects turned brighter still when the USSR disintegrated later the same year. The Muslim republics of the former Soviet Union, most of them with Turkic roots, would be targets for influence, with the West encouraging Turkey to keep them free of Iran's fundamentalist contagion. The prospect of an enormous new sphere of influence for Turkey stirred some long-dormant yearnings for empire, and the Turks began to take a more active military role in the neighboring dispute between the culturally Turkic republic of Azerbaijan and Christian Armenia.

The war also brought severe problems. The shutdown of the oil pipeline cost Turkey billions of dollars in revenue, depriving the impoverished Southeast in particular; the UN sanctions against Iraq were retained after Desert Storm, so the revenue losses persisted year after year, buffeting Turkey's economy. More acute was the chaotic Kurdish crisis at the end of the war. President Bush had called for a Kurdish rebellion against Saddam, so when the U.S.-led coalition quit the war short of Baghdad, Saddam turned his wrath once more against the Kurdish peoples in the north. Two million Iraqi Kurds fled across the border into the Taurus Mountains of Turkey. Özal pleaded with the United States to intervene, and world opinion, aghast at yet another abandonment of the Kurds, forced Bush's hand. A safe zone was created and enforced by Western military forces, and a massive humanitarian-relief effort was mounted. The immediate crisis passed as many refugees returned to Iraq and Saddam retreated.

But the aftermath was hardly satisfying to Turkey. A new political entity, a semi-autonomous "Kurdistan," was now coalescing on its southern border; enabled by U.S. military power, it threatened to inflame Kurdish separatism in Turkey as well as in Iraq. New attention was focused not only on the plight of the Iraqi Kurds but on the Turkish Kurds and their long-festering grievances. The creation of a Kurdish entity enabled the PKK to operate with impunity from northern Iraq. A seemingly open-ended military initiative by the U.S.-led coalition to protect the Iraqi Kurds, Operation Provide Comfort, was based in Turkey. So the outcome of the war was a net loss for the Turks: the rise in stature was not bankable, while the sudden loss of trade and the sharp escalation of the "Kurdish problem" were all too real. The U.S. tilt toward Iraq, aimed to hurt Iran, was now harming another American ally on Iran's periphery, a wound that would not heal throughout the 1990s.

Whether as a response to Iran or simply from a natural desire for profits, the arms business picked up after Desert Storm and again became a most prominent feature of the postwar landscape. The United States sold the equivalent of a billion dollars worth of arms a month to Middle Eastern countries in the four years beginning in August 1990, accounting for 72 percent of all sales to the region. When the Desert Storm forces went home, they left behind armaments worth tens of billions of dollars. Countries now favored by the United States were those that border Iraq—Saudi Arabia, Kuwait, and Turkey—and two long-standing allies who supported the war, Egypt and Israel. By 1992 the three recipients of the most U.S. military assistance were Israel, Egypt, and Turkey, while the Saudis—who could pay, or so it seemed, for their imports—were the highest purchasers.

Nearly ten years of war in the Persian Gulf had left the region in a stupor of exhaustion and ill will. Close to a half million people had been killed, with many more wounded, homeless, imprisoned, impoverished. The ecological damage was incalculable. The financial cost of war to the combatants ran into the hundreds of billions of dollars. The political configurations had changed, but barely: Saddam Hussein remained in power, the Islamic revolution was firmly in control in Iran, and the imperial prerogatives of the ruling clans of Kuwait and Saudi Arabia had not diminished. For every positive sign—a coming Israeli-PLO agreement, Soviet withdrawal from Afghanistan, and cooperation in Desert Storm—there were negative corollaries: the bitter civil war among the Afghans; Kurdish militancy and fratricide; Syrian hegemony in Lebanon; and Islamic militancy on the rise. The arms industries of the world enjoyed a mind-boggling decade of prosperity. And the wealth and influence gained by the arms merchants further enhanced their ability to ply their trade.

It would be an exaggeration to say that the decade of carnage in the Gulf should be laid at the door of the United States' misguided support of the Shah in the 1970s, but such a thought is nonetheless haunting. The lavish arming of the Shah, "like giving a confirmed alcoholic the keys to a liquor store," as one observer put it, led to an arrogance of power, a decadent corruption, which stimulated a radical, anti-Western outburst. That revolution stirred a coup in Afghanistan and an attack on Iran from Iraq. Faced with this sudden, unexpected, and alarming turn of events, the United States persisted with its policy of promoting military "solutions"— arming the *mujāhedīn* rebels in Afghanistan and supporting Saddam Hussein in Iraq. Those maneuvers eventually led to a bloody takeover by Islamist militants in Afghanistan, and the second Persian Gulf war on the Arabian peninsula. Militarism begot militarism. The American policy was a near-total failure. But the brain trusts in Washington were eager to give it another chance.

17

DEFENSE DEPENDENCY TAKES ITS
TOLL IN CONNECTICUT

Desert Storm gave America's defense communities a lift of false hope that the tide of military cutbacks could be reversed. A quick infusion of orders during the crisis was followed by a fresh round of sales to Israel, Saudi Arabia, Egypt, and Turkey in the wake of the war. But most knew the flurry was not sustainable, and not enough. "Desert Storm was a good news–bad news situation," said Donald Fuqua, president of an aerospace trade group, shortly after the war ended. "The good news, besides the amazingly low casualty rate, was that we didn't lose much equipment. But for defense contractors, that's bad news because there's very little inventory to replace. It won't mean much new business." The slide was inevitable, particularly as the Soviet Union took its final fall and the populist democrat Boris Yeltsin took the helm in the Kremlin. And the Bush Pentagon persisted with its plan to cut the defense budget by 25 percent over five years.

The slide in spending was beginning to affect Connecticut. In 1990, United Technologies' flush military contracts slipped suddenly to $2.8 billion, a drop of 20 percent from 1986. UTC was hemorrhaging money, taking a loss of more than $1 billion in 1991. Its "peace dividend" to the state of Connecticut, delivered by chairman Robert Daniell in January 1992, was to sharply downsize the company.

"STATE STAGGERED BY UTC JOB CUTS," the *Hartford Courant* blazed across its front page on the morning of Wednesday, January 22nd. Nearly 14,000 jobs were eliminated, about half of them in Connecticut and most of those in the Pratt & Whitney divisions around East Hartford, where engines for the F-16 fighter jets and other aircraft were made. Hundreds of subcontractors would also be affected, and some would go under. It was not the company's first layoff, to be sure—the UTC workforce in the state had already declined by 9,000 workers to 47,000. But coming as it did in the midst of a recession, in tandem with other defense layoffs and the steady erosion of blue-collar jobs in other industries, the announcement was a startling blow to a state that had seen 90,000 jobs disappear in the previous thirty-four months. "In the almost thirty years I've been in Connecticut," observed a Yale social analyst, "I've never known the mood to be grimmer than today. It's not a ripple effect; it's a chain reaction. You can't put that many more people on the unemployment and welfare lists without having a further degeneration of what is already a horrendous situation."

"One statistic says it all," Senator Christopher Dodd remarked that day. "In 1982, Pratt & Whitney delivered seven hundred fifty jet engines to the Pentagon. In 1993, they will deliver fifty. You don't need to hear much more than that to know why a decision like this was inevitable." But although Pratt & Whitney's domestic sales were down sharply, its exports of engines for the F-16 were rather healthy. In the previous year, 46 F-16s were sold to Egypt, 120 were sold to South Korea, and 18 were on their way to Thailand. New sales were on tap for later in 1992 to Taiwan, Singapore, Saudi Arabia, and Greece. Some of these sales involved coproduction, and not all Pratt engines are manufactured in Connecticut. But whatever the arrangement, however hot the F-16 was at the time, the exports did not do enough for the Connecticut workers at this largest UTC division. Robert Daniell shocked the state with his layoff declaration.

Daniell, a former Sikorsky engineer, was apparently distraught by the impact of the UTC downsizing. "The real tragedy today, compared with some previous reductions, is that the work environment and the number of opportunities are just so few and far between," he told a reporter. "It's just very, very disturbing to figure out how these people are going to find employment."

At Sikorsky, the layoffs were mild. True, 350 white-collar workers had been sent packing four months earlier, and another 200 jobs would be lost in the UTC downsizing. Sikorsky had had its ups and downs in the years before Daniell's announcement, but the Army contract for Black Hawks remained intact. And just the year before, a Navy procurement of twenty

Super Stallions, the heavy-lift helicopters, and research money for the new scout helicopter, the Comanche, were saved by Chris Dodd from the budget ax in Congress.

And exports were looking up. Sales of the Black Hawk to South Korea, Saudi Arabia, Mexico, and Morocco had come through in the past year. The Black Hawk was the company's star—its share of total sales climbed to about 60 percent of Sikorsky's total—and its fate, given the shakiness of the Super Stallion and the Comanche, could spell the fate of the firm and its 12,000 workers, already down from a peak of 14,500. Everyone knew that the Army contract and the export market were the keys to that fate. But for now, in the shadow of the Pratt & Whitney massacre, nearly everyone in Stratford's Sikorsky plant could breathe a sigh of relief.

Their breathing was eased by two foreign deals in particular: Turkey and South Korea. The immense modernization of Turkey's helicopter fleet was not a done deal but looked promising. South Korea was in the bag, though it presented some new difficulties.

The South Korea deal was a problem mainly for Jack Powers. A Vietnam war veteran and assembly-line worker, he rose to the top of the Teamsters Local 1150, the only union to represent hourly workers at Sikorsky plants. Powers looks like a union boss from Central Casting: square jaw, thick mustache, strong build, silver hair parted in the middle, chain-smoking L&Ms. He was clearly at ease in his enormous trophy-lined office, the centerpiece of the Teamsters' cement-block office building in Stratford's light-industry neighborhood between Sikorsky Memorial Airport and Interstate 95. The office displayed models of helicopters, pictures of Powers with famous politicians, citations of various kinds, and a suitable collection of patriotic folderol.

His ascent was not easy. After a bad injury from a truck accident, Powers was out of work for several years until he got taken on at Sikorsky as a hydraulics technician—"a glorified plumber"—working on aircraft for more than six years. He became active in the union during the mid-1980s and was elected to head the local in February 1989. Just eighteen months later, he had to face down his men on the Korea deal.

"It was our first major foreign project," he explains, "and there was a lot of resentment among the guys who were Korean vets or children of vets. Still a lot of feeling about Vietnam, too. I knew things were drying up with the defense cutbacks; I knew if we didn't get foreign sales, we'd put

Sikorsky on the extinction list. I had a hard time with rank-and-file guys who wanted to fight it out, lobbying against it and vowing to put me out of office. We had a meeting where I told them that we'd do this job no matter what."

Resistance to the deal was not just hostile residue from the Korean War, it grew from the structure of the agreement: the Black Hawks would be assembled in South Korea. About eighty Black Hawks were expected to be built in partnership with Korean Air, bringing Sikorsky $500 million over five years.

"When it came time to work and other firms were laying off, they worked," Powers asserted in a 1995 interview. "They never asked questions anymore. If we had not made that move in 1990, half of us would not be here now. Sikorsky would have gone overseas. The Korea deal," he said proudly, "is still going today."

The UTC layoffs seemed not to ruffle Stratford, which by the early 1990s had reached an equilibrium of sorts. Its population, which grew steadily from World War II to a high of just over 50,000 in 1980, had declined by a little more than a thousand by the 1990 census—reflecting the decline of population in Connecticut generally. It was a home-grown town, with three of every four residents born in the state; the same number owned their own homes. The Stratford workforce of 26,000 was high-toned: half were in management, professional, or skilled-labor jobs. Stratford's small-town atmosphere, its long and cherished history, and its apparent prosperity all belied an unease, however, an undercurrent of tension whose root was economic uncertainty. The town was on the brink of bankruptcy. The famed Shakespeare festival, which lent Stratford a pleasing self-importance, had faltered and closed, its grand old wooden theater overlooking the Housatonic shuttered. The town's income levels and unemployment were scarcely better than those of the state as a whole. Its population was aging. Almost half its tax base was tied to just two military contractors. And it bordered two of the nation's worst urban basket cases: Bridgeport to the immediate west, and New Haven twenty miles east.

A long tradition of dominance by suburban politicians in Connecticut had punished New Haven, Hartford, and Bridgeport: in a wealthy state, the three major urban centers were among the ten poorest cities in the nation during the 1980s. Bridgeport in particular was devastated by the flight of corporations from the unionized, property-tax-heavy Northeast and the general decline of smokestack industries that beset so many communities in America's East and Midwest. The vast General Electric plant in Bridgeport, which once employed 10,000 people, was by 1992 nearly empty. Carpenter Steel was gone, its plant demolished. Bryan-Henco, a division of Westinghouse, closed its doors in the late 1980s. Most symbolically of all, Bridgeport Brass, which once employed 4,000 and was the anchor of "Brass Valley," had closed as well, its production moved elsewhere, the plant in shambles.

With its tax base so badly eroded, the City of Bridgeport filed for bankruptcy in June 1991, the largest municipality in America ever to do so. Unemployment was double the national average; one out of eight people were on welfare. Real estate values plummeted. The largest employer in the city was Bridgeport Hospital, and the second largest was St. Vincent's Hospital. Sikorsky, with its small Bridgeport shop still open and many workers from the Stratford plant residing in Bridgeport, was becoming a "salvation for the city," as one community activist put it. The number of Sikorsky employees living in Bridgeport rivaled the hospitals' rolls.

The importance of Sikorsky to Bridgeport was minor compared with the company's position in Stratford. Although Stratford's reliance on Sikorsky for employment had declined over the previous twenty years or so, Sikorsky still accounted for 20 percent of its corporate tax base and perhaps somewhat less of its jobs. "There was a saying that when Sikorsky coughed, the rest of the town caught pneumonia," the town manager, Mark Barnhart, observed. "That's no longer the case. They're a major presence, and if they're hurt, the town is hurt. But defense downsizing is more a regional problem, a state problem, than one of a single town like Stratford."

Even though Sikorsky's workforce was declining very slowly, Stratford and surrounding communities faced a more immediate shock from the defense drawdown: the tank- and helicopter-engine plant near the Sikorsky airport was facing closure. Built on the original site Igor Sikorsky chose for his move from Long Island, the plant was occupied by Chance Vought when it merged with the Sikorsky company (and Sikorsky moved full time to Bridgeport) until Vought moved to Texas. The Stratford site was purchased by the Army, and, in fact, the Army owns it to this day, though it has been operated by a string of private contractors—Lycoming, AVCO, Textron, and Allied Signal. Its last major assignment for the Army was the engine for the state-of-the-art Abrams tank. But tanks were not long for the post–Cold War world; armored land divisions seemed to symbolize a passing era of military combat. The future belonged to air power, and though the old Army facility in Stratford did make aircraft engines, its bread and butter was tank engines. Employment there had declined from a high of about 11,000 to just 1,200 by the early 1990s. And the federal commission created to close unneeded military bases had that plant on its hit list.

The Lycoming plant—as many old-timers continued to call it, after one of its longer tenants—had not worked for the Pentagon alone. Its engines for Bell Helicopter found their way throughout the world, particularly in the flush of the export business in the 1970s and early 1980s, when the Huey was king and the U.S. government opened the financing and licensing floodgates. Three hundred Huey engines to Iran, 100 to Israel, and 125 to Turkey; 30 to El Salvador, 14 attack gunships to Chile, 60 to Argentina, and 112 to Argentina's rival Brazil; a total of 65 helicopters to Ethiopia, Liberia, Uganda, Zaire, and Nigeria—all in the ten-year period between 1973 and 1983, all Lycoming engines in Bell helicopters. It was a heady business, and it kept the Army plant running at full steam. But despite the export business, its days were numbered.

The unique position of the Stratford plant—its location in a defense-dependent community, its status as both a publicly owned facility and a private defense production firm—lured Connecticut's conversion advocates. They wanted to use the Army Engine Plant as the laboratory for their ideas about making plowshares out of swords. Again, the Reverend Kevin Bean was at the forefront.

In July 1989, Bean became director of the Naugatuck Valley Project. This group was created just a few years before by a United Auto Workers organizer, Ken Galdston, a graduate of the school of community organizing inspired and developed by Saul Alinsky. The project took on a broad set of issues of industrial decline—runaway shops, layoffs, worker ownership—in the Naugatuck River Valley, which runs down eastern Connecticut to just north of Stratford. Seeing military dependency as a part of a larger problem of deindustrialization held several advantages: by beginning with concern over worker security and by joining with the unions and other community leaders to seek concrete solutions, Bean and like-minded peace activists were able to transcend the moralizing, and alienating, rhetoric of recriminations that had produced virtually no positive results for the defense conversion movement.

Kevin Bean was well suited to the task. He looked more like an all-American football hero than a clergyman. He was associate rector of St. Luke's (wealthy) Episcopal parish in Darien, and he could draw on that resource both as a door-opener and as a tradition of social activism. Other churches, including the Catholic archdiocese in Hartford, were supporters of the Naugatuck Valley Project. And Bean had a bachelor's degree in economics; he could combine the ethical standing of the clergy and the networking ties of the church communities with nuts-and-bolts knowledge.

The Naugatuck Valley Project had earned a solid reputation of its own. It was credited with saving hundreds of jobs, protecting pension benefits, and pushing through legislation to help finance worker buyouts of closing factories. It was widely viewed as a pioneer of community-based advocacy of this kind, spawning at least thirty other such projects around the country.

Bean recognized that it was precisely this model of organizing that could most usefully address the defense dependency of Connecticut. By the time he moved into the project's office in Waterbury, the U.S. defense drawdown was in full swing, and his early-eighties prediction—that the roller-coaster ride of defense dollars would take a sharp dip by the decade's end—was coming true. He set his sights on a town that had exceptionally high defense dependency and was ripe for a quick fall: Stratford. The task, as he saw it, was to convert the Army facility occupied by Textron Lycoming to stable, peaceful uses.

The plant was losing contracts and laying off workers at an alarming rate. By the winter of 1989–90, the facility was down to 4,000 workers, taking a hit of 300 layoffs in January. Worse was on its way: the Abrams tank contract was due to expire at the end of 1992, and further layoffs were already scheduled. With such bleak prospects, the shop's union representative, Joe Ciuci of the United Auto Workers, readily accepted Bean's offer to seek alternatives. An "optimum use committee" that included four senior managers was set up to investigate other commercial possibilities. The prospects for conversion actually seemed better than for most defense firms. The gas-turbine engines made at Lycoming could be adapted to several uses, making motors, as Ciuci put it, "for anything that moves."

The effort to convert Textron Lycoming was set back by a sudden uptick in defense orders wrought by Desert Storm, but the ultimate fate of the operation was no less dismal. By 1992, layoffs were continuing as the Army contracts and export orders were drying up.

The Lycoming project was one of the more sophisticated efforts at conversion in Connecticut. It could, in theory, benefit from the fact that the facility itself was owned by the Army. Base closures actually offered the best route to conversion, since the bases were frequently turned over to local governments for commercial redevelopment. There was a promising track record of such conversions: from the early 1960s to the early 1980s, some one hundred bases had closed, with a net gain in civilian employment. But in the post–Cold War environment, too many bases were closing at once, states and municipalities were financially strapped, and the national economy was weak. Conversion of bases would take much longer. And time was not on the side of the remaining Lycoming workers.

Nor did it appear as though time would heal the pain of the UTC layoffs statewide. Pratt & Whitney's East Hartford plant was careening down to 2,500 workers from 11,000 a few years before. Norden and Hamilton Standard were issuing pink slips, too. UTC's method of relieving defense dependency had long been to diversify by purchasing nondefense companies, not by converting its defense divisions. At the time of UTC's massive layoffs in January 1992, the inadequacy of that corporate strategy was becoming apparent. "As defense budgets shrink," wrote a Hartford economics columnist, "neither the contractors nor the government is prepared to take the thousands of highly skilled machinists, engineers, welders, programmers, designers, and managers now being put out to pasture and put them to work building things Americans need. The UTC plan calls for streamlining and reducing existing operations—not developing new products and new markets." At the same time, Kevin Bean was called to a meeting of defense contractors, unions, and the state's two U.S. senators, Chris Dodd and Joseph Lieberman, to discuss alternatives to the Pentagon. "It was the kind of summit we should have had five or six years ago," Bean said. "Now that it's really pouring, people are starting to get worried about the climate."

Over at Electric Boat in Groton, the Seawolf submarine contract was in constant jeopardy. Even if it was saved—a third Seawolf was promised by presidential candidate Bill Clinton—more layoffs were inevitable. Its former workers were increasingly gravitating toward to the area's one booming business—the enormous casino opening nearby, courtesy of the remnant of the Pequot Indian nation. Bridgeport, just then in the throes of its bankruptcy crisis, would soon look upon the casino enviously, hoping to build one of its own.

Up Main Street in Stratford, the Sikorsky managers weren't thinking about casinos or conversion. "Whereas we used to turn out a new kind of helicopter every few years, it now takes a generation to develop a new aircraft," said a former Sikorsky engineer. There was a new commercial helicopter on the drawing board, but the familiar ways of the defense industry were stronger lures. "With a long history of fat military orders," *Business Week* observed, "Sikorsky has nearly ignored the commercial helicopter market. Buckley even cut the company's commercial marketing staff by half" in the late 1980s. "For now, the best Sikorsky can hope for is increased foreign military sales."

1 8

THE DEAL OF THE DECADE,
PART TWO

The Pentagon's shrinking procurement did not seem to worry Gene Buckley. "Cutbacks mean they'll cry out for more helicopters, not less," he predicted in 1991, believing in the Black Hawk's post–Cold War potential. As recently as the middle of 1990, the Army had been hedging again. "There's no procurement money in the program for Black Hawks," an Army official flatly stated. "If the Army procurement ends, Sikorsky would have to let production-line workers go." Every Black Hawk required about 17,000 worker-hours in Stratford, so the loss of the Army contract would punish the workforce. As everyone knew, moreover, the production of the helicopter could drop just so low before it would become too costly to continue at all. A total output of just 10 or 15 helicopters a year drives up the price for every component, including those for subcontractors, the GE engines, the avionics packages. "The only way to bridge the gap," the Army officer said, "would be to have an unforeseen boost in sales to foreign countries."

No one in the business by 1990 considered U.S. procurement as "the market," least of all Gene Buckley. Widely regarded as a tough, smart executive, Buckley joined Sikorsky in 1976 after a career that took him to Grumman Aerospace, Republic Aviation, and Rohr Industries. His rather bland, balding appearance belies a fierce competitor. "He's the driving force at Sikorsky," an Army aviation general said in describing Buckley. "He's a hard taskmaster, but he's also polished and charismatic, a real leader. He always gives the most rousing, patriotic, and innovative speeches when he addresses the Army." A native of Brooklyn, a graduate of Brooklyn College, and an Air Force veteran, he took over the Black Hawk program, among other assignments, until ascending to the company's top job in July 1987. Almost immediately he oriented the Stratford plant toward the overseas business. Buckley explained to a reporter in 1991 that he saw several areas of growth to take Sikorsky's foreign sales from 5 percent of business in the mid-1980s to 40 percent by the early 1990s. "That's South Korea, Japan, China and, very slightly, in the Philippines. There are competitions in several other countries which I will not mention," by which he meant Turkey, the largest potential sale but one. "In the Middle East, I think there will be great action, the *Al Yamāma* deal is going to happen. I wish I could say when it is going to happen."

Al Yamāma, or "the Dove [of Peace]" in Arabic, was the $80 billion arms transaction involving some dozens of Black Hawks and many other aircraft, weapons, and firms in Britain, which was negotiating this "deal of the century" with Saudi Arabia. The Black Hawks were meant to be sold through the Westland Group of Britain, which was partially owned by United Technologies and licensed to assemble and sell Black Hawks. The gargantuan deal was long delayed, and it began to dampen Sikorsky's foreign-sales hopes. "Our experience in the international marketplace is that everything takes longer than you think it will take from the start," Buckley explained. "Westland is a good company. We are pleased with the relationship. We could be more pleased with a big Black Hawk order but I think that will be coming. The equipment is identified and we think Westland has taken all reasonable actions to get that contract. I have been there with their president and I think they have taken it very seriously."

Possibly too seriously, as it turned out. Shortly after Buckley's optimistic interview, a Sikorsky executive publicly accused the company of bribery and other illegalities in the Saudi-Westland deal. Thomas F. Dooley, a lieutenant colonel in the U.S. Marines stationed in Saudi Arabia, was recruited by Sikorsky in 1984 to break into that lucrative market, which Sikorsky had repeatedly failed to do. Dooley's mission was to sell Black Hawks to the Saudis. He did that, but he also went public in 1991 with astonishing charges against Buckley and other company bigwigs, claiming that they had bribed Saudi Arabian princes to secure the 90-Black Hawk deal and connived with Westland to arm the Black Hawks in violation of U.S. law. (Dooley alleged that Westland was in part purchased by UTC specifically to circumvent Congress when selling in the politically sensitive Middle East.) Dooley, who was suing Sikorsky for $130 million in damages because, he alleged, they had punished him for raising ethical questions, spoke of secret rendezvous, subterfuge, and international intrigue: clandestine meetings at the Paris Air Show, private jets flown to Connecticut for a dinner meeting in a Greenwich hotel, a memorandum that fingers U.S. personnel in Riyadh and mentions a U.S. assistant secretary of defense ("Armitage involved. Very concerned"). Twelve Black Hawks were indeed delivered to the Saudis in 1990, financed by the Foreign Military Sales (FMS) program. But the larger deal, supposedly meant to go through Westland, fell through because of the scandal.

Dooley's allegations ranged widely and painted a tawdry picture of bribes engineered through a phony firm in Saudi Arabia, designs to help "Saddam Hussein build up his war machine," the involvement of the Saudi ambassador to the United States, Prince Bandar, and a mysterious Pentagon override of an Army aviation officer's uncovering of the entire scheme. At one point a Sikorsky executive allegedly told Dooley, "We must be careful, this is an FMS sale"—meaning, of course, that it would earn more scrutiny than a commercial sale. After numerous meetings with Sikorsky lobbyists, the State Department helpfully amended an export license in 1988 to allow Westland to put Hellfire missiles on the Black Hawks and thereby circumvent congressional review.

Buckley, Westland, Sikorsky, and the other defendants denied the allegations and the case was settled out of court in 1993. While the allegations certainly raised questions about the lengths to which Sikorsky would go for a significant foreign sale, how desperate Buckley and his colleagues were to break into the Middle Eastern market, and how much influence they wielded in Washington and foreign capitals, these allegations would remain untested in view of the settlement.

Despite the imbroglio, exports did look promising. First of all, the U.S. Army contract for Black Hawks, which had gone through constant replays of cancellations and reorders in the late 1980s, was revived by Saddam Hussein's invasion of Kuwait and refreshed U.S. demand for the versatile chopper. The 450 Black Hawks deployed in Desert Storm came through with flying colors. They worked especially well in "hunter–killer" teams with Apaches, and the Army saw, after the war ended, that the Black Hawk could be the command–and–control partner for the attack force, which they believed would "revolutionize" the Army's lethality. So just three months after UTC dropped its layoff bombshell on Connecticut in January 1992, the Army renewed its plans to purchase more Black Hawks—300 more birds over the next five years, a $1.5 billion contract. "It helps all their international marketing efforts on Black Hawk," said a defense market analyst, "because it maintains production at an economic level, which helps them in pricing competition overseas." It gave Buckley some breathing space to expand his overseas market, make up for the *Al Yamāma* deal, and position Sikorsky for the inevitable drop in demand from the U.S. Army. There were also promising signs from Greece and Taiwan, Japan was ordering Seahawks, and Mitsubishi was fashioning a sizable licensing arrangement. But Turkey was the primary opportunity.

The Turkish market opened up in two stages. In September 1988 and again in late 1990, the Turkish Jandarma, the national police force, ordered six armed Black Hawks, with each order worth $40 million. The second of these orders was especially significant, because it came as part of the larger Turkish helicopter deal and directly resulted from James Baker's visit to Ankara in August 1990.

When Baker met with Özal on August 9, one week after Saddam had occupied Kuwait, Turkey's participation in the anti-Iraq coalition was not certain. To induce Turkey to go to war with its neighbor, Baker offered Eximbank financing, now available thanks to Chris Dodd's amendment of the year before. Eximbank, still reluctant to open this door to military exports, had it pushed open by President Bush. Bank president John Macomber, who only the month before had expressed his opposition to the scheme in a letter to the Senate banking committee, was not about to set off on this controversial course without a presidential directive, and on the day Baker went to Ankara, Bush provided just that. The Eximbank guarantees— which enabled Turkey to buy six Black Hawks immediately—provided Baker with one of a number of financial goodies for Turkey, including help both in securing loans from the major international banks and in joining the European Union. As announced by Macomber, the Eximbank approved $1.37 billion in guarantees for the 200-helicopter purchase.

In Stratford a few days later Chris Dodd told an audience of Sikorsky workers and executives, "We're getting our clock cleaned around the world by people who don't play on a level playing field." He said that while the Eximbank was balking at approving the loan guarantees, the

Gulf crisis had turned their head, and major White House players like Brent Scowcroft, the national security advisor, and John Sununu, the chief of staff, had taken up Dodd's cause and forced Eximbank to act. "We think we're in a strong position to win this contract," said Gene Buckley at the same gathering. "Without the Export-Import Bank's decision, we would have had no chance of pulling this thing out." The decision was encouraging to others besides Sikorsky. "Defense industry lobbyists," a trade journal reported that month, "have been watching the Sikorsky sale as a test case for future defense export financing."

While the Gulf war was a strong motivator—"We had to do something quicker than usual," Macomber said—the Bush administration was contemplating a policy, modeled on Dodd's efforts, to use Eximbank more aggressively for arms exports. Lawrence Eagleburger, the deputy secretary of state, had been instructing embassies all summer to be more helpful in promoting arms sales, and just after Christmas he met with Macomber to convince the Eximbank president—still a reluctant partner—to dance with State and the White House on this issue. Macomber relented, and six weeks later, in the midst of Desert Storm, the White House announced it would push for such authorization—$1 billion per year for loan guarantees.

The fullest explanation of the change in Administration thinking came during a March 18 press briefing by the president's spokesman, Marlin Fitzwater:

Question from a reporter: How does this fit with the president's desire to now limit the proliferation of arms, particularly in the sensitive areas and the countries that he listed?

Fitzwater: Well, it would mesh completely in the sense that these would be for certain military sales that would be consistent with whatever the overall policy is of arms reduction. But certainly, that's the process. . . . We've never said there would be no arms sales, only that we wanted to diminish.

Q: It seems to me that you're stepping up arms sales all over the world since the war.

Fitzwater: No, that's not the case, we're reducing it.

Q: It would be difficult to meet the criteria of regional stability, wouldn't it?

Fitzwater: No. Why?

Q: In the Mideast? Anywhere in the Persian Gulf.

Fitzwater: For what?

Q: If the President is attempting to control or to balance, at least, and reduce arms sales to the area, you've got a tinderbox there—

Fitzwater: Right.

Q: Okay.

Fitzwater: What's the question?

Q: The question is, how does it meet the criteria of regional stability immediately following upon a war the president says was exacerbated by extreme arms sales to the area.

Fitzwater: As we have said, we're not talking about cutting off all arms sales. We're talking about a balance and stability in the region. And that requires that a number of companies [*sic*] have the military capability in order . . .

Q: That's true, but the president has also said reduce and balance.

Fitzwater: That's true. But sometimes you've got to make reductions, sometimes you have to build up. It goes both ways. . . . It's in our interest to be able to provide weapons in cases where we think it's in the national security interest.

Q: Eximbank officials opposed this program. Is that correct? And can you explain how the program comes to be going ahead if that is correct?

Fitzwater: I'm not aware of any opposition to it. I would say, this is a pilot program to guarantee commercial credits for defense exports. It is intended to enhance the competitiveness of U.S. industry in the international market. The goal is to establish a market-oriented program that would extend the U.S. defense exporters the same consideration now given to civil use exporters, and create a more level playing field for them vis-à-vis foreign competitors. Two factors make some form of financial support for commercial defense exports timely. The financial support for defense exporters provided by foreign competitors such as France, the United Kingdom, West Germany and others, and a declining U.S. defense budget which over time could seriously erode our defense industrial base and reduce our ability to produce the arms we need. . . . Defense exports have become more important to our own defense industrial base as U.S. defense procurement declines. Maintenance of a viable U.S. defense industry is critical to our ability to respond to the challenges of the future. The survival of a number of important programs is already tied to foreign sales, including the M1-A2 Abrams main battle tank, the UH-60 Black Hawk helicopters, Hawk missiles, and KE-3 aerial refueling tankers.

Q: Marlin, isn't this based more on providing economic stability and helping the U.S. arms manufacturers survive than it is to providing some sort of national security?

Fitzwater: It's both. It's all tied in together. You can't separate it out. This is a program that's been going on a long time. I don't know—it's not that big a deal . . .

Q: What nature does he want nonproliferation to take?

Fitzwater: He wants nonproliferation to take the form of—one is being able to achieve a balance and security that will lend to the national security interests of the world . . . Two recent examples in Turkey demonstrate the difference that the availability of Exim financing can make. FMC Corporation was forced to enter into an extensive work-share arrangement with Dutch and Belgian firms in order to gain approval for an EC-blended financing package. The EC funding proved vital to FMC's win of a one-billion-dollar contract for the armored infantry forces vehicle. By contrast, Bell and Sikorsky were able to stay in the competition for the sale of Black Hawk helicopters without European commercial participation after Ex-Im agreed to support American exports with loan guarantees.

And as I said, there is a process. Applicants must have obtained a munitions export license and would be approved according to Eximbank standards in order to conclude a sale under the program. All guarantee proposals will be reviewed by an interagency board on a case-by-case basis after the sale has been licensed through the U.S. munitions export licensing process, which means the U.S. government makes those determinations about military uses. The board would review all proposed guarantee recipients for their creditworthiness, the role of a guarantee in winning a sale for the United States, and any policy considerations. Policy considerations regarding such factors as sales to Middle Eastern nations or Greece or Turkey would have to be taken into account when deciding if a guarantee was in the national interest. Additionally, technology transfer issues would have to be considered as well as regional stability and human rights concerns.

The long exchange signaled the administration's newfound concern for the "defense industrial base" and its relatively loose concern about arms proliferation, despite its vow, during the run-up to the Gulf war, to stem the arms trade. He asserted the United States would approve the uses to which the military technology would be put. The emphasis on human rights, technology transfer, and regional stability were repeated twice by Fitzwater, but the sales on tap would run against those very promises. And Fitzwater's examples all revolved around Turkey.

"Cold War thinking about Turkey was one-dimensional, all about the military, U.S. basing rights, containment of the Soviets," said a White

House advisor at the time. "It was easy to get attention around the White House for Turkey. The president and Brent Scowcroft always had time for Turkey. It was clearly pro-West. It was a no-brainer."

What got the attention of Turkey, and the Bush administration, was the intensifying civil war with the Kurdish guerrillas. Through the spring and summer of 1992, the guerrillas and the army clashed almost daily; many of the most vicious battles occurred at military stations along the borders with Iraq and Syria. The Turkish government routinely claimed overwhelming victories in these confrontations, such as the shootout in Shirnak on August 18, when four soldiers and four civilians were killed, while 211 PKK fighters were captured, and another 139 "terrorists" were arrested after a security sweep of the city. But not all the news was good for Ankara: a September 29 battle along the border left 36 Turkish soldiers dead, while 200 PKK were reported killed. The imbalance in the numbers of casualties hardly comforted Turkey's leaders, and their sense of insecurity became obsessive as the national press trumpeted each clash with banner headlines.

In Washington, the response was tentative. "I was there at the beginning of the transition from the Cold War," recalled Morton Abramowitz, U.S. ambassador to Turkey in 1989–91, "and everything was still related to NATO. Comes the end of the Cold War. Military assistance becomes questionable. The new rationale for assistance was based on two things: uncertainty over Russia, and Turkey's bad neighborhood. The new rationale was less convincing."

Through 1992, however, the Turks were talking not about Russia or the "bad neighborhood," but about the PKK. "It was a significant concern to us, because the Turks thought it was so," said the president's advisor. "The general view in the White House was that the problem of PKK terrorism was conjoined with Kurdish identity, a problem which emerged over time and was exacerbated by strong economic deprivation in the Southeast and the Turkish government's approach to identity—that is, that everyone in Turkey was Turkish. We thought that a military solution was insufficient. It needed a political, social, and economic dimension.

"We said to the Turks: Killing people must be part of an overall strategy to overcome the PKK, a larger view that does not rely on the military solution alone. This got some response from the Turks. But there was a lot going on at that time, a lot of flux. We asked Turkey to be a responsible member of the West, and they would say, yes, but isn't there a double standard?" Ankara's standard response to criticism of their use of force in the Southeast was to point at Britain's brutish handling of Northern Ireland. "We kept asking about human rights and they would get indignant. We insisted on judicial reform, social enfranchisement, and so on, that they should not treat their people this way. Human-rights activists, like Amnesty International, came in and would in effect ask us to stake the U.S.-Turkish relationship on the human-rights issues. That was not acceptable to us. Blood is thicker than water, and the U.S.-Turkish relationship is like a blood relationship: the U.S. is Turkey's very best friend in the world."

So the Bush administration did not see the PKK insurgency as a Marxist revolutionary movement that justifiably could be crushed by military force, with the force supplied from America. It tended to see the situation rather clearly as an "identity crisis" that required political means to end the war. But the actions of the Administration tended, as always, to support the military option all the same. And the symbol of the actual policy was the deal for assault helicopters.

That deal, the 200 or 720 or whatever the Turks would eventually buy, was astir again shortly after the Gulf war ended. The lengthy process of bidding, which included 8,000 pages of technical data shaped for Turkey's needs, test flights, and the complex arrangements for coproduction, were submitted to the Turkish defense ministry in late April 1991. The test flights in the eastern part of Turkey were conducted the previous summer, with special attention to the choppers' ability to handle the rough mountain topography and the heat of the Southeast. Given its superior technology, Sikorsky was sure to outfly competitors like Aérospatiale's Cougar or Bell's upgraded Huey. The winning bid, then, would hinge on the architecture of the deal—the size and attractiveness of the offsets, the financing package, the overall price of the helicopters and the add-ons like maintenance, and the details of coproduction. The last would include how much helicopter technology would be given to the Turkish partners, how many local manufacturers would participate, and what a longer-term relationship would look like. Every bid was a mind-numbing exercise of balancing each factor, calculating the rewards, squeezing the governments for maximum help with licenses and financing, and guessing how each competitor might deal those same cards.

Bell made the case that the upgraded Huey was a bargain. "We're half the price but we do five-sixths of the mission," said Nick Primis of Bell. "Sikorsky's Black Hawks cost $8 million-plus each; ours are $4 million each. So we're saying to Turkey, the Black Hawk is a great machine, it's wonderful. But it's $8 million. If you could buy two of ours for one Black Hawk, it makes sense to buy ours." He also insisted that Huey maintenance costs were less than half the costs of the UH-60. "The only organization in the world which can afford to operate the Black Hawk is the U.S. Army." He also promised a 100-percent offset. "To pay for this program, Bell will find companies who will buy Turkish products," he offered. "We would try to find an American corn company to buy Turkish corn, who would give the money in dollars to the Turks, who in turn would pay us for the helicopters with these dollars." Sikorsky's Gene Buckley countered with a promise to "build the product" in Turkey, to "ultimately have an in-country capability when the 10-year program is over," in effect selling the Turks the chance to make nearly the whole aircraft.

The bidding war erupted into the press shortly after the documents were submitted in Ankara. Aérospatiale's president, Jean-François Bigay, charged that the Dodd amendment providing $1.37 billion in financing guarantees was unfair competition: France's export agency, Compagnie Française, had only tentatively offered to cover twenty helicopters of the 200-chopper deal. (Aérospatiale actually had the cheek to apply for Eximbank financing through its American subsidiary, but was flatly turned down.) And Germany was providing no special financing for its manufacturer's bid. Sikorsky's vice president for Turkey, James Satterwhite, was promising that production would be transferred there "as fast as Turkish industry can absorb it." Sikorsky was also offering re-export rights, though that would theoretically be subject to State Department approval. Aérospatiale upped the ante on all counts: full transfer of all technology, unrestricted re-export rights, and the chance to manufacture any helicopter in the company's line.

Intangibles, mainly political clout, were also in play. Sikorsky had an ace they used at will: Alexander Haig, the former United Technologies president and secretary of state, was still on the UTC board and visited Turkey frequently on Sikorsky's behalf. "Haig was there a number of times," Mort Abramowitz recalled. "You roll out the assets you have. Most senior defense officials put in a plug for the American firms. I lobbied hard; I wanted to make sure the U.S. could make its case. It's like being a P.R. firm for Uncle Sam." Haig was revered in Turkey for his past stature as supreme commander of NATO, and because he bolstered the Turkish military during the junta when he was Reagan's first secretary of state. "Haig was still a hero there," said a United Technologies executive who accompanied Haig to Turkey. "He worked fourteen-hour days, socialized a lot, saw government people, had many technical talks. The embassy didn't play much of a role; the Turkish decision makers have relationships with the arms dealers, and they don't need the embassy."

The French could roll out their assets, too. President François Mitterrand visited Turkey in April 1992 in part to promote the bid of Aérospatiale, which was headed by his brother. It was widely rumored at the time that France would support Turkey's candidacy for membership in the European Union, and that Mitterrand had made such a promise in exchange for the helicopter contract, but the rumors were never confirmed. Mitterrand did tell a banquet audience in Ankara that France supported the Kurds' cultural rights, but he also opposed a separate Kurdish state and backed the Turks' fight against terrorism. There were also rumors about French bribes, but these, too, were never confirmed. A former Pentagon official suggested that some Turks were skimming money from the defense modernization funds, and there was speculation that Sikorsky was paying off Turkish officials as well. But such unsubstantiated allegations always accompany enormous arms deals. And in the age of offsets, when the buyers can finagle legal *bakhshish* for favorite domestic businessmen, the "need" for outright bribery is diminished.

The deal was delayed again by the national elections in October 1991, but a sense of desperation was setting in. "We urgently need more and better helicopters for use in the Southeast," said one parliamentary leader. And Vahit Erdem, the defense undersecretary who would negotiate the transaction, insisted just after Süleyman Demirel was re-elected prime minister that "this is a very urgent, high-priority project. It is practically ready for decision. All the bids, within a small margin, meet our military requirements. The important thing now is how they will serve our objectives from the industrial and technological point of view." The group making the decision included Erdem, President Özal, Prime Minister Demirel, Defense Minister Nevzat Ayaz, and the chief of the General Staff, General Doghan Güresh.

By the summer of 1992 the casualties in the civil war had reached 4,500, and Erdem was promising that the deal would be consummated within weeks. All that summer and autumn, too, Turkey was getting the "excess defense articles" from U.S. stocks in Central Europe, freebies like 1,057 M-60 tanks and ten Cobra attack helicopters. Those additions and the purchase of the assault choppers would bolster the Turkish military's capability dramatically. The cascade of old NATO equipment did not bring the advantages of coproduction and offsets, and no Black Hawks—essential to the type of war Turkey was waging in its Southeast—were shipped in from the European front.

Finally, in a September 21 meeting of Demirel, Güresh, Erdem, and others, Sikorsky was selected for final negotiations. If details could be worked out, the Black Hawk would be the winner of the competition that was now five years old. "We were up against the toughest international competition there is, and our Black Hawk team won," Gene Buckley exulted after the announcement. The French were miffed and complained of undue pressure on Ankara from Washington; they thought they had the deal sewed up. Apparently, however, no extraordinary measures were taken to capture the Turks' hearts. "My gut feeling was that the Turks respected the Black Hawk more," said one of Sikorsky's dealmakers. The intended negotiation, however, would only be for 75 helicopters, with a possible follow-up order of 125 more. Fifty were to be assembled in Mürted from "kits" of components manufactured in Stratford, with the remaining 25 shipped immediately from Stratford. The negotiation would be completed by late October, the Turks promised, and coproduction would begin within eighteen months. The total price was expected to be $855 million. It was still a very large deal, the largest foreign sale in Sikorsky's history, and the promise of more to come was a sweetener.

Within a few days of the announcement, Prime Minister Demirel "urgently" requested that an additional twenty Black Hawks be acquired immediately. The civil war was going badly, and the Turkish military was pressing for the versatile helicopters. The armed forces had taken high casualties in the Southeast, and the added mobility of the UH-60s was considered a must. "We could prevent many ambushes and foil many attacks with helicopter gunships," said General Güresh during a September trip to the Southeast. The General Staff did not want a commercial deal; they cared little about the coproduction and offset dimension, and much more about getting Black Hawks quickly. Vahit Erdem and the industrial-minded Turks involved in the deal wanted all coproduction and its fruits for local businesses, but "the military prevailed in getting the first forty-five Black Hawks off the shelf," said an American close to the deal, "because of the situation in southeastern Turkey." There was no mention of Turkey's "bad neighborhood" of Iranians, Iraqis, or Syrians—just the Kurds. Clearly, the Black Hawks were to be used mainly, if not exclusively, in Turkey's civil war.

The negotiations then focused on details, particularly the offsets, according to a United Technologies vice president involved in the talks. "As a dealer you have to consider what kind of work they can do, if they have the technical base, the skills, the quality control, and so on," he explained. "They're looking for jobs, technology transfer, and coproduction. In making a bid, you have to figure out what's important to the buyer. You have to sit down with them and philosophize about their needs and a five- to ten-year strategy. Do they seek air superiority, ground cover, or what? Lots of time and effort is put into this by lots of people, including think tanks, war colleges, and the like. It takes three to four years to prepare for a sale. We used all available resources to get the deal done."

The U.S. government had no objection to the sale. "We never had a problem selling to the Turks back then," Glen Rudd, the Pentagon official, explained. Approval for a license to export came quickly from Bush's State Department, and no one in Congress challenged the deal, as they have the right to do for any export worth more than $14 million. All that was left was for Sikorsky to wrap up the details with Vahit Erdem, and the Black Hawks would be on their way to a base near Diyarbakir.

The sticking point in the negotiations was how the coproduction would be designed. "The offset is the discriminator," said a UTC vice president. "The Black Hawk is a great technology, but had we not thrown in the offset, we wouldn't have gotten the deal." Glen Rudd, who had dealt frequently with the same Turks as head of the Defense Security Assistance Agency, said the details would also involve the balance between hardware and support: "The question is, do you want more rubber on the ramp or do you want money for spare parts, maintenance, and training? Lots of countries just want more rubber on the ramp, and it's not always for parades."

The negotiations between Gene Buckley and Vahit Erdem were universally described as hard bargaining. Buckley, the streetwise Brooklyn-born scrapper, was a good match for Erdem, the British-educated Turkish technocrat who looked like a fierce tribal chieftain just off the steppe. Intense pressures drove them together toward a deal: Buckley was operating in a buyer's market and knew that Erdem could turn to Aérospatiale at any moment; Erdem was criticized in Turkey for letting the helicopter modernization program languish for five years through six bids and three governments. Both were motivated to find common ground and, within a few weeks of beginning face-to-face meetings in mid-October, they did just that.

On December 8, 1992, Prime Minister Demirel, Defense Minister Ayaz, American ambassador Richard Barkley, Vahit Erdem, and Gene Buckley gathered under a portrait of Kemal Atatürk to announce that the deal had been struck. "The contract by the Turkish government for Black Hawk helicopters," Buckley said, "is further evidence that the Black Hawk is the world standard." He thanked Demirel for his confidence, and he singled out Chris Dodd for his role in enabling the Eximbank financing, without which the deal would not have been possible.

The 150-page contract stated that Turkey would purchase 45 Black Hawks for immediate delivery for $485 million; the partners would then coproduce 50 more UH-60s in Mürted for $615 million. Another 55 were an option for coproduction. The Turks would contribute 18 percent of the final assembly initially, with that participation rising to 50 percent at the end of the assembly period, though Demirel said, "I hope that in the end the rate will be 90 percent." And Turkey would also realize $250 million in "indirect" offsets having little or nothing to do with the choppers, whose details were never specified. In all likelihood, they were of the kind General Dynamics swallowed in the F-16 deal—marketing Turkish products in the United States. The total deal, excluding offsets, was worth $1.1 billion, living up to its reputation as the "deal of the decade."

Other influences at work on the deal were the standard desire of the General Staff to have what the U.S. Army has; the fact that the F-16s were using General Electric engines assembled near Mürted, and G.E. makes engines for the Black Hawk; and the technology itself, such as the aircraft's extraordinary lift and climbing rate, which, in the words of one expert involved in the talks, makes the UH-60 "the best helicopter for mountainous regions like the country's Southeast." The helicopters, everyone agreed, would be used in the Southeast to fight the terrorists.

The deal was a closely watched train, and when it came in, everyone had his own spin on the significance of its arrival. Chris Dodd's timely intervention in 1989 was often noted. (The importance of the Eximbank guarantee was underscored when Citibank prepared the syndicated credit, 80 percent of it covered by Eximbank, for the billion-dollar loan: "Most bankers laughed when asked about the credit," reported a banking newsletter. "'Oh, no, you mean the Turkish one?' said one banker. . . . 'Who wants to take Turkish risk?' said another, echoing the sentiments of most bankers who had heard of the credit.") Others drew out the broader implications. "The Turkish buy was proof positive of the effectiveness of this kind of mechanism and the need for it," said the industry's chief lobbyist, Joel Johnson. "You've got a billion dollars worth of jobs in Connecticut that otherwise would be in France or Germany." Dodd wasn't available for comment, but Senator Joseph Lieberman hailed the deal, saying it "means job security for many Sikorsky workers and a very positive ripple effect in the state's economy." In fact, a Sikorsky spokesman remarked that no new workers would be hired to fulfill the contract, but "it does help ensure the stability of the workforce," the 1,500 men and women exclusively devoted to the Black Hawk line in Stratford. Within the sprawling plant along the Housatonic, however, the Turkey deal was greeted as if it were the second coming of the Gulf war.

After the deal was penned, Gene Buckley flew back to Stratford, where he was greeted on the night of December 10 like a conquering hero. He gave, according to an eyewitness, "a fiery speech" on the plant floor to 400 workers on a late shift who were outfitting Black Hawks for use in Somalia. "As far as I'm concerned, this is the first part of a major alliance between Sikorsky and Turkish industry," he proclaimed. "It was the most ferocious competition, it never stopped until the moment we signed the contract." The deal could expand by a factor of five, Buckley told the workers, and would give the Black Hawk an edge in winning other Middle Eastern orders.

It was especially comforting to the Sikorsky workers in view of a Pratt & Whitney layoff of 1,400 earlier that week. "We're all in good spirits now," exulted an engineer savoring Buckley's triumph. And a manager nearby said, "it makes it a little easier to do some long-term family planning."

Within a few days, the Sikorsky workers loaded five Black Hawks onto a C-5 Galaxy cargo plane to be flown to Ankara, where they arrived on December 23, the day before the Turkish parliament was to vote on extending Operation Provide Comfort. Ten more would come within weeks. By mid-January, the Black Hawks were flying missions over the Southeast against rebel Kurds. "Officials said combat helicopters," reported the Anatolia news agency, "including newly purchased Sikorsky Black Hawks, were used against the PKK camp in Serik." One hundred fifty people died in the raid.

19

COPING WITH THE DRAWDOWN

While Sikorsky enjoyed a reprieve from the gathering momentum of the defense drawdown, the public clamor for a remedy for massive layoffs in the industry—a "peace dividend" for defense workers—built quickly after the Gulf war and the final collapse of the Soviet Union in 1991. The idea, however vague, was a popular notion, but the business community was dead set against any defense relief plan.

"Why should communities harmed by the loss of defense installations be treated more generously than those that suffer the shutdown of an auto or steel plant?" asked *Fortune* magazine. "True, unemployment will increase because Washington has changed a policy. But when the Fed raises interest rates, carpenters and bricklayers get tossed out of jobs as families stop buying homes. Government doesn't pay them top rates to do useless work." Similarly, the journal *Business Economics* pointed to the "worker adjustment programs" created in the 1980s to cope with the new global economy as being "adequate to handle the defense-related downsizing; if new programs were to be introduced, they are likely to be counterproductive," taking years to implement. And experience shows, the magazine insisted, that "targeting such programs for selected groups of workers tends to retard necessary adjustments to economic change. The key to successful workforce adjustment is economic growth."

George Bush seemed to be listening, because his response to the crisis of defense layoffs was nearly nonexistent, misreading again the lessons of his vastly more popular predecessor. Reagan spent government money wildly

on defense, boosting employment and lending the U.S. economy the appearance of health. Only a 1992 bill pushed through by the Democratic-
controlled Congress addressed the drawdown. The Defense Conversion Act
earmarked nearly $1 billion to provide job counseling, retraining, and other
benefits, but limited the programs to former military personnel and defense
workers. It was a small drop in the considerably larger sea of spending cutbacks. And it could not address the niggling questions about retraining—for
what jobs? Did workers even want to be retrained? But it was more than
what Bush himself could conjure up. He was convinced that Washington's
"help" for military firms was just more pork-barrel politics, or worse still,
the foot in the door for industrial-policy advocates. As an interagency report
put it, "Conversion legislation mandating the reuse for civilian purposes of
defense industrial facilities is not needed. Moreover, prior experience has
shown that conversion as such does not work, even when initiated by the
private sector." Bush's line on conversion stayed steady throughout his
1989–93 term: do nothing.

As the scale of the disaster was becoming apparent soon after Connecticut hit its defense peak in 1989—some thirty to fifty thousand defense jobs
lost in the early 1990s—the "do nothing" attitude was a nonstarter. Only
half of those laid off found new jobs within thirty months, and the rest either left the state or simply fell off the charts altogether. Those who did
find new jobs were paid much less than they had earned at United Technologies or Electric Boat. More than half moved into service jobs. Bruce
Olsson, a union organizer at Machinists Local 91, which represents Pratt &
Whitney workers, told of the awkwardness in defense communities. "I've
seen some guys working in convenience stores. You don't know what to
say. A lot are still unemployed."

Connecticut wasn't the only place hurting, of course. Hard times were
suddenly setting in Fort Worth, despite the continuing popularity of the
F-16 abroad. The U.S. drawdown and the iffy foreign market had a harsh
impact on the bleak landscape of Forth Worth. In the mid-1980s, nearly
two-thirds of Tarrant County's manufacturing jobs were tied to military
production. Hundreds of retailers fed off the high wages of F-16 workers,
as well as those at Bell Helicopter and three other sizable defense firms in
the city. By 1995, some 26,000 county residents had lost their jobs in military production—roughly five out of every seven who had them in the
good times of Ronald Reagan's presidency.

Fort Worth Mayor Kay Granger ordered a study of the unemployed. It estimated that those who found new jobs took pay cuts of 20 percent, but noted that more than a quarter of the former defense workforce could not find jobs and stayed unemployed for three years or more, many of them falling into the dark category of "discouraged workers" whose numbers do not show up in unemployment statistics. "We were surprised at the number of people who were without work," was Mayor Granger's peculiarly innocent reaction. Job retraining seemed to be the answer, she said, but the jobs available in Fort Worth were still likely to be defense-related, and the cycle of sudden joblessness could be sparked again at any time.

It was job losses like those in Fort Worth that finally brought the coproduction gambit into the spotlight. A General Accounting Office analyst told Congress in 1994 that such deals "reduce the employment, defense industrial base, and other economic benefits that normally accrue to the United States from weapons exports." The practice was especially hard on subcontractors, some of whom had gone bankrupt because their work was transferred overseas. But the market for arms makers is such that, in the words of one Lockheed executive, "if we don't export, there's no business. If there's no business, there're no jobs."

But exports weren't keeping many jobs alive. In Southern California more than 100,000 aerospace workers lost jobs between 1989 and 1993, and 60 percent of those failed to find new jobs or left the state; another third took jobs that sliced their annual wages by an average of $22,000. "They ended up at low-wage firms in the retailing sector and the service sector," said a UCLA researcher, "where they often did not have health insurance." The psychological impact was equal to the financial trauma. "Suddenly, I was Mr. Mom," said one unemployed engineer. "No matter what I did to land a job, it didn't seem I was working hard enough. I wasn't bringing in any money."

The closer to the pain, the more pressure there was to do something. California unveiled a program, Calstart, which was meant to use the energy and talent of the aerospace industry to develop an electric car and re-employ some of the 300,000 laid off in the Los Angeles Basin. Calstart was not just "make-work," but aimed to solve both California's persistent curse of air pollution and America's oil dependency. The program got off to a slow start, but still held open some hopes for a viable industry by the end of the century.

Hartford was far less ambitious, but the state's politicians, so slow to take note of the oncoming disaster, finally did commit resources to a conversion strategy. They transformed an old agency into Connecticut Innovations, Inc., to help businesses figure out how to diversify and to provide some small venture capital to help businesses take the first steps toward making commercial products from the fruits of military R&D. Then, in 1991, the legislature created a Defense Diversification Fund of $22.5 million to invest directly, to create civilian products to be made by defense-dependent firms. Other services, including a broad array of technical assistance, were implemented with federal funds.

The investment in conversion was, of course, what advocates like Kevin Bean had been advertising for years. Now, in the midst of a recession and the panicky mindset that accompanies all disasters, it would be more difficult to achieve. But they tried. Among the investments were $3 million to Kaman Corporation for "risk financing" to develop a new commercial helicopter, and another $3 million to a division of United Technologies, Turbo Power & Marine, to help develop a commercial engine. United Nuclear Corporation got $100,000 to identify business opportunities. Other grants were meant to improve defense contractors' ability to get contracts or become more efficient. And the Lycoming plant in Stratford picked up $3 million to help it win an engine contract for a British commercial jet.

No one knows if the state's money actually did much good. Companies like Kaman and UTC had learned the hard lessons of military cutbacks in previous decades—Kaman almost went under after losing a Navy contract in the 1960s—and had diversified before the Reagan buildup. But the lure of the Pentagon's dollars was irresistible, and now, in the early 1990s, they were hurting again. The $3-million state grant to Kaman helped develop a heavy-lift helicopter, the K-MAX, and Charles Kaman claimed that the money, while a pittance compared with his company's $210-million net worth, was essential in moving the project along quickly. Few others made such claims. UTC's project never seemed to go anywhere, and the Lycoming effort did not work out, either. Could the state's small grants make a real difference to corporations whose bottom lines reached into the billions?

The conversion advocates were skeptical. "We believe this is a federal problem, not a state problem," said the Machinists' Bruce Olsson, "and the state simply does not have the resources to cope with it. Connecticut makes a good effort, but how much can it do? Look at Electric Boat. It can't do better than 10,000 layoffs in next few years, and that's the optimistic case. The best some of those guys can hope for is to be dealers in the Indian casino."

Kevin Bean was equally skeptical. "The companies that I really worry about are the billion-dollar contractors, the ones that don't want to horse around with million-dollar contracts," he explained. He saw the answer in a federal initiative. "We need a more diversified industrial policy. You start with a new set of priorities in this country by spending in another area. You claim the peace dividend by spending it."

Connecticut's program also suffered from its penchant for looking to other federal contracts as a salvation, and the creation of new levels of state bureaucracy. "We think there is a problem with the state program," says Olsson, who acknowledges that his union suddenly discovered the logic of conversion when Pratt was losing jobs by the thousands. "In its grants, it doesn't consult at all with the unions, only business executives and state bureaucrats. Connecticut spent hundreds of millions of dollars, and created 620 jobs net." Mark Barnhart, Stratford's city manager, remembered looking in on a state-sponsored conference for subcontractors: "There were about thirty people there from the state offices, and six subcontractors showed up." Kevin Cassidy, a conversion expert who teaches at Fairfield University in Bridgeport, surveyed the state's results and concluded that little of value could be shown for the effort. And Jeff Blodgett, head of research for Connecticut's Department of Economic Development, which runs many of the programs, noted wryly in 1996 that its Defense Information Services Network, meant to advise firms on commercial possibilities for defense contractors, "does not get many inquiries anymore."

The large defense firms had their own coping strategies, of course, and they rarely had anything to do with conversion. The winning tactic was "right-sizing," the industry euphemism for layoffs. But the strategy went deeper than simply showing workers the door. The major primes had to re-engineer their production, not least to keep the per-unit cost down so as to remain competitive. At the F-16 plant in Forth Worth, for example, the managers wanted to keep the price of an F-16 to $20 million— difficult to do while the Air Force was reducing its purchases—to stay competitive in the world market. They were able to do so through a number of devices, including "outsourcing" work to subcontractors. The president of the plant is fond of recalling the "Gucci rivet machine" they had on the Fort Worth factory floor, an amazingly expensive way to meet the Air Force's requirement that they manufacture *all* their components—right down to the rivets. When they started contracting with small shops for that kind of work, they saved millions. By 1996, an F–16 cost 6 percent less than it did five years earlier, when the Air Force was buying four times as many. Normal business practices were finally being applied to the defense industry, and they were achieving economies that had always been available but were never demanded in the profligacy of the Cold War.

Sikorsky also took up the challenge of reinventing its workplace. In the clean, well-lighted place that is the Sikorsky factory, dozens of Black Hawks and other airframes are neatly arranged in rows in the surprisingly small space, with work teams adding the 35,000 parts that gradually make the whole chopper. Arrayed around each bird is a myriad of electronic equipment, technical manuals, and tools. "I love the shop," Gene Buckley proudly told a touring reporter. He had instituted new concepts of team-work where employees learn many jobs, heightening cooperation, innovation, and the ability to shift workers around as needed. The improved efficiencies, just as at Lockheed, kept the Black Hawks more sellable over-seas. "The good Lord smiled on us," Buckley said. "That would not have happened had we not put all the improvements in place."

Other defense contractors were searching for other kinds of efficiencies. Pratt & Whitney demanded of new governor Lowell Weicker concessions on taxes, workers' compensation, and other costs of doing business. A few days after the rancorous meeting with Weicker the demands leaked to the press, and the lieutenant governor of Georgia came to UTC headquarters to make a pitch for moving the entire operation to the land of Sam Nunn and Newt Gingrich. Weicker caved in to the demands, as did the Machinists' Union, which had to serve up "givebacks" to Pratt to avoid even more layoffs.

Very few major contractors bought into anything resembling conver-sion. "To the extent that it's happening, it's among the smaller, second-tier firms," said Don Nakamoto, a leading union expert on conversion in Los Angeles. "The prime contractors have the resources and technology to convert. The second tier, unless hit very hard by loss of defense contracts, can also convert. But the third- or fourth-tier companies don't have the re-sources. Looking for money for conversion into new technical products is very hard. The feds put them in this position through defense dependency, and they feel that the feds should help them convert. Is that a viable alternative? It's limited. They don't have the large engineering or marketing staffs; some may have only two engineers. They have no established links beyond the one or two customers that purchase their product.

"These companies are in a state of paralysis," Nakamoto concluded. "They're trying to figure out what to do. One wrong step is deadly. They're fearful."

Those lower-tier firms, the ones that would make a few components for a major contract—an electronics package for the Black Hawk, for example, or a fuel-system component for an F-16—were the ones being bloodied by the defense cutbacks. The primes could still obtain the contracts and downsize their workforce to remain profitable; they also merged with each other, as Lockheed did with Martin-Marietta to form the largest defense corporation of all. "So much for that projected bull market in high-tech plowshares," business columnist Michael Schrage wrote at the time of the merger. "They'll stick to their swords, thank you very much." Citing the odious comment of Norman Augustine, the new Lockheed Martin chairman—"Attempts at defense conversion are largely unblemished by success"—Schrage said, "The industry has become an even more devout group of defense fundamentalists."

The smaller firms could not benefit by mergers, and had none of the same resources or political clout of a Lockheed Martin or a United Technologies. The empty industrial parks and machine shops around Stratford and Fort Worth bore testimony to the high death rate among the feeder firms.

Had the big players decided to utilize their vast technology base more inventively, many of those smaller companies, and their workforces, would still be alive. "If the prime contractors put some resources behind it, they could be very successful in conversion," Nakamoto contends. "Defense contractors have been producing the finest technology in the world. Hughes has 3,500 patents; Lockheed, McDonnell-Douglas, and the others probably have the same number. They haven't taken steps to find commercial applications. Meanwhile, the Japanese export agency has approached DOD to get access to defense technology.

"Most prime contractors' attitude is to fight it out because that's what they do best. If they diversify too much, they believe, the government won't view them as serious defense players."

The shrinkage of the workforce is not due to the cuts in the military budget alone, the Machinists' Bruce Olsson explained; it also has much to do with Washington's attitude. "Jobs are lost through foreign competition and partners for UTC, like coproduction. And innovation, which is the AIDS of employment. To the extent the U.S. does have an industrial policy, it's through the Pentagon. New manufacturing technology—automation, robotics—is supported in various places. Pratt had a plant in Georgia to make parts of jet engines, which is very automated. GE has a 'plant of the future' that is fully automated. Some are looking at 'virtual companies' that bring different corporations together to do a project, after which workers are laid off." What is happening more generally in the American economy is also affecting the military firms. "Conversion is much broader than the defense industry," Olsson offered. "It's about economic development."

The lamentations of the defense workers almost always turn to the "Feds"—what is Washington doing to help? Often "Washington" is viewed as an enemy, not just because the Pentagon's budget is being cut—most workers realize that was inevitable—but because they see the government always siding with the corporate bottom line. Olsson's example of the manufacturing technology is a case in point. Mergers and acquisitions, which invariably cost jobs, are encouraged by the Pentagon with bonuses, whereas conditions to develop commercial products are never imposed on the merging primes. Another example was offsets in exports, which peaked during the Bush administration.

So many jobs were being exported with the sales of helicopters and fighter jets and tanks that the unions, who were rather sanguine about the practice in the salad days of the 1980s, were now in an uproar. George Kourpias, the head of the union that organizes the F-16 plant in Fort Worth, addressed a rally of cheering workers in 1992 just outside the gates of the plant. "We've had enough of this company and others like it, and this government selling off our technology, our skills and our jobs to foreign countries and then laying off American workers. Enough is enough!" But President Bush, when earlier given the chance to take some action on offsets, simply released a short statement stating that offset policy "resides with the companies involved."

The companies involved wanted two things from George Bush and his successor, the first two post–Cold War presidents. First, they wanted help in exporting, especially the kind of financing that Chris Dodd wangled for

Sikorsky to sell the Black Hawks. Second, they wanted the Pentagon to keep the factories running, even at a low level. "History will tell you we will not have a peaceful world," observed Sam Iacobellis, Rockwell's chief, just before the 1992 election, "and if defense technology is allowed to dry up, we will lose our leadership in weaponry. We should take the so-called peace dividend and spend it to develop high-tech weapons to keep our intellectual talent employed." That argument, fully developed by Les Aspin, the Wisconsin Democrat who headed the House Armed Services Committee, was the case for preserving the "defense industrial base." Bush was equivocal about that idea, which would be reasserted by Aspin when he became secretary of defense after Bush was voted out of office.

But the other idea, the financing for exports, came to be more to Bush's— and Congress's—liking. Building on Dodd's 1989 gambit, Bush supported a $1-billion fund through the Eximbank, and in 1993 the Democrats, now in control of the entire federal government, passed a bill proposed by a Republican senator from Idaho, Dirk Kempthorne, which diverted money from conversion funds to support export financing. Kempthorne, among others, credited Dodd for blazing the trail for the new law. "It was all the same crowd working together," said one Senate staffer. "Dodd opened the door to this kind of financing."

The incoming president, Bill Clinton, seemed to adopt the opposite of Bush's positions: skeptical about what became known as the Kempthorne amendment, supportive of Aspin's desire to sustain the defense industrial base, and enthusiastic about conversion. As a candidate, he made rather bold declarations: "Take the money and use it to rebuild our transportation systems, our communications systems, our environmental cleanup, to develop new technologies." It was the standard-issue philosophy of turning swords into plowshares, and in the new, boomer-generation White House the emphasis was on high technology. At last, it seemed, the defense worker would have an active friend in the White House.

The scale of the retooling effort in the ensuing years was paltry compared with the need, however. The new team in Washington at first talked about infusing the idea with $60 billion over five years, but the number kept shrinking as the realities of budget constraints and Capitol Hill politics set in. The new team did begin, as their major initiative, a Technology Reinvestment Program to invest in a form of conversion—but that left many dissatisfied. The sourness stemmed from the TRP's insistence on "dual use": technologies having both civilian *and* military uses. In the eyes of its critics, such dual-use requirements placed the bar too high for conversion, and would eliminate many possibilities for moving the lower-tier players from defense dependency to commercial profitability. The primes were still getting much of the dough: in February 1994, for example, a round of TRP grants in Connecticut was announced, and the winners were Pratt & Whitney and Electric Boat, which were teaming up on projects with the likes of IBM, Boeing, Martin Marietta, and DuPont. And after Congress turned Republican in 1995, these small efforts were under attack. "At least it was something," said Don Nakamoto. "It was serving to pull together most firms interested in conversion, along with company partners, academics, labs, et cetera. It was a galvanizing thing."

The other mantra chanted in Washington was worker retraining, but this too encountered dour responses in the ranks of defense blue collars. "We're disappointed with Clinton," Pratt & Whitney organizer Bruce Olsson complained. "Robert Reich and the Department of Labor focus on training programs, but we say, job training for what? Jobs create training programs, not the other way around. We've gotten millions for displaced P&W workers for readjustment. Guys used to be tool-and-die makers are now driving trucks. It deskills the worker."

None of the conversion efforts in Hartford, Sacramento, or Washington were matched to the size of the task, and perhaps none could be. The primes and many of the major subcontractors were not interested, and without their enthusiastic participation, classic conversion—taking defense technology and refashioning it into commercial products—could not succeed. The mentality of the primes, shaped by decades of fat cost-plus contracts from the Pentagon, proved harder to reform than the Kremlin. The only consistent help that Washington would offer to the shrinking defense industry, obtained with the industry's legendary lobbying skills, would be billions in procurement contracts for no other reason than to keep the assembly lines moving, and more subsidies to export weaponry to our stout allies and democratic friends, like the Republic of Turkey.

20

NEW TUNE, SAME DANCE

Washington, 1993–1995

On a cold, brilliantly sunny day in Washington, the American presidency passed from George Bush to Bill Clinton. What Bush passed to Clinton in foreign policy was essentially a hodgepodge. His principal legacy in the Middle East was the unstable fulcrum of Iraq. Operation Provide Comfort was in full swing, but an exit strategy was nowhere in sight. The Kurds of northern Iraq—the tribal chieftains Talabani and Barzani—were bickering ceaselessly. Saddam was typically defiant. Turkey grumbled that it was losing billions of dollars in trade with Iraq, especially from the oil-pipeline shutdown, and that the autonomy granted by the UN to Iraqi "Kurdistan" was providing a haven for the PKK. Islamic militancy was gaining ground in Saudi Arabia, Egypt, and Pakistan. Afghanistan had descended into a state of violent chaos. The peace process centered on the Israeli-Palestinian standoff seemed stalled. Very little looked promising in this volatile mixture.

The Clinton team brought to this situation three new impulses. The first was to correct the Bush administration's naïve reliance on Iraq as a counterweight to Iran. This need had been evident for eighteen months, of course, but a new theory or doctrine was required all the same. Second, the emphasis on trade as an engine of foreign policy was a mantra of the 1992 campaign and would be given its due in the new administration: export growth was seen as a panacea for the long decline in manufacturing and workers' wages. The trade portfolio would include military technology, as this was one of America's most advanced commodities. The third impulse was human rights, intentionally neglected for twelve years under the Republicans, who had sneered at Jimmy Carter's supposed embrace of a rights-based foreign policy. Each of these fresh impulses would have a significant impact on Turkey and the region.

President Clinton got off to a bad start with the Turks, when Özal's visit to Washington in the late winter of 1993 turned into a public-relations fiasco. The Turkish president and hero of the Gulf war was snubbed at first by the White House, then granted just a fifteen-minute audience. When Özal died in April 1993, only a low-level U.S. delegation attended the funeral. In the eyes of the Turks, these were insults to a great ally that was continuing to make enormous sacrifices for the sake of American interests.

U.S. policy was changing, but in two contradictory directions: toward more heavily armed allies in the region to protect U.S. interests, and also toward restraint, based on budget-deficit penury and spasms of human-rights concerns. The first policy direction endorsed the traditional American view of Turkey: staunch ally in a bad neighborhood, geostrategic linchpin of U.S. interests. When Secretary of State Warren Christopher visited Ankara in June 1993, he pledged U.S. support for the fight against the PKK and agreed to provide ten Cobra helicopters. He made the usual noises about increased economic investment and strategic partnerships. This rhetoric, combining the grandeur of Turkey with its aching vulnerability, appealed to the Turks' deep pride and their equally strong feelings of persecution. The appeal was later summed up by Richard Holbrooke, the assistant secretary of state for Europe: "In Turkey, we seek the further development of a democratic, secular state with a prosperous economy, a supportive approach to Western interests, and high human-rights standards. . . . Our interests are considerable. Turkey stands at the crossroads of almost every issue of importance to the U.S. on the Eurasian continent—including NATO, the Balkans, Cyprus, the Aegean, Iraq sanctions, Russian relations in the Caucasus and Central Asia, and transit routes for Caspian oil and gas. Our policy reflects the continuity of shared security interests and intensive security cooperation."

"Shared interests" and "cooperation" were soon defined by the new president's answer to Bush's failed Persian Gulf balancing act. That answer was an attempt to isolate the bad boys of the Persian Gulf, Iran and Iraq. Both had provided treacherous footing for the U.S. security establishment. The Nixon-Kissinger-Ford-Carter strategy of propping up the Shah had catastrophically collapsed. The Reagan–Bush policy of strengthening Saddam as a counterweight to Iran had catastrophically exploded. Some new theory, a fresh conceptual framework for U.S. security policy in the region, was needed.

Bill Clinton, himself unschooled in international affairs, had assembled a team of advisors that seemed up to the task of redefining American globalism in the post–Cold War world; indeed, his was the first presidency of that new world. The new secretary of state, Warren Christopher, was not known as a conceptualizer but as a wise head who could readily counsel the young president. The national security advisor, Anthony Lake, an academic who served at the NSC during the 1970s, was widely seen as progressive, intelligent, open, and unassuming. The defense secretary, Les Aspin, the longtime Wisconsin congressman who had headed the House Armed Services Committee, was the giant among them—the most assertive, in any case—and he brought a sharp group with him to the Pentagon as well. It appeared that Aspin would take the lead in redefining the security vision of the United States: that was his predilection, and he had shown a flair for big thinking in the House. At the second level in these three venues of policymaking were other formidable minds—Bill Perry, Richard Holbrooke, Ashton Carter, Joseph Nye, Mort Halperin, Tim Wirth, and Brian Atwood, among many others. It was a dream team of intellectuals set to play for the United States in the post–Cold War arena.

In the first months of the new presidency, however, the policy construction job went very badly. Aspin foundered as defense secretary, proving ill-suited to the regimen and unable to make decisions. A few weeks after the death of eighteen soldiers during the peacekeeping mission in Somalia, he resigned. His only contribution to a new security vision was the two-front war strategy—the "need" for the United States to be prepared to fight two major wars simultaneously—a concoction of a military brass worried about the prospects for a peace dividend at the Pentagon's expense. Thus Aspin became the intellectual captive of the military; that was his only discernible legacy.

Meanwhile, the quieter but determined Tony Lake began to issue the policy statements that would define the American role, particularly in the Middle East. One idea became the focus of all the Administration's thinking: "backlash" states. That, it seemed, was all there was to worry about. The overarching theme for a new policy was "enlargement" rather than the Cold War's organizing principle of "containment"—a clever turning of a phrase. Enlargement of democracy and free markets was a concept with which few could argue. But the backlash states provided more grist for the milling of a new doctrine. "Our policy toward such states," Lake explained in a major address in September 1993, "must seek to isolate them diplomatically, militarily, economically, and technologically. It must stress intelligence, counterterrorism, and multilateral export controls." The states he had in mind, of course, were Iran, Iraq, Libya, North Korea, and Cuba. The grounds for branding them as pariahs were also articulated. "Centralized power defends itself. It not only wields tools of state power such as military force, political imprisonment and torture, but also exploits the intolerant energies of racism, ethnic prejudice, religious persecution, xenophobia, and irredentism." The description Lake offered could easily fit more than the unholy five, and fit some U.S. allies rather closely.

Containment was not out the window altogether, however. Lake articulated a new policy of "dual containment" in the Middle East to deal with both Iran and Iraq. Dual containment signaled a special effort to isolate rogues, and would be backed by the largest military expenditure during the Clinton administration, a $50-billion-per-year deployment of forces in the Gulf region.

The policy's evolution resulted from an unusual display of intellectual clout. The Washington Institute for Near East Policy, a think tank strongly associated with the pro-Israel lobby in the United States, had assembled a stellar group of movers and shakers between 1990 and 1992 to reconsider the failure of U.S. policy in the Gulf. Iraq and Iran had proved especially troublesome for Israel, Iraq having threatened Israel directly and Iran having supported terrorist groups like Hamas and Hezbollah in Lebanon. The Gulf crisis of the autumn of 1990 affected Israel as much as anyone, and those in Washington concerned with Israel's safety naturally wanted to reconsider the long trail of failed U.S. policies toward the two great rogues of the Gulf. The Institute, under its founding director, Martin Indyk, assembled a "strategic study group" to provide some policy recommendations.

Such study groups are common in Washington, and their thinking rarely reaches more than a handful of report readers. But Indyk and his young deputy, Robert Satloff, chose their participants with a deft touch. They included future Clinton appointees Les Aspin, Madeleine Albright, Stuart Eizenstat, Sam Lewis, and Walt Slocombe, plus a handful of sympathetic columnists and such perennial power brokers as Sam Nunn, William Cohen, and Daniel Inouye, all U.S. senators, former secretary of state Alexander Haig, and former defense secretary Donald Rumsfeld. The group met several times, but as is usual in these cases, the institute staff led the discussion and prepared the three reports. "There was an ongoing in-house discussion of this," Satloff recalls. "We perceived Iraq as a rogue state long before August 1990. By about 1989 to '90, after the end of the first Gulf war, we thought the U.S. no longer needed to tilt toward Iraq and that the tilt lived on too long. The senatorial delegation [to Iraq in the spring of 1990], which included Bob Dole, was a symbol of that tilt."

The group issued three reports, the final one in 1992. In fact, the reports were vague with regard to any grand revision of strategy, apart from isolating Iraq. What they did, more likely, was to establish the need for a revision of strategy in the Gulf. But the key point of influence was not the reports but the entry of several of its authors into the Clinton administration most significantly Martin Indyk.

An Australian by birth and still sporting an Aussie accent, Indyk in appearance was a throwback to the days of Dean Acheson, with his gaunt, silvery features and pencil-thin moustache. He assumed a post in the National Security Council, in essence becoming the president's top White House advisor on Middle East issues. The power of NSC staffers derives from their access to the president and from their filtering of information and policy prescriptions coming from the rest of the vast national security bureaucracy for the president. Indyk thus had the best of all worlds: a pivotal position close to the one person, Tony Lake, who stepped forward with a new strategic scheme, and with powerful friends in State and Defense who had been part of the Institute's study group just months before.

By May, Indyk was ready to unveil the new concept of dual containment, fashioned at the institute by himself, Satloff, and staffer Patrick Closson. At a conference organized by the Washington Insititute at the Sheraton-Carlton Hotel, Indyk gave the keynote address outlining the Administration's approach to the Middle East. His "shorthand" description of that approach: "'Dual containment' of Iran and Iraq in the east; promotion of Arab-Israeli peace in the west; backed by energetic efforts to stem the spread of weapons of mass destruction and promote a vision of a more democratic and prosperous region for all the people of the Middle East." These objectives, Indyk proclaimed, were feasible "as long as we can rely on our regional allies—Egypt, Israel, Saudi Arabia . . . and Turkey—to preserve a balance of power in our favor in the Middle East region." Turkey, Indyk said, "is coming to play an important role not only in Central Asia but also in the Middle East," particularly through Operation Provide Comfort.

In unofficial policy circles, the new framework earned a rather sharp rebuke. The barometers for commotions on arcane policy matters are the prestigious journals *Foreign Affairs* and *Foreign Policy,* and both were moved to publish articles denouncing the policy. "Dual containment explicitly disavows the need for any kind of political relationship with Iran or Iraq," wrote one prominent analyst. Its essential military character also places a burden on the Gulf states. "The higher the American military profile in these countries, the greater the risk that it would become a lightning rod for domestic discontent, as happened many times in past decades in the Middle East." The embargo on Iraq, perhaps the most sellable dimension of the initiative, began to suffer public-relations setbacks; its harshness was measured in impacts on ordinary Iraqis, as when *60 Minutes* showed hospital wards of malnourished children and claimed that 500,000 youngsters had died as a result of the West's action. America's longtime allies in Europe bitterly complained of the policy, seeing U.S. embargoes against Iran, Iraq, and Cuba as motivated by domestic politics rather than by any strategic imperative.

In fact, when President Clinton announced a trade embargo on Iran in the spring of 1995, he did so in front of a major Jewish organization. Indyk himself soon departed Washington to become U.S. ambassador to Israel (taking out American citizenship just before being sworn in as ambassador). Ethnic politics has always played a large role in American foreign policy, and for a time it seemed to be escalating in the post-Communist era. Turkey itself is relentlessly needled by the hectoring of prominent Greek- and Armenian-Americans.

But the formulation of dual containment expressed the essential continuity of U.S. policy. Noxious anti-Western regimes would be "contained" by military means, with the help of surrogates—Turkey, the Gulf sheikhdoms, and Egypt. The prospect for democratic "enlargement" being enhanced by militarizing already repressive regimes was not explained. But the key point was the reliance on military means, including enormous shipments of military hardware to these "front-line" states.

That Iran remained the central obsession of U.S. policy was due in part to the presence of so many Carter-era veterans in the Clinton administration. Warren Christopher in particular was frequently rumored to have an obsession with Iran, because of how the 1979–80 hostage crisis consumed him as deputy secretary. Throughout the first term of Bill Clinton, Iran made quiet overtures toward reconciliation, which were rebuffed by setting tough conditions for dialogue on Teheran. It was politically more appealing to isolate and excoriate the Islamic Republic. But it had a cost. Europe and Japan disliked the policy, and continued to trade with Iran. The Russians were forced to withdraw a nuclear-reactor sale, a public humiliation for proreform forces in Moscow. The radical mullahs in Teheran clearly gained new life as a result of the U.S. belligerence. Militant groups like Hezbollah were activated, as were opposition groups in Egypt and Saudi Arabia. U.S. facilities were frequently targets of terrorist acts.

The turmoil—and the doctrine—provided a fresh rationale for the second major characteristic of the Clinton administration, a quiet resolve to export weapons. By the time Clinton entered the White House, the drawdown was already an alarming fact of life for the defense industry. Clinton's early budgets projected a sharper cut in military spending than had Bush's, and procurement would take a noticeable hit. There was much talk about a federally led effort to convert defense industries to commercial production, probably headed by Vice President Al Gore. But Clinton had shown his hand as a candidate during the previous autumn when he endorsed F-15 fighter-jet sales to Saudi Arabia and F-16s to Taiwan, both rather obvious political gestures to save jobs in California and Texas. These sales undermined talks among the so-called P-5 (United Kingdom, United States, France, Russia, and China) to limit high-tech arms transfers to the Middle East.

It was that campaign impulse that defeated loftier ideas of conversion throughout Clinton's first term. Two origins of the policy were evident. The first was Les Aspin's insistence that exports could bridge the gap between generations of weapons. As the manufacturing of tanks, aircraft, and the like withered owing to lower demand from the U.S. armed forces, that "defense industrial base" would not be available for the next generation of weapons—perhaps a decade away—or in the event of serious security threats, such as a renewal of the Cold War.

The second, and probably more powerful, impetus came from a pro-trade outlook that overwhelmed the far weaker voices of restraint. Secretary Christopher cabled U.S. embassies in the spring of 1993 emphasizing that "commercial interests must be one of your highest priorities," and among those, one of his deputies flatly stated, were defense exports. The king of promoters, however, was Ron Brown, the new commerce secretary, a wheeler-dealer of the old school whose hyperkinetic mission was the overseas sales of all products American made. Brown was known to request meetings in foreign capitals with the heads of defense ministries on his frequent trips abroad. In the summer of 1993, he was the first U.S. commerce secretary to attend the Paris Air Show, the Grand Bazaar of the arms trade. He even interpreted the brief enthusiasm for defense conversion to mean federal support for exports ("a critical piece of the defense conversion puzzle," he cold a congressional panel, "is helping firms find export markets"). A defense industry honcho marveled that he couldn't "think of a Secretary of Commerce in the past who associated himself more with defense exports."

The influence of the industry itself, wholly dominant during the Reagan-Bush era, scarcely waned in the Clinton years. The major advisory groups—one in the Pentagon, another in the State Department—were chock full of defense industrialists. The Defense Trade Advisory Group at Foggy Bottom, for example, included 57 industry members out of a total of 60 people on the panel. It would routinely hear from State Department officials. For example, Lynn Davis, the undersecretary responsible for nonproliferation, told them at their October 6, 1993, meeting of the government's "commitment to actively support U.S. manufacturers' efforts to increase their exports," and that the government would consider "a proposed export's economic consequences and effect on the industrial base."

Early on, the White House—possibly trying to find a seam of difference from Bush's foreign policy—promised a major review of the arms trade, which turned into that quintessential Washington fixture, the formless, toothless, and tardy committee report. The interagency exercise, which began in the autumn of 1993, was spearheaded from State, with a few key people just below the secretary level tasked to the review, including Lynn Davis and Tom McCarthy, the assistant secretary for politico-military affairs, State's most hawkish desk when it came to arms trade.

The interagency review ran into few obstacles; only the Arms Control and Disarmament Agency, with its coterie of arms-restraint professionals, had problems with the pro-export orientation of the document. The nearly final policy statement was on Clinton's desk in September 1994—but it languished there for several months. Clinton himself had to resolve one dispute: whether or not a new loan guarantee fund, similar to Eximbank's backing for the Black Hawk deal to Turkey, would supplement the $4 billion already provided by the U.S. government. In a move widely described as the sole setback to the defense industry, he declined to approve such backing. Finally, the policy statement—Presidential Decision Directive 34, or PDD-34—was issued in mid-February 1995. The actual document remains classified, but the White House released a fact sheet, with no fanfare and little press attention, outlining the policy. Five goals were articulated: "(1) To ensure that our military forces can continue to enjoy technological advantages over potential adversaries. (2) To help allies and friends deter or defend themselves against aggression, while promoting interoperability with U.S. forces when combined operations are required. (3) To promote regional stability in areas critical to U.S. interests, while preventing the proliferation of weapons of mass destruction and their missile delivery systems. (4) To promote peaceful conflict resolution and arms control, human rights, democratization, and other U.S. foreign policy objectives. (5) To enhance the ability of the U.S. defense industrial base to meet U.S. defense requirements and maintain long-term military technological superiority at lower costs."

The five standards could readily have been borrowed from the Bush or Reagan administrations. Nothing in PDD-34 indicated the slightest change of policy. "I think it's pretty clear that for other major suppliers around the world their companies have the very active support of their governments at all levels," a department spokesman said at the time. "Our goal here is simply to level the playing field for American companies." He made no mention of nonproliferation as "our goal."

Arms-control advocates jumped all over the statement as a reneging of candidate Clinton's vow to be tougher than Bush on arms trading, but given the Administration's record to that point—record levels of sales and transfers in 1993 and 1994—the dovish comments of the Arkansan on the hustings in 1992 seemed long ago and far away. The outrage was summed up by one of the most trenchant critics of arms policy, Lora Lumpe of the Federation of American Scientists: "Lacking the courage to take on weapons corporations, the Commerce Department, and the Pentagon, and lacking the vision to devise new security paradigms, the Clinton administration has failed to seize the opportunity afforded by the end of the Cold War. Rather than seeking to reduce reliance on the use of force—and building up reliance on the rule of law—the White House is risking not only much more warfare to come, but killing and destruction at much higher levels."

In Washington's "K Street corridor" and in the Capitol Hill suites of the industry, the mood was jubilant. The Clinton directive, said Joel Johnson, a top aerospace lobbyist, is "the most positive statement on defense trade that has been enunciated by any administration." Sales were booming, against the expectations of many in the aftermath of the Cold War: in 1993, government and commercial deals (including deliveries and agreements) for American manufacturers totaled nearly $60 billion, nearly twice the total in the post-Gulf-war year of 1992; and 1994 had seen a solid $38 billion. Regulations for exporters were being streamlined; the industry advisory groups at State and Defense were successfully making it easier to do the paperwork and expedite government approval. By the midpoint of the Clinton administration, the United States was selling 75 percent of the supply of arms to the Third World. And Dodd's dream for a grand financing mechanism came to fruition in the Defense Export Loan Program, a $15 billion fund in the Pentagon that Clinton accepted from the new Republican Congress in late 1995.

The White House liberalization of arms trading was not getting by unscathed, however, particularly where Turkey was concerned. The mounting onslaught of human-rights groups was gradually taking a toll. Foggy Bottom and the National Security Council were filled with veterans of the Carter administration, and while those longtime-in-the-wilderness few (Christopher, Lake, Aspin successor Bill Perry, Madeleine Albright at the UN, among others) were wary of looking like Carteristas reborn, they were naturally prone to emphasize rights. Even Clinton had done so in the campaign, using Haiti and China as examples of Bush's moral deficit. When a former head of the American Civil Liberties Union, John Shattuck, was made assistant secretary of state for human rights, the die was cast: Turkey's deplorable record of abuses would be placed firmly on the bilateral agenda.

The election of a Democrat also had the peculiar effect of liberating some Republicans on Capitol Hill who were inveterate critics of Turkey, especially Senator Alphonse D'Amato, the voluble New Yorker, with his big Armenian-American backers, and Representative John Porter of sub-urban Illinois, whose unusually vociferous criticism of Turkey's Kurdish policy was largely driven, many believed, by his high-profile activist wife, Kathryn Cameron Porter. With pressure from the Hill and from within the Administration, Turkey would surely be under exceptional—indeed, un-precedented—pressure to repent.

The anti-Turkish forces on the eastern end of Pennsylvania Avenue mounted their campaigns quickly. A central player in their game was the slightly obscure Commission on Security and Cooperation in Europe (CSCE), a bipartisan and bicameral committee composed of nine representa-tives, nine senators, and three members from the executive branch. It derived from the organization of the same name in Europe, a result of the so-called Helsinki process that drew in all the nations of Europe and emphasized human rights. The Helsinki commission, as it was often called, included Turkey critics John Porter, Al D'Amato, and representatives Steny Hoyer (D-MD), and Christopher Smith (R-NJ), and would convene hearings every few months that brought witnesses from Turkey's Southeast to describe the increasing horror of the civil war in the region. The panel was nothing if not bold: testimony from Kurdish nationalists and harsh criticisms of U.S. pol-icy were commonplace. Ample attention was given to Kurdish members of the Turkish Parliament jailed for advocating a political solution to the civil war. No one paid much attention to these hearings, which were drowned out in the hubbub of talk that is official Washington, but the commission was a platform for the Turkophobes on the Hill, and the staff were strategists in Congress and a point of entry for the NGOs hoping to block arms sales and military assistance to Turkey. "Dear Colleague" letters, speeches for the record, various sorts of condemnations—all could be hatched by the commis-sion. It was an amazing spectacle in the imperial city: Republicans openly aligning themselves with radical Kurds—some of them, no doubt, Marxists—to incessantly harass an ally widely beloved by the Republican establishment and accepted by the Democratic president.

The panel's Democrats were not without their own measure of indigna-tion. When chairman Dennis DeConcini, an Arizona Democrat who was soon to retire from his Senate seat, visited the Southeast of Turkey in the au-tumn of 1994, he used the bully pulpit of the commission to needle Ankara. "It was discouraging to note," he said upon his return, "that rising national-ism is fueling present government policies, accounting in part for the inability of Turkey's leadership to take meaningful steps toward a nonmilitary resolution of the Kurdish issue. . . . Open debate about the fundamental problem confronting Turkey—much less discussion of compromise—is increasingly impossible, even though many admit that the present policies are not working." The report made no waves in the United States, but it was widely reported in Turkey—particularly since Prime Minister Tansu Çiller refused to see DeConcini. And it sent another salvo down to the Hill, for among the executive members of the commission was John Shattuck.

Congress was far from all smoke and no fire when it came to Turkey, however. In the summer of 1994, the U.S. aid was "conditioned"—a dreaded word to all aid recipients—on the Kurdish issue. Ten percent of aid was withheld pending an inquiry by the State Department into the accusations of human-rights abuses by the Turkish government. State was required to investigate and produce a report in the coming fiscal year. This was the distilled essence of the Helsinki panel's reports and exhortations. In the midst of a campaign that would turn Congress over to the Republicans, the action still had a tempest-in-a-teapot appearance, but it was real enough to the Turks, who indignantly said they would not take the 10 percent under any circumstances. (The other 90 percent, however, was accepted.) Aid to Turkey had been converted from grants to loans in fiscal year 1993, and the overall numbers were dropping too. But that had less to do with anti-Turkish sentiment than with general austerity in the foreign-operations budget.

Off the Hill, the pivotal role of human rights was most visible in Clinton's presidency because of John Shattuck's presence. The tall, professorial Shattuck, with his unruly, thinning gray hair and earnest countenance, cut a strong profile in the State Department. He had run government relations for Harvard University before coming back to Washington, and he knew bureaucratic politics as well as he knew the human-rights agenda. Apart from China and Bosnia, Turkey became the overriding concern of his bureau.

The interest stemmed not only from human-rights abuses: the long-standing practices of torture, proscriptions on tree speech and organizing, disappearances, judicial irregularities, and the like; Shattuck worried about the very stability of the regime in Ankara. Perhaps alone in a national-security bureaucracy that was habitually blasé about Turkey, Shattuck and his deputies saw the war against the Kurds as weakening the secular, pro-Western government. The displaced Kurds and even those remaining in the Southeast were voting in record numbers for the Turkish Islamic party

Refah; they were radicalized and alienated from the secular Turkish state. At the same time, the economy was in ruins, fueling discontent among Turks. The status of rights in the Turkish Republic was more than a moral cause; it was fundamental to American and Western interests.

This concern was manifested in several ways, beginning in 1994. Shattuck took two trips to Turkey, one in July and the second in November. Both created a sensation there—here was a senior American official not only "inspecting" the country for its human-rights record, but suggesting openly that a political solution to the Kurdish crisis needed to be pursued. He met with human-rights groups and independent intellectuals who could provide a powerful account of the deterioration of politics, especially Refah's gains and the war's costly brutality. Higher-ups in the U.S. government—Christopher, Talbot, Lake, the Pentagon—weren't engaged. So Shattuck began to wage a quiet campaign to bring a sense of realism to the Administration's rote determinations about Turkey.

Top officials routinely expressed sentiments to their counterparts in Ankara about torture, the Kurdish issue, and such, but Turks could normally brush off such comments as the necessary folderol of diplomacy. "What do you do after you've done all the talking?" asked a senior State Department official. "The denial of arms sends a clear political signal that we consider what's happening in the Southeast as unacceptable." Shattuck himself was convinced that the arms-export handle could be utilized to send stern messages to Ankara without embarrassing them. They were, after all, important allies, and one didn't want to fuel anti-Western sentiment by publicly humiliating the government. But he also had to find incentives for Turkey to improve its behavior. The key seemed to be Ankara's desperate yearning to become part of Europe. "Since we began to engage this issue," Shattuck commented privately in June 1995, "there have been no cluster bombs, no SuperCobras, et cetera, transferred to Turkey. As to enforcement, the Turkish interest in the customs union is leverage we are using. We're not shouting this from the rooftops, but it is a conscious effort being done through positive inducements."

The denial of arms was suddenly made easier by the report Congress had mandated the summer before. Shattuck's bureau was required to assess the use of U.S. arms in human-rights abuses against the Kurds and in Cyprus—the latter, of course, remaining an obsession of the powerful Greek lobby. The report was written over several months and drew heavily on dispatches from the field gathered by the U.S. embassy's human-rights officer, Janice Weiner, and the final draft was crafted in Washington by Kate Schertz, a foreign-service officer who had served in Adana and Izmir. It was somber, unemotional, and systematic, describing the crisis and how the Turkish government organized itself to mount the campaign against the Kurds. Detailing the weapons America had supplied, the report noted that Black Hawks, for example, "are used for reconnaissance, observation, supply, evacuation, and command and control of operations." Actual abuses weren't detailed, only the general categories of weapons use were mentioned (abduction by helicopter, forced evacuations of villages, etc.). The reporters could not procure first-hand information, because Weiner was escorted around the Southeast by the Turkish military. Villagers were unlikely to speak to her, and she didn't seek out the displaced in the major cities. But by simply *mentioning* the weapons systems, by linking them to probable use in these most egregious human-rights violations, Shattuck possessed an invaluable tool to deny Turkey future arms transfers. Bureaucratically, the report was found gold.

Already two significant sales were being held up. Cluster bombs, pernicious weapons in which shrapnel is dispersed at high velocity over an enormous area, were requested by the Turks in 1993; the sale, however, was quietly held up in Shattuck's office until Human Rights Watch discovered the deal and mounted an effective public campaign to defeat it, relying on Hill activists and a suddenly righteous press. A new batch of Cobras was also slated to be sold to Turkey, and the usual lobbying ensued, with Texas congressmen pushing hard for the Fort Worth product. Again, however, delay in licensing the attack copters allowed the public-interest groups—tipped off by a source in the Pentagon—to make a strong public stand against. "The human-rights bureau can be ignored," a longtime political operative said of the episode, "but Turkey proves that they're not." A sale of tactical missiles was approved by State in late 1995, but only because they were unlikely to be used in the war against the Kurds.

In public, however, Shattuck differed little from the rest of the Administration on Turkey. The uniform approach was to stress Turkey's importance to the United States and to accept, regrettably, its war against "terrorism." The Clinton administration, alone among Western allies, endorsed an April 1995 cross-border invasion by the Turkish military to root out PKK camps in northern Iraq, a month-long operation that failed to do much beyond further damaging Turkey's reputation. Coupled with the release of the report on Turkey's use of U.S. arms, the invasion of Iraq stirred new anti-Turkish sentiment on the Hill. Following the summer recess, Shattuck appeared before the Helsinki Commission in Congress to defend Ankara's improving record on human rights and the export of American weapons to Turkey. "Human rights violations have occurred in the course of operations," Shattuck's prepared testimony read, "but those operations appear to have been undertaken for a purpose authorized" under the Arms Export Control Act. The United States must support "Turkey's legitimate struggle against terrorism." Along with Marshall Adair of the European bureau at State, Shattuck stressed the good news from Turkey, the move toward some constitutional changes and toward freer speech in particular. But the congressmen were not impressed. "I've been dealing with this for ten years, and if you ask me, the situation in Turkey has gotten much worse in the last few years, not better," said John Porter. "U.S. policy sounds bankrupt to me."

The Administration's line echoed the longtime pattern of U.S. behavior toward Turkey: don't rock the boat. "The support for Turkey over forty years has remained strong, essentially unaltered, even as the rationale for support changes," notes one longtime observer. The uniformity of official opinion in 1995 reflected the fundamental truth about Washington-Ankara ties: the Clinton team wanted to keep the conservative parties in power in Turkey and to help Turkey enter the European customs union. ("Holbrooke is cracking heads all over Europe to get Turkey the vote," a U.S. diplomat said privately.) But just weeks after the customs-union vote, a Turkey watcher at State admitted that the human-rights situation had deteriorated badly, with an accused torturer installed as Interior Minister and new fighting in the Southeast. The U.S. strategy of public approval for Turkey, making arms sales there with just occasional interruptions, and Turkey's refreshed position in the pantheon of U.S. strategic interests was wobbly, stumbling toward a nasty fall.

2 1

AMERICANS IN TURKEY

There is a saying in Turkish that might shed some light on the nature of Turkey-U.S. relations," a Kurdish activist told a congressional panel. "It goes something like this: 'Give a man a hammer and he will think all problems are nails.' Turkey has been supplied with plenty of hammers by the United States government, and it is the Kurds who are being ruthlessly pounded like nails." The United States gave Turkey $6 billion in military assistance—most of it weaponry—in the decade from 1984 to 1993, making it the third-highest recipient of American largesse, after Israel and Egypt. No nation in the post–World War II era had closer ties to Turkey than the United States. Washington supplied four-fifths of Turkey's military imports, which from 1991 to 1995 were the largest in the world.

But by the 1990s, the Americans in Ankara felt they had, astonishingly, lost much influence with the Turkish government. Despite unstinting political support, the growing American business investment in Turkey—$1 billion a year, a close second to Germany—and the generous provision of "hammers," Ankara felt wounded by the ethnically driven excoriations from Capitol Hill, the mild rebukes on human rights emanating (almost exclusively) from John Shattuck's office, and the scattershot condemnations of Turkey in the *New York Times* and the *Washington Post*.

So the Turks began to play hardball with the one maneuver available to them: the military relationship. Since this was the rock upon which Washington had constructed its ties to Ankara, it naturally became the lever for Turkey's discontent. The two principal deals brought into play were Operation Provide Comfort and the purchase of helicopters.

The war against Iraq in 1991 was the precursor to a new phase of America's relationship with Turkey, and Operation Provide Comfort, the consequent mechanism to supply and protect the Iraqi Kurds, became the enduring manifestation of that post-Cold War phase. U.S. policy toward Turkey from the 1950s to the 1980s "was very simple," recalls Morton Abramowitz, the American ambassador from 1989 to 1991. "Turkey was a NATO ally, a flank state, and served as an important deterrent to the Russians. Comes the end of the Cold War. Military assistance becomes questionable. The Gulf war was just a hiccup in that; we paid Turkey for its support with another tranche for the F-16, which was linked to Özal's determination to build a big defense industry. The new post-Cold War rationale for assistance was based on two things: uncertainty over Russia, and Turkey's bad neighborhood." And no one was badder than Saddam.

Provide Comfort was nearly invisible in the United States. But it was very much on the minds of the Turks. The embargo on Iraqi oil was in fact a larger matter, the nonuse of the oil pipeline running along the south of Turkey to the Mediterranean costing the Turks $6 billion or so each year. But Provide Comfort—essentially part of the same policy as the embargo—was even more sensitive than financial loss. The protection of Iraqi Kurds—former subjects of the Ottoman Empire—by the U.S. Air Force was troublesome in at least two ways. The Kurds in Iraq were creating a quasi-state, virtually autonomous from Baghdad but not quite sovereign. But sovereignty could be just around the corner, and this prospect Ankara opposed and feared: many Turkish politicians saw a U.S. conspiracy to create a new Kurdistan; at a minimum, Kurdish aspirations in northern Iraq could stir Kurdish nationalism across the northern border. Bülent Ecevit, the social democratic leader, echoed Turkish anxieties when he asked the Grand National Assembly, "Are we going to commit suicide just to please the United States?"

The second problem was the PKK. The Iraqi Kurds, while dependent on Ankara for protection and supplies, were prone to give sanctuary to the guerrillas, and, inconsistently and tempestuously, often did. So the Turks required compensation for the political upkeep of Operation Provide

Comfort (which needed a thrice-yearly vote of their parliament), and that came in the form of military assistance, loans, and sales, political support for transborder raids, and intelligence data. The last, generated by the airborne force assembled to keep Saddam in line, served up to the Turkish military information on the PKK, including targets to hit with fighter jets and helicopters. But each year the vote in the Grand National Assembly was harder to win; as the Islamic party became stronger and the governing coalitions weakened, the American position became less tenable. Turkey was not willing to be the pliant ally if its own interests—admittedly difficult to define—were part of the price.

"Provide Comfort? Well, there's no exit strategy," a senior American diplomat in Ankara acknowledged. "The fate of Saddam is the fate of Provide Comfort. The Turks are very suspicious, they think we want a Kurdish state in northern Iraq—which we do *not*. But the Turks won't make us leave. They don't want all those refugees."

The more enduring part of the U.S.-Turkish military relationship was arms supply, and on this Ankara was bristling at the repeated suggestion that weapons should be denied because of their abuse of the Kurds. The first unambiguous signal of a change in American policy was the conversion of U.S. foreign aid from grants to loans. In train since the autumn of 1992, the switch was doubly hurtful to Turkey when the interest on a $400 million package was altered in 1993 from "concessional" to market rates, a very considerable burden on a government that was already neck deep in debt. From 1993 to 1997, loans and economic support funds—cash not directly related to military aid—steeply declined to around $150 million. U.S. officials in Ankara repeatedly urged Congress not to alter the generous terms of our military assistance, siding, as usual, with the Turkish military's desire to upgrade its weaponry. The Turks viewed the change with equal measures of equanimity and distrust: the more even-tempered saw foreign aid generally declining, not just aid to Turkey, but there was always the suspicion that the Armenian and Greek lobbies were behind the cuts. What rankled more, however, was the stalled sales of weapons. Having come to rely so much on high-quality American aircraft, the Turks wanted more—as if 10 more Cobras, 50 more Black Hawks, or a few thousand cluster bombs would transform the "Kurdish problem." But militaries are nothing if not thirsty for more technology, especially when facing an adversary who simply refuses to quit.

"The PKK is giving us an armed fight and Turkey would give them a fight with whatever arms it could find," insisted a former government minister and current member of parliament, Altan Öymen. "The American equipment, like the helicopters, are pretty advanced, so obviously they have aided in the fight against the PKK. The control in the Southeast has been facilitated by the U.S. arms. It has been brought under control faster than it would have been. But Turkey buys from France, Germany, even from Russia."

And that was the counterpunch to the human-rights jabs from Foggy Bottom. The French and Russians could both supply helicopters, and the Germans could provide armored vehicles and tanks. France was the most visible supporter of Turkey's bid to enter the European customs union, and in return the center-right government of Tansu Çiller in early 1995 ordered twenty of Eurocopter's Cougars from France during Çiller's visit to Paris. This was done without giving other companies the chance to bid on the contract—earning a loud protest from the Sikorsky chief in Ankara—but it was clearly done as a tribute to French President Jacques Chirac, as a diplomatic gesture of gratitude.

With the French as an alternative, the Turks could complain long and hard about the U.S. proclivity to press them on human rights. (The Russian supply of transport helicopters turned out to be a bust—poorly made, difficult to maintain.) "The United States should not hurt the Turkish public by lecturing about human rights or the Kurdish issue," President Demirel declared in a 1995 interview. "It should understand these issues correctly. It should not allow itself to be led about by its media, or the data provided by certain lobbies."

Privately, Turkish officials were more blunt. Gündüz Aktan, a longtime fixture in the foreign ministry, was particularly articulate. An elegant and educated man, Aktan has served Turkey in both Europe and the United States, and he understands Turkey's troubled relations with both. "Europe and the U.S. condemn terrorism, then instead turn to the last act of the security forces," he said in a 1995 interview. "Condemning terrorism is no big deal. Nobody really denounced the PKK as violent in a democratizing country. No violence is permitted to promote cultural rights. And the PKK aimed at dismembering Turkey, one-third of the country. Öcalan didn't hide his intentions. What we expect of the U.S. and Europe was to check these demands of Öcalan against the principles of self-determination. We've never heard from the U.S. or Europe that self-determination doesn't work here. Öcalan went to Syria and took money and sold drugs for arms. Syria uses the PKK as a proxy to put pressure on Turkey. None of these countries has denounced Syria for harboring the PKK."

While Turkish sensibilities are constantly upset by this perceived double standard, one that is not applied, they say, to Britain's treatment of Catholic rebels in northern Ireland, they maintain an appreciation of American support. "We have nothing to complain about with the Clinton administration. In northern Iraq, on NATO, Bosnia, economics and trade—it's all been very good and helpful. Holbrooke and Grossman are excellent," Aktan continued, reflecting the widespread Turkish view that Assistant Secretary of State Richard Holbrooke and Ambassador Marc Grossman formed a pro-Turkey axis against the anti-Turk cabal of Shattuck and Deputy Secretary of State Strobe Talbott. "But we are not happy with the human-rights reports. U.S. actions on human rights are harmful in most cases. Some in Congress use very harsh language, and their comments are almost immediately reflected in the Turkish press, which makes it hard for the U.S. in Turkish public opinion.

"In terms of the amount of U.S. aid to Turkey, it is not important, but it helps. One needs foreign credits. Symbolically, it's important because it represents U.S. support for our defense. Coproduction is most significant: F-16s, armored vehicles—investment in Turkish technology transfer shows the U.S. trusts us. We have to buy European matériel also because of the political situation, our entry into the customs union. But most major weapons systems are American. For all but Refah, the military relationship with the U.S. is very important."

Aktan's frank views are nearly carbon copies of those inside the American embassy. The boxy, U-shaped building on Atatürk Boulevard in Ankara is an unassuming place, looking more like a military compound and with security to match. (In that look it reflects Ankara itself, with its modern, garrison-like atmosphere, its feel of a postwar East European capital, and a skyline dominated by Atatürk's martial mausoleum and, as a reminder of that other cultural heritage, the Saudi-donated Kocatepe mosque.) Inside the American embassy only the ambassador's office is at all resplendent; most of the political and economic officers work in cramped, dreary quarters. The Foreign Service has been battered in the 1990s, slashed and abused by right-wing isolationists in Washington, but its importance to U.S. interests is very much in evidence in places like Turkey.

"We've been trying to change the conversation with the Turks," a senior

U.S. diplomat in Ankara explained in the late summer of 1995. "I say it's to take risks for stability and democracy. It's important for peace in this region. We want to be able to support democracy and the territorial integrity of Turkey. We say, 'The more you change, the more we can support you.'"

Clinton's Commerce Department had designated Turkey as one of the ten biggest emerging markets, and this began to alter the purpose of the embassy from a purely Cold War and regional-security bastion to an economic-operations center, in keeping with the fresh emphasis on trade. So the sporadic human-rights complaints by the U.S. government, long tempered by Ankara's front-line status as a military ally, were now muted by Turkey's potential as a market. "U.S. assistance has fallen to such a low level that it doesn't open doors. Turks understand this," the American diplomat continued. "Trade and investment is what matters now; the Caspian Sea oil pipeline is far more important than $20 million in aid."

The embassy was "outraged" by Congress's threats to not fund military training programs for the Turks, the IMET program that costs just one to two million dollars a year. "There's a whole strata of military leadership at the top that was trained in the U.S.," the diplomat contended. "Now the majors and lieutenants are training in France and Germany. Those guys will be buying the aircraft and tanks in the future.

"Human-rights activism from the states has a big impact because of the arms embargo of 1975–79. The Turks don't hear the nuances of tactics in Congress, the NGOs, and so on. What they hear is 'arms embargo.' They say 'You're hypocrites, we'll buy from the French and Germans.' It doesn't have any impact on the human-rights situation. What's caught their attention on human rights is the customs union, because you can't buy that anywhere else. It's a hundred times more important than denying them cluster bomb units. There'll be a lot more leverage if they're in the customs union. Sure, there'll be backsliding. It's about where you set the bar. This isn't Switzerland.

"The countervailing forces are pro-Greek, pro-Armenian, pro–human rights. So do we give them incentives or do we slap them around? The objective is a country that supports our kind of values. I'd rather have them on our side than not."

A week later, Ambassador Grossman was in Washington speaking to a conference convened by a pro-Turkish lobbying group. He mentioned five objectives of the U.S.-Turkish relationship. Better performance on human rights and democracy in Turkey and a political solution to the Kurdish crisis were not among them.

If the Kurdish insurrection gained little public mention from Americans in Ankara, it was partly due to lack of trying. The embassy was not set up to monitor the civil war beyond the assurances they received from Turkish officials and the sketchy press reporting. "We never knew much of what was going on the Southeast," recalled ex-ambassador Abramowitz, "nor did we have the means to acquire it. There was a lacuna of information. We couldn't really trust the Turks' statements. You have to live there to know what's going on."

When Human Rights Watch came to Turkey in late 1995 to release a report on the use of U.S. weapons in the war against the Kurds, the project director, Joost Hilterman, did not get a warm welcome from embassy officials. But he found among the dozens of NGOs he briefed a willingness to take on the arms sales as a key human-rights issue. They "lauded us for saying things that, had they themselves said them, would have landed them in jail," Hilterman told his colleagues in an internal memo. "All who spoke commended us for our report, emphasizing that no one had looked at the arms issue before."

A few prominent Turks recognized not only how America's military aid was fueling the war, but also how Washington's big-carrot-and-little-stick policy was not working. "It's obvious that U.S. military technology has been essential to the war in the Southeast," observed Cengiz Çandar, an adviser to Özal and a columnist with *Sabah,* a leading Istanbul newspaper. "I told John Shattuck that if you want to stop human-rights abuses do two things—stop IMF credits and cut off aid from the Pentagon. But don't sell the weapons and give aid and then complain about the Kurdish issue. Shattuck said that with aid cutoffs the human-rights situation could worsen. I said that's our business. You do your part, we'll do ours. We'll pay the price for that. But don't tell us about human rights while you're selling these weapons."

But the mounting pressure on the Turks was taking a toll: they constantly threatened to take their business elsewhere. When the Cobra helicopter sale was stalled in Shattuck's office in 1996, the Turks began to make more explicit threats. They revived plans to buy 200 helicopters, including perhaps more Black Hawks—Gene Buckley lobbied Turkish officials in July to breathe life into the coproduction deal for 50 armed Black

Hawks—but the Cobra snag was unnerving. "If the U.S. deal fails, the Americans can be sure that it will be very difficult for them to take part in Turkey's future helicopter projects," a Turkish official told *Defense News,* a trade journal. "If the United States is not willing to sell those helicopters, we will get their equivalent elsewhere, probably from Eurocopter." And they did, canceling the Cobra buy in late 1996 and ordering thirty copters from France soon after.

So the purchases from the French and Russians in the early to mid–1990s were perhaps a precursor to a more lasting military relationship—just as the American defense industry had long maintained. "If they don't buy them from us, they'll get them somewhere else, and all we lose are jobs," was the stock answer to denial on moral grounds, and this assertion seemed to be coming true in the case of this most-stalwart ally. Few would argue that the French technology was better than Cobras or Black Hawks, and the notion that the Russian hardware was equivalent was laughable. But it was better than nothing, in the official Turkish view. And they kept announcing bigger plans to entice U.S. weaponeers: $150 billion of arms imports over thirty years, Ankara declared in late 1996, three times the annual rate of the world-leading pace Turkey set in the early 1990s. (Dozens of attack helicopters were on the list, and Sikorsky would bid to sell Turkey the Comanche even before the new chopper had been ordered by the U.S. Army.)

The growing controversy over U.S. arms sales to Turkey gradually brought the question of American strategy in the region into sharper focus. Turkey's "front-line" status was forged in the Cold War, but was now reconfirmed as a bulwark against Muslim radicalism, whether it be Saddam's version of Arab nationalism or Khomeini's Islamic revolution. Vast quantities of money in the Middle East and political capital the world over were being expended in the name of that policy. A defining American foreign-policy goal was at stake, a goal, in the case of Iran, stretching back to 1979, revived and reshaped by every U.S. president since. "Yes, dual containment is one objective of our relationship," the senior American diplomat in Ankara insisted. "The 'bad neighborhood' argument is a cliché, but look around."

Most Turks would disagree. Relations with Iran were always wary, rooted in centuries of dynastic and Sunnī-Shīʿī rivalry. Khomeini's revolution unsettled the Western-oriented elite in Ankara, and the 1980 coup was in part the panicked reflex of the stoutly secular military. But Turkey-Iran relations remained intact—Turkey was even a supplier to Iran during its eight-year bout with Iraq—and while at times the ties were shaky, particularly when it appeared that Teheran was arming the PKK or supporting the more radical Islamic groups inside Turkey, diplomacy and trade continued more or less normally. So, too, with Iraq: the Turks didn't like Saddam, certainly, but Ankara resolutely supported a unified Iraq and was willing to accept Saddam's survival and his political control over northern Iraq.

When push came to shove, Turkey wanted to have no part in isolating either country. It fought the United States time and again on the Iraq embargo and only reluctantly agreed to Operation Provide Comfort. Surreptitious and then open, even flagrant trading across the Turkey-Iraq border was encouraged by the government. Turkish diplomats helped engineer the UN's partial lifting of sanctions to permit Iraqi oil sales for humanitarian purposes.

Ankara's attitude toward Iran was even more dismissive of "containment." President Clinton's trade embargo of Iran, flouted by the Europeans, wasn't given a second thought in Turkey, not even by the resolutely pro-American Çiller government. "Although Turkey is acutely aware that Iran has a different regime," one Turkish official explained when the embargo was announced in 1995, it has "good economic ties with the country and [Turkey] wanted to maintain good neighborly relations." Like the complex support for Iraq, Turkey's steadfast pursuit of diplomatic stability with Iran hinged on the Kurdish issue; neither wanted to stir up the other's Kurdish population. And the relationship with Syria was tempestuous precisely because Assad was harboring Kurdish guerrillas.

So the question was brought into sharp focus. At the key moment of dual containment, the key country was rejecting it, however quietly. Islamic fervor was on the rise. Successive pro-American regimes in Ankara were unable to survive. Flagrant human rights abuses persisted. The PKK guerrillas were undaunted. The Kurdish population was under seige from a military stocked by America. To the Turkish military, the "bad neighborhood" for which it needed more weaponry was its own Southeast. Still, to the Americans in Ankara, this was "a country that supports our values."

22

STRATFORD GETS BLUDGEONED

For Stratford, Connecticut, the year 1995 was one to forget, to wish it had never happened. The village that English settlers took from the Pequots and Igor Sikorsky built into an aviation mecca was sliding toward the fate of its decrepit neighbor, Bridgeport. The town's major employer was facing cutbacks in its Army contract for Black Hawks and the new-generation Comanche. If it lost both—a harrowing possibility—the company would be reduced to supplying parts for the 2,000 Black Hawks it had already sold to twenty-one countries. And Stratford's other major defense contractor, the army engine plant in the old Sikorsky factory down river, was on the short list for closure. If both military firms were hit this year, it would devastate the local economy and send the town reeling toward bankruptcy.

"The town was on the brink of financial ruin when I got here," Mark Barnhart, the boyish town manager, said one gray winter afternoon early in the year. "There was a $2 million deficit in a $100 million budget in 1992. We never quite got on the 'watch list' of Connecticut's basket cases. Property taxes were shifting from industrial to personal, which did not make people happy. We had underfunded pension funds, and the town's bonds were being downgraded. Rating companies look at defense cutbacks and its effect on the local economy, and they were worried by the army engine plant."

Like most city administrators—and he was a well-trained and skilled practitioner—Barnhart had few choices. "I imposed stringent spending controls and layoffs, including forty-five jobs from public works," he explained. "The town has deferred maintenance. We're still in a downsizing mode."

The impact of the two defense companies was not easy to gauge. Together they paid only about 15 percent of the town's taxes, down considerably from a few years earlier, and the workers were spread out around the coastal towns of southeastern Connecticut. But the giants' maladies were felt all the same. A town of small shops and luncheonettes like Stratford depends on its big employers well beyond the cold statistics of taxes paid and workers living in town. "The town, without realizing it, became very dependent on Sikorsky Aircraft," said Lew Knapp, a retired Sikorsky engineer and town historian. "At one time in Connecticut, one in ten people worked for United Technologies, and when you counted in the multiplier effect, it was one in four. The same was true for Sikorsky and Stratford. People are very anxious about dependency on Sikorsky, but we don't know what to do about it. We're amateurs. Just in the last two years has this realization come upon us."

That reality was brought into sharp relief by the precarious status of the Lycoming army engine business, now run by AlliedSignal, a major defense contractor based in Phoenix. The Army had owned the plant since the 1940s, and was threatening to close it down as part of the post–Cold War reduction. The number of bases had proliferated ridiculously during the Cold War—providing yet more payola from the Pentagon to make members of Congress happy by situating bases in their districts—and now the piper had to be paid. Congress, unable to make the painful choices itself, set up a Base Realignment and Closure commission, or BRAC, to act on the Pentagon's own recommendations for shutting down bases.

Even though base closures in the past had resulted in a net gain in local employment for the communities affected, the massive closures of the 1990s—some 500 bases were closed by BRAC—combined with the desultory economic conditions of slow or no growth, struck fear and anger into the heart of every city with a military base. And Stratford was no exception. The army engine plant had seen jobs flow away for years, from a high of 12,000 during Vietnam, when it made engines for Hueys and Cobras, to just a tenth of that in 1995. It had already been through a boom-and-bust cycle, declining to 2,500 employees in the aftermath of Vietnam. Even though the plant had built more helicopter engines than any other in the world, and had exported thousands of helicopters to Iran, Egypt,

Turkey, and elsewhere, its prospects were dim until Lee Iacocca, in restructuring a nearly moribund Chrysler Corporation, sold its tank-engine business in 1976 to AVCO, which then operated the army engine plant in Stratford until Textron took over in 1984 and AlliedSignal in 1994. The assembly line steadily grew back to 6,000 workers by the mid-1980s as the Stratford plant built and repaired engines for the Abrams tank, the mainstay of the land forces along the Cold War's main fault line in Central Europe. The plant was still building helicopter engines, too, including the new design for Sikorsky's Comanche.

"There was the expectation that there would be a follow-on to the Abrams," says Dave Kelly, the president of the plant's union local, the United Auto Workers. "The disparity with the Warsaw Pact countries seemed to guarantee that. Then, *poof!*, it was gone."

The BRAC commission, in its final round of cuts, had the Stratford plant on its list. The town fought it in every way it could. Local congresswoman Rosa DeLauro and Senators Dodd and Lieberman were mobilized, but unlike the machinations over procurement or export sales, Congress's hands were intentionally handcuffed by BRAC. Few options to fight base closures were available. Mark Barnhart tried one: he ordered up an exhaustive study of the impact of closing the base from the Connecticut Center for Economic Analysis, respected econometricians at the University of Connecticut, and they produced some alarming figures.

The Center saw private-sector employment declining over ten years in Fairfield County by 25,404 "job years," and the total economic output in Connecticut drop by $2.6 billion in that same decade if the AlliedSignal plant were closed. The unemployment rate in Stratford would increase by two points, they said, but the number "will be restrained by the large number of citizens leaving the Stratford area."

The real killer, though, was the Center's calculation of the impact of the army engine plant closure *and* planned cutbacks at Sikorsky, taken together. Actual job losses would total more than 15,000 in the county. Thousands would leave Connecticut, and the state would suffer an annual $1.4 billion loss in output each year of the 1996–2005 decade. The totals, of course, measure the "multiplier effect" of defense jobs—many of those blueberry pies consumed in Stratford luncheonettes, for example—but do not capture the intangible losses of engineering talent migrating out of the state, or the staggering financial losses to families selling homes for half of what they bought them for. The study called the Pentagon's plans "devastating."

The BRAC Commission was supposed to take economic impact into consideration, but Stratford also argued the military need for the army engine plant itself. It was, as Dave Kelly pointed out, a state-of-the-art facility, and could not only continue to make Abrams tanks—countries like Turkey wanted to buy hundreds of them—but could also repair the 12,000 engines made for the tanks over their expected 25-year lifetimes. It could overhaul helicopter and airplane engines, too.

Barnhart and his team took this strong case, and a petition signed by thousands of townspeople from Stratford and surrounding villages, to a BRAC hearing in New York City on May 5, 1995. They knew it was their last best hope of saving the facility. "We in this community believe that the Army has grossly underestimated the costs associated with closing this facility," Barnhart told the commissioners. "The economic impact is significantly higher than what the Army has projected." The sobering numbers from the economic study were recited, then Barnhart played another card. "We understand the difficult nature of the task before this commission," he said. "We only ask that you consider an alternative." That option, a plan for shifting the work of the plant toward commercial rehab, was not much different from the vision articulated by Kevin Bean's conversion ideas of a few years earlier: use the "technology base"—the skills, know-how, and machinery—to do nonmilitary work, emphasizing the gas-turbine engine the workforce had perfected for so many years.

But the card was played too late. In July 1995 the commission upheld the Army's request to close the base. "The BRAC process was preordained once the Army recommended closure," Barnhart said later. "AlliedSignal may have been behind the decision. They wanted to consolidate in Phoenix. People in the community were suspicious of the company's motives. AlliedSignal bought the technology—the know-how—not the plant or equipment."

The UAW's Dave Kelly, a longtime Lycoming veteran whose father moved his family from Vermont to Bridgeport in the 1940s to work in the defense industry, persisted with AlliedSignal, but to no avail. When they bought the operation from Textron in 1994, AlliedSignal wanted to move the commercial operations immediately to Phoenix. "We worked with them to commercialize the plant, redoing the shop floor, making it more efficient commercially and less dependent on the Pentagon," he explained. "We see this as a viable business, and AlliedSignal should unpack its bags. Our piece of the action—overhauling engines—is not going out of business. AlliedSignal said it was moving to Phoenix before the ink was dry on the BRAC decision." Kelly makes a convincing case for the economics of keeping the engine overhaul work in Stratford, but the Army is moving its operation—at a cost of $100 million—to Army depots in Alabama and Texas.

Within weeks after the fatal BRAC decision, Stratford faced another disheartening blow: the Army's five-year contract for Black Hawks at 60 per year was coming to an end in 1996, and inside-the-beltway rumors had the Pentagon forgoing any renewed orders. In August, the Pentagon released its own study on the health of the helicopter industry, finding Bell in the best position and Sikorsky a potential basket case: "Sikorsky, which currently has the largest market share by dollar value of any helicopter manufacturer worldwide, will be most affected by declines in the defense budget." During that same summer, a report in *Defense News*, the definitive trade newspaper, had the Army coming up short with "modernization" funds and unable to renew the contract for more Black Hawks.

The rumors had been building for more than a year, and they were in fact more than just rumors: when the budget for fiscal year 1995 was submitted in February 1994, the Army said that the five-year, 60-copters-per-year contract was its last, reflecting a drop of 50 percent in the Army's acquisition budget. That year the Pentagon also canceled the Seahawk, a $600 million contract with the Navy to produce the same utility helicopter outfitted for ocean duty. The end of the Seahawk was expected, however, and layoffs and buyouts of employees began as a gradual drizzle; but the end of the Black Hawk contract would unleash a deluge of unemployment. At one point, Sikorsky offered severance packages for 5,000 workers, though only some 200 took the offer. There was little else to fall back on, because Sikorsky's ratio of military-to-commercial sales was nearly twenty to one. In 1994, despite Gene Buckley's boasting about Sikorsky's capturing a chunk of the civilian market, they delivered a grand total of eight commercial helicopters.

The Army already possessed more than 1,300 Black Hawks, and did not need more. Its aim to buy 1,700 UH-60s was based on its revised plan to maintain fewer divisions, down to 15 from the Cold War level of 20. But even that number, which would keep the Stratford plant in business until the Comanche was ready, was controversial. The Army had other modernization priorities, including the Apache. And some analysts insisted that the Hueys remaining in inventory could satisfy the military's needs. "The Army orchestrated an anti-Huey campaign," contended one industry expert. "The Army has an antipathy toward Bell, because the Bell stuff is off the shelf. Those Hueys could be maintained for more than thirty years. UH-60s are doing jobs the Huey could do, transporting a general from point A to point B, medevac, things like that." Some 450 Black Hawks were used in Desert Storm, and the current "requirement," while trimmed from Cold War highs, still reflected the generous assumptions of Aspin's Bottom-Up Review, which necessitated enough hardware to fight two major wars simultaneously, a strategy most regarded as excessive. Another Pentagon watcher suggested that the Army was employing a "Washington Monument" strategy, including a budget cut that Congress would never allow—like proposing the closing of the Washington Monument—and that the Army brass never intended to stop buying the Black Hawk. Whatever the assumptions and gambits of Washington's Byzantine procurement politics, the Black Hawk was on the chopping block. Whatever was saved for the UH-60 might come out of other companies' hides, and the competition for the Army's dollar would be heated. "It's a matter of survival," said one Sikorsky competitor. "There's blood in the water."

It was during that shaky year, the year the Turks began to back out of the coproduction deal for the 50 Black Hawks, that lobbying for a new U.S. Army contract began in earnest. The strategy was to argue that the operational gap between the end of the Black Hawk production in 1997 and the beginning of the Comanche production in 2006 would break the back of the company: there were too few orders to keep the plant running. Skilled workers would be let go, probably leave the area, and not be available to Sikorsky when the Comanche buy was ready to go. Just as important, foreign sales would be dealt a body blow: without American military purchases, the cost per chopper skyrockets, making the Black Hawk too expensive to compete with Eurocopter's Cougar and other foreign brands.

The peril to the company was imminent. Not only were Pentagon bureaucrats saying no more Black Hawks after the five-year contract expired, but some were even saying that the final year of the $350-million annual contract would not survive cost-cutting in the Army. The loss would be staggering, ensuring that the gap until Comanche production began—itself not a certainty—would widen, probably forcing Sikorsky to close, merge with another helicopter maker, or drastically downsize into a repair shop. "People that give away their ability to make things give away their souls," Buckley said of the latter prospect. Jack Powers, the local Teamsters head, predicted a 50 percent layoff if the Black Hawk and Comanche were both canceled. There was talk of a Pentagon-forced merger with McDonnell-Douglas, maker of the Apache attack helicopter.

So United Technologies Corporation set its considerable D.C. influence machine in motion. The tactics were varied. In house, UTC would create a "murder board" to float ideas and then let their corporate executives try to murder them. The battle-tempered gambits would then be sent along to its Washington office a block from the White House and the Eximbank.

The Senate Armed Services Committee restored the Black Hawk funds absent from the Clinton budget, but the full fare for 60 copters was still doubtful by autumn. By September, only half the appropriation for the 1996 buy seemed secured. Lieberman, Dodd, and DeLauro had to go to work with UTC to save the '96 purchase and extend the chopper for the remainder of the decade. They had allies: Sikorsky and UTC have plants in other states, and their members of Congress were mobilized as well. The need for a Black Hawk assembly line to be "kept warm" until the Comanches started up was a much-discussed problem in defense circles, and new defense secretary William Perry had signaled his attention to it earlier that spring. Senator Howard Heflin, the voluble Alabama Democrat, asked Perry to tell him if the Sikorsky component plant in Alabama would be "left hanging for six years and would no doubt have to close." Perry gave him an unusual promise. "The secretary understood the problem," Heflin told a reporter, "and assured me that if the sale of Black Hawks to U.S. allies is not adequate to keep the work going, the Army will consider buying additional Black Hawks."

Perry had by now succeeded Les Aspin as defense secretary, and while the two friends were strikingly different in manner—Perry a methodical, soft-spoken technocrat, whereas Aspin was a disheveled, gregarious intellectual—they shared the gripping concern of the defense intelligentsia: how to maintain the "defense industrial base" while sharply cutting orders for new weapons. Nothing illustrated the dilemma more clearly than

Sikorsky. And the "solution," however patchworked and improvised, went to the root of the agonizing problem of jobs and exports.

The outcome was a three-way circuit. For the Pentagon, making sure the new-generation Comanche would be built was paramount. Helicopters were the key to the Army's mobility and lethality in the post–Cold War world, as pivotal a technology as any in the American arsenal. The Pentagon would press for more money in their modernization budget for Black Hawks. They knew that if the Black Hawk line went cold, the chances of prying the Comanche out of a reluctant Congress would be diminished, because the costs of start-up would increase if Sikorsky had to lay off its skilled work force. For Sikorsky, the extension of the Black Hawk contract not only would be profitable in itself, but would bolster the firm's new emphasis on exports (while helping its repair shop, too, since more birds mean more maintenance over many years). Keeping the Comanche alive could have the company humming until the year 2030. And for countries like Turkey, Egypt, and Saudi Arabia, their costs in purchasing the world's best helicopter would be kept low by a new U.S. Army contract, and their purchases would in turn help save money on each copter the American military procured as well.

At least for the shaky 1995 purchase, the arguments worked: the final budget decision gave Sikorsky another year of a 60-Black-Hawk production run. No one was saying whether lackluster sales abroad had anything to do with the Pentagon's reversal of its early 1994 decision to cancel. But Bill Perry's promise to Howard Heflin resonated when it became apparent that the Turks were getting cold feet on the second half of their deal to assemble 50 Black Hawks in Turkey with parts made in Stratford. They didn't have the money (not least because they were spending so much on the war against the Kurds), they were demanding more offsets from Sikorsky than the company could afford, and this biggest-ever helicopter trade was coming apart at the seams. So the Turkey deal, which had rashly raised Sikorsky's expectations for exports, fortuitously came to its rescue later in the decade via its half-failure: the absence of strong sales abroad convinced the defense secretary to step in to save the company with another domestic purchase of Black Hawks, saving it not only for American uses (the Comanche), but for the Turks and other "allies." The cost of the 1995 Black Hawk procurement was $321 million.

The drama played out in 1994 was repeated again in 1995, only this time it was even more dire for Stratford and possibly even for Sikorsky.

The big contract—60 Black Hawks a year—was certainly not to be renewed at that level. And the Comanche was still fighting for its life. The Pentagon had decided to keep pressing for its development, but its progress was slowed by budget woes. Only two prototypes were being built in Sikorsky's West Palm Beach plant, and the congressional critics of Comanche were relentless.

Again the lobbying bandwagon was set in motion. The height of the campaign came during an elegant dinner for the movers and shakers of Congress and the Pentagon, a $350,000 feast at one of the world's great museums, the National Gallery of Art on the Mall just below the Capitol. The ostensible occasion—which of course was tax deductible, as nearly all lobbying is—was an exclusive first viewing of the hottest exhibit to be mounted in America in years, the few extant paintings of the Dutch Renaissance master Jan Vermeer. Getting a hearing from the decision makers is the first priority for anyone in the lobbying business, and a night like that icy December evening of candlelight, caviar, and exquisite paintings would turn any politician's head.

It was not a typical evening, of course, but it typified new UTC president George David's aggressive style of winning business for his company. An old Sikorsky veteran, David sent longtime aide Bill Paul to Washington to pilot the corporation to new contracts. "This year, a veritable SWAT team has worked to ensure future helicopter work for Sikorsky," wrote Michael Remez of the *Hartford Courant,* citing the vulnerability of Comanche and Black Hawk. "Working with key lawmakers and the Army, UTC lobbyists implemented a plan to add money to the Pentagon budget for both projects." The company's 39 full-time lobbyists helped Senator Lieberman and Representative DeLauro lay "the legislative groundwork in hearings before their respective defense committees." The effort was aided by a video sales pitch from novelist Tom Clancy, who had used the Comanche in his recent thriller *Debt of Honor.*

The lobbying strategy took many routes. At the high end was Vermeer. At the low end was political money and Teamsters. "I have a federal PAC and a local PAC fund," Jack Powers boasted earlier that year. "In this country it takes votes and money. Dodd and Lieberman have been the best. Rosa DeLauro is one of the hardest working ladies I've ever met. Sure, I go to see people on Capitol Hill. We lobbied with Sikorsky to save the appropriations." UTC has a Political Action Committee, too, dispensing nearly

$500,000 in the 1995–96 election cycle and, separately, providing $200,000 in "soft money" contributions. The Connecticut delegation soaks up some of that juice, of course, but they need no further incentives when thousands of jobs at home are at stake. Contributions to others on congressional committees can be decisive, however; one study suggests that a mere $3,500 can turn a congressman's vote. And UTC lavished money on key legislators—for example, $10,000 to Bob Livingstone (R-LA), chairman of the House Appropriations Committee, and another $10,000 to Ted Stevens (R-AK), who heads the same panel in the Senate. Certainly the Republican majorities ruling on the Hill did not need much convincing to spend more money on the military, and with Chris Dodd now leading the Democratic National Committee (DNC)—the wellspring of campaign money for Democratic incumbents—his wishes on Black Hawks and Comanches would be fulfilled.

So the Black Hawk contract was saved again, though the jury stayed out until March 1996. Word came down that 36 Black Hawks would be ordered by the military in 1997, and possibly the same number in each of the next five years. It seemed to be lifesaving news for Sikorsky. But in February 1997 more bad news befell the company: the Army decided to buy just 18 Black Hawks in 1998, 12 in 1999, and none thereafter. "We argued the hell out of this inside the building here," said Gilbert Decker, an assistant secretary of the Army. The conclusion: "We would not jeopardize readiness for some time to come . . . if we just didn't buy any more Black Hawks." The decision also pivoted on the Army's revised view of the worldwide market. "We don't need to buy for sustainment of the helicopter industrial base," Decker explained.

Even the new contract for 36 Black Hawks, rather than 60, meant that 2,000 workers at the Stratford plant would be losing their jobs, a 22 percent cut. The new procurement cut would cost another 1,000 jobs at least. Buckley brought Dodd and DeLauro to Stratford for a rally after the Army's devastating announcement. "I can guarantee we are going to fight tooth and nail to restore those 18 helicopters in the budget," Dodd told the Sikorsky workers. "I happen to think that fellow in the White House owes me a little bit," he proclaimed, referring to his leadership of the DNC, which just then was wracked by charges of being "bought" by special interests. Three other bridges to the Comanche procurement were possible: an unbudgeted wish of the Army National Guard to purchase 586 Black

Hawks, a planned buy of the Navy for 134 of a new version of the UH-60 beginning in 1999, and, of course, more exports. None were certain.

Equally uncertain was Congress's commitment to the Comanche, which was already under renewed fire in early 1996 from a Congressional Budget Office report asserting that the new helicopter program was not worth its $35 billion price tag. The Black Hawk contract had to be stretched out until the Comanche could be produced—if it ever is—and the willingness of Congress to spend $200 million or more annually for a decade to procure Black Hawks was doubtful. Even before the drop in Army orders, Sikorsky was producing fewer helicopters—a total of 158 in 1994, down to an expected 120 in 1996. Foreign orders were trickling in—the largest recent order for 15 Black Hawks came from Israel in early 1997—and Gene Buckley hoped such sales would account for 50 percent of Sikorsky's business in the remainder of the 1990s. But the market overseas, especially in the all-important Middle East, was becoming saturated, and while exports could reach half of all production at the Stratford plant, it would be half of a much smaller loaf. Hopes for the S-92 civilian helicopter, based on the Black Hawk design, were tenuous: production would not begin in earnest until 1998, and the commercial craft's prospects were iffy at best; it was openly belittled by Bell Helicopter, which said it was too big and would surely fail.

Failure of any kind reverberates first through the workforce, and the Sikorsky workers were on pins and needles. "We're all scared," said Terry, a veteran of the shop floor, "not so much for the paycheck, but for the lifestyle. When you get laid off, a guard and two supervisors come up to you and tell you to collect your stuff and leave. Just like that. I've seen guys crying as they leave. It's a shock." The threat of layoffs is a constant worry to workers and their spouses. "Everybody knows what's going on. Sikorsky was overextended. There's a gradual shrinking of the company." One persistent story in the plant: a coworker was driving around rural North Carolina and saw an old sign that said, "Future Site of Sikorsky Aircraft."

When layoffs come, the Teamsters post some available jobs but do little else. "The union doesn't help much with the layoffs," Terry pointed out. "They don't give money. Jack Powers knows where there'll be layoffs, and moves around his favorite people to sections that aren't gonna be laid off."

Mike, another Sikorsky worker of ten years, spoke of the same kinds of anxieties. Living in a modest little house in Stratford with his wife, who works part time, and three children, Mike has often been moved around the company and now works on quality control. "Now I'm concerned about layoffs, which I never have been," he said in the spring of 1995. "They're collapsing eighty-seven work groups into twenty, which makes everyone vulnerable. If I got laid off, I wouldn't wait to be called back." His section was being cut.

The insecurity stems in part from the uncertainty. "There's no notice of layoffs," Mike explained. "You're usually walked out the same day. A big layoff, more than 250 maybe, you must be notified ten days in advance, but they walk out the guys who're laid off right away and give them two weeks' pay, to prevent vandalism. We talk about job security with our friends, always, yes. There's an undercurrent of tension. And all new hires are friends and family of the management."

Still another worker, a middle-aged white man who complained publicly about affirmative-action hiring at the plant, said his wife "worried all the time about me being laid off," so much so that he left Sikorsky for a lower-paying job at a computer firm nearby.

Jack Powers is concerned about his workers, but protecting jobs, in his view, means working with Gene Buckley and the other Sikorsky management. "I do not have an adversarial relationship with Sikorsky, but I did when I took over. I put a demonstration on the street to protest the firing of a union steward. We had supervisors threatening us, calling in police. The younger guys thrived on it, the anger. The older guys were tired of it. I realized all the craziness had to stop.

"The younger guys who are laid off and then brought back, some swear that 'after this time, I'm outta here.' They're frustrated. A lot of them will try to get on with airlines as mechanics, but the airlines are downsizing, too. I do think I'm going to lose a lot of these guys. A lot will leave the state. We had people from the state and local governments, United Way, and so on, helping our people with their resumés, how to get aid for fuel bills, how to get retraining. Some got a lot out of this, some are still stunned that they're laid off.

"You know, labor costs of the Black Hawk is only seven percent," Powers pointed out, as if to say there are other ways to lower the price and save contracts. "Engineering is the main cost. The military makes changes all the time. The specifications are crazy."

The workers who wanted to leave—and Connecticut was one of only two states to experience a population decline in the early 1990s—faced dicey job markets elsewhere, but also suffered what Connecticut economist Jeff Blodgett calls an "equity meltdown." They bought their homes during the Reagan defense boom, which was accompanied in New England by wild inflation in the real-estate market. After housing prices dropped by 30 percent or more in the late 1980s, many of these Sikorsky and Lycoming workers were stuck: they can't sell their homes, they can't refinance them without jobs, they can't take on the debt that selling for a huge loss would mean.

For Stratford, the shock of losing the army engine plant in 1995 gradually turned into a grudging awareness of how precarious all the defense business in the area was likely to be. UTC profits remained very strong throughout these successive crises, as it followed the industry's trend of sustaining profitability by discharging workers. But the town's prospects were far bleaker.

"There's tangible evidence of the defense cutbacks," said one of the Sikorsky workers, "There're shops closing. The second-tier subcontractors are hurting; metal finishers, for example. Outside machining is brought back into the plant. You can see the empty buildings that used to have those firms."

The town was cautiously optimistic about putting new businesses in the Lycoming plant once the Army moved out. It is an enormous space: 58 buildings, 90 acres, 1.7 million square feet of factory floor. It could, if reconfigured, attract the kind of light manufacturing gradually replacing the big smokestack industries that once dominated this area. Mark Barnhart acknowledged that he was not totally unhappy that the facility would be available for new tenants—tenants who would be paying property taxes. But problems loomed. Given the kind of work the Army contractors did there for so many years, toxic wastes such as solvents and other petrochemicals are likely to be plentiful, and an enormous clean-up headache looms.

"The Army Corps of Engineers will do an environmental impact statement," Barnhart explained in early 1996, just as AlliedSignal was winding down its work. "We don't know yet if there are problems. It is a big question, especially if there isn't federal money available to clean it up. There was open dumping in the river. They called me one day to ask if they could burn some low-level radioactive waste as an exercise to 'train' employees to put it out. I said 'I don't think so. You guys wouldn't be doing this just to get rid of your waste, would you?' So we know there's some radwaste there." The federal government is notoriously dilatory in providing the funds needed to clean up military toxic wastes, which could run into the trillions of dollars nationwide. And the old plant at Stratford will have to queue up for funds that may take a decade to come through.

Jeff Blodgett, the economist, is not so optimistic about the Stratford site. "Big industrial spaces have not been recycled much," he says, "since there's not a lot of demand for manufacturing space." The space is not easy to reshape for new tenants, and the town itself has no redevelopment authority that could finance the redesign. Private investors will have to take on the job, and they won't move until the site is certifiably clean. It's a logjam that might not become unstuck until well into the next century.

For Sikorsky, the town really has no coping strategy. The company gives them no information that can help them plan; no number of Sikorsky workers living in Stratford; no list of the subcontractors, who are even more vulnerable to the vicissitudes of the defense market. "I've never met Gene Buckley," Barnhart says of the Sikorsky president. "He doesn't live here. Sikorsky has been a good corporate neighbor, though they've been more aggressive recently in appealing their tax assessment. We had extreme difficulty getting information from them for the base closure hearing, even after a direct appeal to them from Lieberman."

After the AlliedSignal plant was scheduled for closure, Barnhart was not feeling good about the town's economy. Next door, Bridgeport had voted to build a casino, envying the success of the Indian money machine across the state near New London. "I had mixed feelings about that," Barnhart said of the casino, which was being blocked by the state legislature. "We're tied to the Bridgeport economy, like it or not." But his more immediate concern was the shutdown of the army engine plant, to be completed at the end of 1997, and the steady erosion of jobs at Sikorsky and its suppliers. "The multiplier effect for local retailers will mean tough times ahead," Barnhart said. "Our tax list has not grown in the last four years. It's a mature community. It's not 'green' enough for corporations—it's a blue-collar town. The economy overall, well, it's not a good situation."

The human situation was troubling, to be sure, as invisible as it is to the statisticians and defense analysts. But the UAW's Dave Kelly sees it every day. "These guys were getting eighteen, nineteen dollars an hour," Kelly said of the army engine workers. "There are no equivalent jobs around here. The lucky ones may get jobs in small machine shops for $13 an hour with no benefits.

"Most are foundering. I get calls all the time, 'Dave I'm gonna lose my house, can you help me out?' I don't know what to tell them. It breaks my heart." For Kelly and the AlliedSignal workers, time and options had run out.

"The Army and their contractor pals, they don't want to hear from us. They don't count the human cost—lost jobs, lost homes, broken families."

2 3

THE TERRIBLE RECKONING

Turkey's "White Genocide"

Lost jobs, lost homes, and broken families were by 1993 becoming a way of life in Turkish Kurdistan. The toll of the civil war in 1992 was so alarming, the stories of PKK attacks and army reprisals so brutal, that no one could be optimistic about the new year. Although Prime Minister Demirel and President Özal had acknowledged the "Kurdish reality," the drum-beating in the Turkish press and the conservative parties, demanding a harsh, militant response to the PKK insurgency and any expression of Kurdish independence, was steadily overwhelming more conciliatory notions. The issue was engaged on two fronts: the war against Kurds in the Southeast, now to be fought with superior numbers and technology—the Black Hawks were arriving—and the war against Kurdish*ness* in the cities and towns, any signs of opposition to the war and sympathy with the insurgents.

The war was being pursued by government fiat and extralegal terror—much as in previous years. *Özgür Gündem,* the pro-Kurdish newspaper in Istanbul, was closed on January 15, 1993, less than nine months after its birth. The financial pressures were too great to bear, said owner Yashar Kaya. One of every five issues had been confiscated by the government; Kaya had been fined $16,000 and others on the editorial staff, including editor Ramazan Ülek, had been fined and threatened with prison. The death toll for *Özgür Gündem* was far worse: six journalists, three distributors, one vendor, and a driver had been murdered since publication began. None of the murders was investigated. The staff was still reeling from a brutal December 10 raid on their offices by Turkish police, and the leaders of the periodical had to regroup. "The newspaper was accused of separatist propaganda," Ramazan recalled. "We criticize the policy of the Turkish state and promote the right of the Kurdish people to live freely. The government can only think of war, and it leaves no breathing space for oppositional views." The journalists reopened their newspaper in April under a new banner, *Özgür Ülke* ("Free Country"), and the State Security Court promptly set upon them again, confiscating the first issue and forty of the next seventy. Later that spring, several staff members of the new daily were arrested, detained, or beaten by police.

The war in the Southeast was being pursued with equal intensity. To many observers it appeared that the Turkish armed forces were finally gaining the upper hand. The guerrillas were suffering large losses, and persistent reports were circulating of division in their ranks. New vows from the General Staff to vanquish the PKK by the end of winter suddenly seemed like more than routine assurances.

On March 17, without warning, PKK leader Abdullah Öcalan announced a cease-fire. "I met with Öcalan and publicized the cease-fire offer," recalled Cengiz Çandar, the journalist and adviser to Özal. "Öcalan knew I would take the message to Özal. My interpretation is that Öcalan was in the hands of Syrian intelligence. He was looking for a way out. With the cease-fire, he put the ball in Turkey's court."

In the eyes of the government and most of the news media, the cease-fire offer was a sign that the guerrillas were on the verge of collapse. But Öcalan, while facing a difficult military situation, was replying to Özal's gradual overtures, begun during the second Gulf war. The Iraqi Kurds, too, pressed for a rapprochement between their Turkish cousins and Ankara; their survival depended on Turkey, and the bitter civil war was doing them no good. "The cease-fire was not done by Öcalan just because the PKK was weaker," Çandar insists. "It was a genuine peace move."

The hope in both camps—those of Öcalan and Özal, that is—was to engineer a graduated series of steps to bring the PKK down from the mountains and, through periodic government amnesties matched by increasing PKK moderation, convert the guerrillas into a political party as their modest demands were satisfied. With this strategy in mind, Öcalan renewed the cease-fire on April 16, asserting that Kurds "should be given our cultural freedoms and the right to broadcast in Kurdish. The village

guard system should be abolished and the emergency legislation lifted."
The PKK leader was asking for cultural and political rights in Turkey, not
for a Kurdistan. His demands were well within the boundaries already established by more liberal Turkish politicians and opinion leaders. Öcalan, it
seemed, was coming down from the mountain.

But fate willed it otherwise. The day after Öcalan made that offer,
Turgut Özal suffered a massive heart attack and died. Hopes for a quick
end to the war would be buried with him. More than any political leader
in Turkish history, Özal recognized the injustices visited upon the Kurdish
people and tried to break through Turkish indifference and hostility to
forge a new reality for them. He evolved from a conventional politician
doing the military's bidding to a leader willing to confront the Kurdish
issue openly, revise the language proscriptions, and pursue quiet diplomacy
to end the PKK insurgency. To be sure, Özal was cautious, and the position of president did not give him enough leverage to act at will; the prime
minister's remained the more powerful position, and Süleyman Demirel
was both unmoved by Özal's Kurdish initiative and weaker in the face of
the military's constant intimidation. In the West, Turgut Özal is remembered for two achievements: an insistence that Turkey abandon Atatürk's
étatism in favor of market economics, and the prominent positioning of
Turkey as a geostrategic player. Neither contribution helped the Kurds.
Özal left two legacies on the Kurdish question itself: a small opening for
politicians to cope more realistically with the fact of Kurdish grievances,
and a military strategy that relied on overwhelming force in the Southeast
and deportation of Kurds from their homelands. The second legacy was
more durable.

Demirel quickly reversed any momentum created by the cease-fire. The
armed forces stepped up their campaign to root out the PKK and Demirel,
moving into the presidency, entertained no serious hopes of a dialogue
with Öcalan or the increasingly vocal Kurdish parliamentarians, who were
also agitating for a political solution. The new prime minister, elected by
the governing coalition in June 1993, was Tansu Çiller, an attractive, articulate, American-educated economist. Çiller, like many Turkish politicians,
made some comments early in her administration about settling the Kurdish issue politically; she even ventured to suggest a "Basque-like" autonomy arrangement—which was condemned in much of the press and
Parliament within hours of her uttering the idea. Within a few weeks she

was disciplined by the General Staff and began to speak more militantly about eradicating PKK terrorism than her predecessors ever did. Çiller's role as prime minister was relegated to her supposed strengths: managing the privatization of the economy, and leading a charm offensive in Europe and the United States that utilized her Western connections and graces (in sharp contrast to a millennium of Turkish leaders): her winning smile, quick wit, excellent English, and pretty pastel wardrobe. The military would—as always—take care of the Southeast and "the Kurdish question."

The stepped-up military campaign quickly earned an embittering reprisal: on May 24, a bus carrying off-duty soldiers was ambushed by the PKK in the Southeast. Thirty-one Turkish soldiers and five civilians were killed, another two dozen wounded. The incident rocked the nation, and calls for an all-out war on the Kurdish rebels reached a frenzied pitch. There were many observers who believed that the ambush was not as it appeared— either not carried out by the PKK at all, or a set-up of the PKK by those in the military or its many civilian allies who wanted to inflame the situation. Öcalan clearly did not order the attack; if it was done by the PKK, the attack was instigated by a rogue commander. But the end result was not in dispute: the PKK cease-fire was finished (Öcalan felt compelled to claim the action as his own), and a new phase of bloodletting was in store.

The war took a vicious turn that lasted for the next two years. The army's strategy was to hunt down the PKK wherever they could be found and to accelerate the control of the villages and countryside. The new mobility afforded by the 57 Black Hawks enabled the Turkish military to chase the rebels into their mountain hideouts, track and outpace their movements, and deploy soldiers quickly into contested areas—just as counterinsurgency doctrine demanded. Unlike a pure attack helicopter, such as the Bell Cobra, a single Black Hawk could deliver eleven soldiers and equipment; but like the Cobra, the UH-60 could deploy awesome weaponry: Hellfire missiles, land-mine dispensers, machine guns and cannon. The Kurds had never seen technology of this sophistication. The new combination of mobility, intelligence gathering, and sheer firepower was as significant as any new *military* factor yet introduced into the war. Suddenly, the hit-and-run tactics of traditional guerrilla warfare were not as effective. Now the army could identify major camps and hit them with F-16s; they could hunt and engage smaller bands of PKK with the Black Hawks and

Cobras; and they could enforce roadblocks and other ground operations with M-60 tanks and armored combat vehicles.

In theory, the Black Hawks could provide a more selective and flexible tool for the armed forces, in contrast to the blunt instruments of F-16s and tanks. Dozens, perhaps hundreds, of indiscriminate bombings of villages and towns had alienated the Kurds. With the Black Hawks, and the Cobras that would follow later that year, the Turkish army could get closer to the rebels without sacrificing much firepower; indeed, the types of ordnance the copters carried was better suited to the task at hand.

Technology and its surgical use alone cannot unglue a rebellion, as Vietnam amply proved, and the Turkish authorities never relied on the conventional uses of technology alone to wage war. For 60 years Ankara had confronted Kurdish restiveness, and its answer always relied on controlling the population through a vast array of means—mainly the promotion of Turkification and the suppression of Kurdishness. As the war grew, control had to be intensified and more firmly enforced. There were the usual means: censoring the likes of *Özgür Gündem,* bullying the mayors, breaking up Kurdish associations, detaining and torturing suspected PKK sympathizers. More vicious methods started to be employed, however, which were also linked to the government. Disappearances and assassinations by the Gray Wolves or other paramilitary gangs became commonplace. In 1992, some 160 Kurds were killed by death squads, several of them journalists who were investigating the links between these shadowy assassins and the Turkish military. The military allegedly supported a radical Islamic group, Hezbollah (the Party of God, in Arabic), in its skirmishes with the PKK as well. Some 100 Kurds were killed by Hezbollah gunmen in 1992, and while rumors of their connections to the government persisted, the government cracked down on the group beginning in 1993.

In the villages, control was exercised through the village guard system and by more direct means. The army would at times deny the use of pasture to villagers deemed to be sympathetic to the guerrillas. A single contact—the sighting of guerrillas in a particular town, for instance—could condemn an entire village to such penalties. Roads might be blocked or savaged, livestock confiscated or killed, access to markets denied. In many of these cases, the new tanks and helicopters were put to special uses. Tanks would block roads, knock down homes, or simply sit in a village square as a reminder. Helicopters would hover menacingly, chase and kill livestock, and deliver officers for a bit of village education. The quintessential technology of counterinsurgency was dedicated to a fierce and relentless intimidation. Counterinsurgency training also had a link to America; hundreds of Turkish officers educated in the United States employed the methods familiar to peasants from Vietnam to Guatemala.

The strategy of control was not enough, however, and once Özal was dead the way was cleared for a new level of military aggression that sought to eliminate the base of support the PKK enjoyed. That would be accomplished through a sweeping evacuation of Kurdish villages. Özal himself had started such a program, though one of smaller ambitions than Ankara would implement. In a February 1993 letter to Demirel, Özal urged that "starting with the most troubled zones, villages and hamlets in the mountains of the region should be gradually evacuated. With this group of PKK supporters, in number no more than 150,000 to 200,000, being resettled in western parts of the country according to a careful plan, logistics support for the PKK will have been cut off."

The more thorough control ceded to the military by Prime Minister Çiller resulted in taking Özal's idea to a harsh and extreme degree. Beginning in the summer of 1993 and continuing unabated for more than three years, the military systematically evacuated and in many cases destroyed more than two thousand Kurdish villages in the Southeast. Army chief of staff Doghan Güresh concisely summarized the strategy: "We have changed the concept. We are now implementing area domination. There is no advancing on terrorists. We now apply 'Let them stay without logistic support—go hungry and surrender' strategy."

To accomplish such an objective required a truly massive operation, one that required the armored combat vehicles, tanks, and helicopters the United States provided. According to tales told by refugees who were forced from their villages, the operation was indeed harsh.

Ali, a fifty-year-old man from a village near Diyarbakir, found his way to a refugee camp in Greece after he was forced from his village in July 1993. His worn and haggard face became animated by a restless anger as he spoke. "When they burned Kaynak, my village, they assembled all the people in the central square. The soldiers made a tour of the village and took valuables, jewelry, et cetera, from the houses, then burned the houses, even with the animals inside. Tanks, helicopters, they are all the time there.

For almost five years, there was a food embargo. In my village they have slaughtered two hundred horses; with these, we carried food. They are so important. There were so many animals in Kurdistan; now you cannot find two chickens. The shepherds are all afraid to do their work.

"In my area, they don't make warnings. They often arrest people, torture them for days. Burn the houses while people are there, while torturing some at the same time. There were a hundred families in the village, but now only ten old people who don't want to leave.

"I have seven children still in Kulp. We were one of the richest families in the village, and now they live in misery. I was selling sheep, and had a field in the village. I cannot tell you how long my family was there, they have been there always. My grandfather and his seven brothers were executed in the Kurdish rebellion of 1925. I was told there were human rights in the world, but very few people came to Kurdistan to find out in detail what was happening there. I don't believe anyone went to the villages to find out."

A young man in his twenties, Kamil makes his living as a marble worker in Istanbul. His strong, square face and cheerful demeanor begin to darken as he tells the story of his Kurdish village, Sirvanikesi Salanzo, near Siirt. The village was evacuated in September 1994. It had 90 houses, and about 400 people, plus two attached hamlets, with ten to fifteen villagers in each. His mother, a young brother and sister, and an older brother with wife and children all lived there.

"My mother called me during the ninth month of the year and told me the village would be burned," he recalled. "The Jandarma told them if they failed to take up arms against the PKK they would burn the village in one week. Most living in the village were old people—the youngest adult was forty-five, next youngest fifty-seven. I had heard things like this but hadn't believed it until then.

"The officers told them to take nothing from their homes, including clothes. Most of the villagers there are related, and many youths from the village living in Istanbul got together to decide what to do. Most people in the village are not interested in politics; I'm about the only one. I said, Let's go to Ankara and notify the state ministry for human rights. I talked to a secretary of the minister, and she said it's not possible to talk to the minister." Kamil had reason to think the minister, Azimet Köylüoghlu, would help; he had been critical of the displacement strategy, later that year calling it "state terrorism." But he couldn't be reached, nor could Kurdish MPs—who were in jail for "thought crimes"—and other politicians Kamil could possibly have access to.

"I remembered there was a history professor at Ankara University from our village; he had been back to the village during my childhood, and he was revered there. We went to see him at a businessman's club, the Anatolian Club, and told him the story. He said, 'The Turkish state will not burn my village.' He had good relations with the governor of Siirt, and called him. The governor of Siirt promised to call the Jandarma. They respected the professor. At this point, the professor did not really believe our story until the governor confirmed it by speaking with the Jandarma. It was Tuesday, and on Thursday the village would be burned. The professor called other ministers to call Demirel; Demirel called the governors. The ministers then got back to the professor and told him not to worry, the village would not be burned.

"I then called the *mukhtar,* the head of the village, and told him the news. He went to the village, was stopped at a checkpoint, where the Jandarma told him, 'What the hell do you think you're doing to try to do something about saving the village?' He hit the *mukhtar,* and told him that they had five days until the burning.

"My mother was in the village. Everyone was trying to get away. They couldn't sell the stock, couldn't harvest the rice, grapes, walnuts. A few clothes were taken, all else was left there. My mother only knew the village. Three families went to the mountain and live in a tent. Everyone wants to go back but no one could; my mother has two daughters in two different villages in that area.

"I went back during the Feast of Immolation. I was searched every few kilometers. I could walk, and if asked I said I was going to the cemetery where my father is buried. It was a Sunday, trees were blooming, all was silence, there was not even a cat about.

"All the houses were shattered, torn down, not a single one intact. Our houses are made of earth and stone, roofs of trees, and they're pretty strong. I think the destruction to each came through the roof, each of them crushed or bombed. I asked and was told they were bombed. Windows were shattered. Doors were broken. Whatever was left was taken by the police for themselves.

"This was my childhood home. It was so strange. Everyone in my father's line lived there. My life passed before my eyes when I saw the fountain where we had played as children; it was crushed. Nothing was left in the village except the schoolhouse, where a Turkish flag was flying. In the health center, where everything had been looted, there was a wall intact which had scrawled on it, 'One Turk is worth the whole world.'"

Kamil said he knew of many other villages in the area that had been bombed or burned. His mother, he insists, was anti-PKK, as were most of the villagers. But they also resisted the village guard system. "In order to get the fish you have to dry out the ocean, says the government. But the government is driving people toward the guerrillas," Kamil says. He became more political as a result, becoming active in the current Kurdish political party, HADEP.

The Kurdish refugees' stories register a harshness by the military that exceeds any conceivable military necessity. Time and again, tales are told of villagers suddenly, usually unjustly, accused of contacts with the rebels and summarily driven from their homes. The hundreds of thousands, if not millions, of Kurdish peasants displaced as a result of the military's depopulation campaign directly violates the Geneva Convention, especially the Additional Protocol II ratified in 1977. "The displacement of the civilian population," states the international law, which Turkey signed, "shall not be ordered for reasons related to the conflict unless the security of civilians involved or imperative military reasons so demand." But those latter reasons, the official interpretation asserts, cannot include "political motives" in order to "exercise more effective control over a dissident ethnic group," and people who are displaced must be provided with "shelter, hygiene, health, safety, and nutrition."

The Kurds of the razed villages on the Turks' list have nowhere to go and have been provided with nowhere to go. Their lives were agrarian, with little cash saved for such an emergency. Their livestock, land, and homes were their only assets, as well as the pivots of their existence. The village was their entire social world. Most of the women do not speak Turkish. The military acted on a concept of collective guilt: you are a Kurd, therefore you are suspect. Where the PKK was active, of course, the reprisals were sharpest.

One such story comes from a 25-year-old woman from the village of Hurse, near Mardin. "We had one hundred houses in the village. Eight people had joined the PKK. Guerrillas would come to the village. So soldiers targeted this place. We like the PKK. If we had a problem we would go to the PKK and they would solve it. We'd be too afraid to go to the government. Even before we had PKK sympathies, the soldiers would harass us.

"The soldiers performed an operation in the village, and two PKK and two soldiers died. They brought all the villagers to the schoolyard. They stripped the PKK and said, "These are not Moslems, these are heretics. Why are you helping the guerrillas? We will kill you all.' They said, 'Look, they are not circumcised,' meaning, they are not Moslems. There are many poor people who cannot afford this. We knew these people, and we did not believe the soldiers. We knew that they were trying to scare us. We were forced to pile the bodies in a shallow grave, with no ceremony. The police shouted warnings at us and left. After they left we dug up the bodies and washed them and gave them a proper burial.

"One week passed. We were preparing for the Nawroz [New Year] festival. Soldiers came to the village. My two brothers-in-law were at home. The soldiers threw a bomb at the house and killed both. They then took all the villagers into the schoolyard and set the whole village on fire. Everything was burned, including the animals. There were ten other villages in the area, and nine of them were also burned to ashes. Nothing was left. We had fourteen children, and they told us, Go wherever you like, but you have no village now. We couldn't take anything from the village. There was one of our cows left, so we sold it to get money to come to Istanbul. The whole family came except for two of my stepdaughters who joined the rebels because of this incident.

"We lived in a tent for eight months. The police came and raided because of the two stepdaughters with the guerrillas. They kept my husband in detention for two months."

The violence came in many forms, and at times the Kurdish villagers were victimized by the PKK's tactics as well. Not all were forced out specifically by government-mandated evacuations; some left because of the general increase in violence. "There was a Jandarma station in our village, which was raided by the PKK," recalls a twenty-one-year-old woman from the village of Dargeçit, near Mardin. "A small fight occurred. In the morning, when it was finished, many more government forces came to reinforce the station. The PKK sent word to the villagers to vacate the village because they didn't want the government to take vengeance on us for the attack. Take the women and children out, they said, because there could be a bigger fight. So many of us left; only the elderly and a few who didn't hear the warning were left.

"I was three months pregnant at the time with my third child. My husband was working in Istanbul. I took the two children and moved out. It was a chaotic night, each person for himself. The commotion was terrifying. My village had seven hundred houses. Everyone was going in a different direction in search of safety with someone they knew. I walked three hours, my feet were bleeding, I was walking through mountain thorns, until I reached another village. I saw one woman give birth as she was fleeing.

"After we left, there was another fight. Five PKK died, and perhaps some soldiers, too. My mother has a lame foot and couldn't leave. She said that helicopters came and circled around the village; there was shooting from the helicopters, shooting indiscriminately. They shot people, livestock, even cats. The animals are very important to us. During this, they killed seven people. Among these seven was a relative. Four of the dead were young, including a newlywed with an infant, and another two who were the shepherds of the village.

"My in-laws' house was burned to the ground by the government. Of the seven who died, one was a guerrilla. But the government lined up all the dead with weapons and then showed them on television as guerrillas. They would not let their families claim the bodies, which were burned. It was harvest time, and the soldiers had burned all the wheat. When we went to find the corpses, there was nothing left in the village. The village is abandoned now; neither humans nor animals."

As the numbers of Kurds who were "internally displaced" grew into the hundreds of thousands, a small number of human-rights organizations began to investigate and speak out. For the most part, human-rights groups were focused on the impediments to free speech—the jailings of writers, journalists, and parliamentarians under the infamous anti-terrorism law—and the long-standing practice of torture in Turkish police stations and prisons. These injustices gained the attention of Europeans, in particular, because Turkey aspired to join the European Union. In fact, its entry into the European customs union—a first step toward full E.U. membership—was nearly blocked in 1995 by the socialists and greens in the European Parliament (the legislature which governs many

European institutions), who objected vociferously to Turkey's human-rights record. But the commotion stirred in Europe over rights issues centered almost entirely on the speech constraints. The Turks had jailed 170 writers and reporters on charges of publishing "separatist propaganda." Fifteen Kurdish parliamentarians in the Grand National Assembly were prosecuted under the same provision, and six were given long sentences. Incidences of torture—much of it in the form of especially gruesome, sexually and mentally abusive practices, such as making children watch their parents being raped—were rising, and the courageous physicians of the Turkish Human Rights Foundation were harassed for documenting it. Most of the rights violations revolved around the Kurdish question, and the desirability of a political solution to Kurdish grievances was stressed. But while the Kurdish issue was on the lips of every leftist in Strasbourg, there was scarcely a mention of the single greatest violation affecting the Kurds themselves—the forced evacuations of Kurdish villages. By the time the European Parliament reluctantly approved Turkey's candidacy for the customs union in December 1995—responding to Çiller's dire warnings of an Islamic revival if Turkey was rejected—the number of Kurdish refugees in Turkey had climbed to two and a half million, among the largest numbers of internally displaced people in the world. Of the major international NGOs, only Human Rights Watch and Amnesty International were paying heed to this disaster.

Later, another division of Human Rights Watch, its Arms Project, conducted an extensive investigation of the U.S. arms used in the war. The report, which caused a stir in Istanbul and Ankara but made scarcely a ripple in the United States, documented dozens of cases of abuse by Turkish armed forces using Black Hawks, F-16s, Cobras, and other American-supplied technology. The uses of the Black Hawks were particularly gruesome. "Helicopters are the backbone of the Turkish counterinsurgency effort in the Southeast," the investigator, Jim Ron, concluded, "and as such are deeply involved in the abuses . . . and illegitimate actions" of the forced evacuations, village strafings, and other violations of the rules of war. The helicopters would be used to ferry troops to villages, but were also used for command and control—Black Hawks were best equipped for that role—in which the choppers identified targets for the F-16s to bomb. They were employed routinely in village evacuations as intimidators, hovering menacingly or shooting at civilians and livestock. At times, the uses of the choppers were even more inventive, as the Human Rights Watch report documented in a May 1994 case near the town of Lice.

Three PKK suspects were picked up by the Jandarma and loaded onto a helicopter, an eyewitness told the investigators. The three alleged guerrillas—Abdurrahman, and two women in their early twenties, Zelal and Bermal—had already been badly beaten. Once aloft, "The sergeant ordered Abdurrahman to stand near the door, told him to 'reserve a place for me in the next world,' and pushed the man to his death." The other captives were ordered to watch. "The Jandarma sergeant then ordered Bermal over to the door and ordered her to take her clothes off. Bermal refused, so the sergeant tore them off anyway," T.P. [the eyewitness] recalled. "He fondled her naked body, made humiliating sexual remarks about wanting to fuck her, and then pushed her out the door." Then the sergeant turned his attention to the other woman. "Zelal was also stripped, humiliated, and shoved from the helicopter."

The 171-page report details case after case of the helicopters' special utility in the forced displacement of the Kurdish villagers. "The helicopters strafed the village"; "The helicopters hovered over the village . . . and there were sounds of machine gun fire"; "Helicopters buzzed the surrounding forests"; "Two helicopters, most probably of U.S. origin and flown by U.S. crews, hovered in the vicinity of the attack"; "Helicopters were frequently used to burn down the forests"; "The 'bad helicopter' arrived first, strafing the village with a machine gun and then 'throwing bombs' at the houses"; "'Soldiers had poured gasoline all around the women,' he recalled, 'and were debating whether to burn them or throw them from helicopters'"; "Helicopters appeared overhead. 'There were three helicopters shooting' . . . all she recalled was 'bombs and more bombs from the helicopters'"; "Eleven missing men . . . were 'taken at different times by military helicopter . . . and have not been seen since.'"

By 1995, the village-evacuation program was working much as the Turkish military hoped it might. Cities like Diyarbakir swelled with villagers escaping the violence, and tens of thousands more fled to Istanbul, Izmir, and Adana each month. In combination with an occupying force of 300,000 troops in the Southeast, the depopulation strategy forced the PKK into smaller areas of control, including northern Iraq, from where they could attack. The number of battles between rebels and government troops fell during 1995. The Turkish military chased them into Iraq regularly, at times creating embarrassments for Ankara through inept raids and even large-scale incursions in the springs of 1995 and 1997 that damaged civilian homes but failed to root out the rebels. The U.S. military supplied intelligence data for the F–16, Cobra, and Black Hawk attacks in Iraq, but the intelligence was not enough for a successful guerrilla war, and the jet and helicopter raids were ineffectual. For the Turkish military, the Kurdish areas of northern Iraq, Syria, and Iran were frustrating sanctuaries—Turkish generals once asked a former U.S. defense official if they could "get away" with an attack on Syria—but the cross-border escape of PKK fighters seemed to be the only flaw in the grand strategy of destroying the villages and emptying the Southeast in order to save it. Öcalan declared another cease-fire at the end of 1995, which the Turks summarily rejected as another ploy of a dying insurgency. Finally, it seemed, the tide had been turned, thanks to the American technology required to execute a winning strategy. "There is no doubt," said one Turkish analyst, "that the war against the PKK could not have been pursued so well without the U.S. weapons."

The strategy was taking another kind of toll, however, a wickedly explosive cost of the pacification program. The refugees from the violence suddenly looked to the politicians like a distinct, alienated mass of discontent, despair, and embarrassment. In the shantytowns and slums of the major cities, busloads of refugees would arrive every day, most of them with little more than a knapsack of belongings and almost no money. A scene typical of the millions of "internally displaced" could be found twenty miles from the American consulate in Istanbul, in Esenyurt. This outer section of Istanbul teems with 100,000 Kurds, thousands of them in shantytowns built illegally to house the most recently arrived. Their homes, without running water, are built with walls of stacked bricks and tin roofs. A few cows and geese drink from a stream blackened by industrial waste that runs through the middle of the settlement. Children roam through the hillside hamlet, unable to attend school because they possess no identification papers and the Turkish government demands a school fee that none of their parents can pay. The parents, too, have fallen out of the system. Afraid to speak up for their rights—voting, housing, jobs—the Kurdish refugees of Esenyurt piece together subsistence lives under constant threat. Gray Wolves harass and sometimes "disappear" political activists among the Kurds. The men can find work only as day laborers on construction crews, uncertain and seasonal work. The local government, excoriating the refugees as PKK, regularly bulldozes the shanties. The Kurds were driven from their homes in the Southeast when the government destroyed them, driven to a marginalized sore of a makeshift village in "Europe," where their homes are destroyed by the government again.

This is not the worst of it, either; tens of thousands live in tents, or in refugee camps in Greece, or in crowded huts in Iraq and Iran. Thousands more find housing with relatives, doubling up in the crowded apartments, hiding out from authorities who they fear may persecute them again. Virtually all find the city a bizarre and frightening experience. "I was a shopkeeper in my town," said Mehmet, a wiry man of forty-eight who was forced to migrate to Istanbul with his wife and ten children. "I wasn't political, but I was a respected citizen. After we left, our house was looted and burned. Now I cannot find work here. My wife is sick and needs an operation. She misses her home. Here we live incognito." A young mother says, "Culturally, it's so different here, I can't blend in. It makes me sick to think about how we will manage here." A mother of five: "The children don't know about cars. One of mine was struck by a car." Another woman: "We want to go back. We can't work here. To feed eight people is very hard, there's no continuous work. We are so afraid for our husbands because the working conditions are unsafe." A forty-nine-year-old man from near Diyarbakir, whose wife was murdered by the village guards and whose home was "shelled by panzers," says of his existence in Istanbul, "I don't even understand my life anymore, I don't understand what is happening to me." Concludes Mehmet: "This is the life we lead, in the shadow of guns, tanks, and helicopters."

Not all the refugees are so despairing. A growing number are becoming radicalized by their displacement. Many of the Kurds from small towns and villages were never politically active. They may have harbored vague sympathies for Kurdish nationalism—why, after all, could they not speak their own language?—and appreciated the fighting spirit of the rebels, but they liked neither the PKK's tactics nor their Marxism. However—when the military destroy their fields and flocks from their Black Hawks, when they bulldoze their homes and set them aflame, when they herd the villagers into the town square and excoriate them as terrorists, when they drag off a few young men to the torture chambers, never to be seen again, then the typical villager's attitude undergoes a transformation.

That transformation is accelerated by their experience in the urban slums, tent cities, and shantytowns. Doghu Ergil, a renowned political science professor from Ankara University, studied Kurdish attitudes in an exhaustive 1995 survey and found growing discontent among the refugees of Adana, Antalya, and Mersin, all towns along the southern coast of Turkey. "In the immigrant populations we see a higher rate of political radicalization," he explained. "In the cities, they are trivialized. They had their gardens and their livestock in the village, and now they have nothing. The mafia gets its manpower from this group, too. There is going to be an urban problem." Ergil's analysis sent shock waves through Turkey's political culture, since his study was sponsored by a prominent business group. He found that among all Kurdish populations, not just the refugees, the PKK was regarded as a useful goad to the system; they wanted political and cultural rights, not separation; and they despised the state-sponsored terror in the Southeast. "Ankara is using its muscle," Ergil concludes, "not its brain."

The PKK recognized this changing battle landscape in 1995 and began to alter its strategy. A rebel leader based in Athens explained in exaggerated fashion that "The Turkish state is having problems in western Turkey with people forced out of their villages. There are four million Kurds in Istanbul, with many, many economic and social problems. We have access to the urban areas, and we are strong. It is not difficult to recruit; the problem is training them all. A good organization has no problem recruiting; I know many youths who want to go but are not accepted because there is not any room for them." But through 1996 and 1997, the war resumed along its familiar lines, with ferocious battles throughout Turkey and northern Iraq.

The restless energy and discontent of the refugees was in part diverted into that force long feared by Kemalists: a vibrant and *political* Islam. Apart from HADEP, the nascent secular political party of the Kurds, there were no strong Kurdish organizations in the cities to capture the refugees politically. That left Refah, the Islamic party, which had constructed a version of Tammany Hall machine politics in many major cities. It was Refah and like-minded Muslim organizations that at times provided shelter, food, jobs, and community to the beleaguered immigrants. At home, many Kurds were devout Muslims of the traditional type: it was a simple, integrated part of their village existence. In the village, they were neither militant nor evangelistic, because there was no need for either. Then, in the cities, they encountered a more active and angry form of Islam, a revivalist faith that was, for the first time in seventy years, challenging the secular, nationalist ideology of Mustafa Kemal.

"Yes, the Kurdish refugee crisis benefits Islam: it's the only thing there to comfort them. I was among the first to say so." The speaker is Abdurrahman Dilipak, a renowned journalist in Istanbul and an unofficial spokesman for the Islamic movement. "The Kurds cannot find security and comfort in the old ways of the village here in the city. People disparage the way they dress, how they hang out their wash. So they find comfort in Islam. They didn't know before what religion meant to them. Now in the city, where it is hard for them, they are made Muslim almost by force. The Turkish government and Westerners have hastened this process."

The attraction of Islam that draws the Kurdish refugee is part of a larger phenomenon, a powerful magnetic field throughout Turkey. "People in this region are searching for their own past—the river is searching for its bed," said Dilipak. "Nothing is from our own past. We are falling into a vacuum. We have to find a way out. Will you find solutions by going back to Islam, by Turkification, or through the West? The Kemalist approach—we are the Turkish nation, the society of Islam, the civilization of the West—is nonsensical. It's like saying 'I believe like an Arab, think like a Turk, and live like a European.' This could not go on. Civilizations must fit within their own reality; therefore we cannot be split in these three different directions."

Tall, elegant, graceful, Dilipak speaks with the calm confidence of one who believes he is riding a wave of history. "Fifteen years ago there were just three catechisms, now there are over two hundred catechisms on how to live an Islamic life," he said, holding up a thick book with listings of Islamic writings. He explained there are now 10,000 titles in print from Islamic publishers; two-thirds of the Turkish book market is books for Muslims. Islamic newspaper circulation now accounts for 1.2 million out of four million newspapers sold in Turkey.

"The atmosphere of conflict, it costs so much in blood and lives, and the Islamic movement is so fragmented. But some significant things are about to take place.

"I don't reject the West, I just don't want to live in it or worship it. The future will not be the emulation of the West. But we must do something that is dedicated to my God. I'd like it to be more democratic, freer and more participatory than Western democracy, and also an avenue that opens new paths into one's own soul. This is my utopia."

The wave Dilipak and his cohorts in the Islamic movement were riding was a revival of Muslim feeling unlike anything seen in Turkey since the late nineteenth century. It was not only the Kurdish refugees who visibly bolstered the status of Islam; it was a society racked by hyperinflation, a growing income gap, and a failing system of secular belief rooted in the person of Atatürk, by now a vague and distant memory for the Turkish people. Ineffectual civilian governments alternating with brutal military governments had wasted much of the good will of the Turkish people. The old-style Turkish nationalism could no longer sustain popular enthusiasm for the mission of the Kemalist revolution. As in many societies in the post–Cold War world, the political culture was fragmenting: business elites, many intellectuals and opinion molders, and secular politicians gravitated toward the Western model. The have-nots, the traditional, the religious, and the doubtful resisted that model, and they resisted it with mounting fervor as Americanization came to appear to be the inevitable path for Turkey. In 1994, in a stunning and unexpected electoral spasm, the Refah Party swept into power in Istanbul and Ankara (and hundreds of other municipalities), electing mayors and city councils in the symbolic capitals both of European Turkey and of Kemalism. Suddenly, an "Islamic threat" was alive and well in Islam's most secular polity.

"A structural change in Turkey is needed to have harmony between tradition and modernity," said Altan Tan in a 1995 interview. Tan is an engineer and Islamic intellectual whose mother was Kurdish and whose father was Turkish. "It can be a model for the Balkans and for Central Asia. Turkey must cleanse itself of its racism, including a solution to the Kurdish issue. Kemalist secularism must be abandoned. It is Jacobite secularism. We need pluralism instead, human rights, democracy—a system that can accommodate Islam, Kurdishness, and the rest of the world. It's not the secular democrats that can accomplish this, but democratic Islamists."

Altan Tan has a jaundiced view of Refah, as many thoughtful Muslims do. Once an up-and-coming party operative, he was imprisoned in 1984 for his Kurdish activism. He added, "Muslim groups have a problem in that they're dominated by certain individuals, such as Erbakan, and sects.

On the Kurdish issue, they are nationalists, Turkish nationalists, and they back the government. This attitude prevents Refah from finding a solution to the problem. It cannot be an Islamic democratic party."

Refah is a successor to the National Salvation Party, which Necmettin Erbakan also headed, and which provided Turgut Özal with a platform early in his career. The durability of Refah is attributable in part to the wily political instincts of Erbakan, but as an *Islamic* vessel the party suffers from his machinations. "It is a proto-Islamic party. They advance some things based on Islam, but the main foundation of Refah is a counter-elite to Kemalism," is the blunt assessment of Aynur İlyasoghlu Leblebicioghlu, an Istanbul intellectual who specializes in the role of women in Islam. "The leading men are coming from traditional villages; it's not a 'revival.' Rather, it's a different kind of elite that seeks to run the country."

But she does see a particular potency in the mixture of the Kurdish diaspora and Islamicism. She says the Kurdish refugees "do not interact with the city. Refah is good organizationally, so it goes to find those who are unengaged, the unrepresented masses of urban poor. These masses can be changed if politicized through unions and other such organizations, but now there is no chance of that—no welfare, no economic development. But Refah works within the system; it is not against the E.U. or the U.S. There is some theoretical rejectionism, done just to capture the nativistic elements in society."

But while these keen observers of the Islamic phenomenon are skeptical about Refah, the party and its successes sharpen the conflict with secularism, heighten the inconsistencies within the Turkish political and social system, and open the door for a more authentic and radical form of political Islam. "Refah is a small boat rising on the sea that is Islam," insisted Abdurrahman Dilipak. "Whatever advantage Refah gains will also benefit the sea. Refah defines itself within the system; but it does show the world something not otherwise represented. This is a school for us; we are learning how to make politics."

"Turkey is embracing the Islamic values and traditions suppressed under Kemalism," added Leblebicioghlu. "It's a part of our social context."

It also soon became a more significant part of the political context. On the night before Christmas 1995, Refah for the first time won a general parliamentary election. Its total share, a mere 22 percent, outdistanced the center-right party of Prime Minister Tansu Çiller and Özal's Motherland Party, headed by Mesut Yilmaz. Refah's "victory" was all the more remarkable given

Europe's and America's active support of Çiller. The vote in the European Parliament to admit Turkey into the customs union, coming just two weeks before the Turkish election, hinged on the Islamic question. Çiller repeatedly and adamantly asserted that a rejection of Turkey from the economic agreement—an important step toward full E.U. membership—would enable Refah to win the election and usher "fundamentalism" into Europe. Even the socialists and greens in the European Parliament were sufficiently spooked by Çiller's dark specter of *jihād* in a NATO member to approve Turkey's candidacy with no conditions—but with a sharply worded rebuke about freedom of speech.

Çiller's threats worked in Brussels and Strasbourg; the U.S. bid up Çiller's stock; the International Monetary Fund provided enormous loans—and she still placed third in the balloting. The defeat could be attributed in part to the Kurdish conflict, particularly to the staggering costs of the war, which was eating up as much as 40 percent of the Turkish Republic's budget and the thin shreds of goodwill toward Turkey remaining in the international community. Investment, privatization, agricultural production—all were being shaken by the war. In 1994, economic activity fell and inflation rocketed by more than 100 percent; in 1995, the economy moved forward, but 80-percent inflation and devaluation more than robbed the average Turk of any gains. Corruption surged, touching every dimension of public life—including the war, where officials profited in myriad ways—and growing into a $45 billion-a-year enterprise, much if it from drugs. Half of Turkey was living below the poverty line; in crowded Diyarbakir, 80 percent were impoverished, half of them desperately so. The war was clearly to blame, and Çiller—the Wellesley economist, America's favorite Muslim—could not escape her culpability.

Refah did not take a position on the conflict—they maintain that all concerned are Muslims, hence Muslim-Muslim ethnic or nationalistic conflict is unacknowledgeable—except to hint that they would seek a political solution. Many of their votes came from the Southeast. Refah's longtime dispute with the military became more apparent just before and after the 1995 election, when the General Staff purged dozens of officers from its ranks for excessive religious zeal. It was a signal, no doubt, to politicians to exclude Refah.

Just as the Kurdish conflict gave Refah a boost toward power in the 1990s, the military had inadvertently sown the seeds of its rise in the 1980s, and that, too, was now bearing fruit. Alarmed by the Marxist-oriented radicalism of the late 1970s, the military began to fund Islamic schools for children to counter the atheistic ideology of the student radicals. The schools flourished. "The military used Islam to block oppositional movements in the 1980 coup," Aynur Leblebicioghlu explained, "using them as an instrument. The schools they created are still growing." The shadowy relationship between the General Staff and the Islamicists is a constant source of speculation and conspiracy spinning. But the support of Hezbollah and the schools is a fact; the part of the national budget still devoted to religious instruction is astonishing, a political gift to the Muslim stalwarts of the center-right parties. Refah itself aligned with the ultranationalist party of Alparslan Türkesh in 1991, revealing its inherently conservative character.

Now that the "Islamic reality" has been acknowledged—the genuine possibility that an elite committed to governance by *Sharī'a* could form a majority government—the character of the next generation of Refah, or a new Muslim party to follow, becomes crucial.

Ending the war by nonmilitary means required a level of public understanding that the government was unwilling to permit. The war in the Southeast was always a few months away from being finished, in the words of successive ministers and generals. The press in Istanbul and Ankara, ostensibly lively, was hostage to the official view. Few Turkish reporters ventured into the war zones—they were at risk from the guerrillas or the ultranationalist death squads—and even fewer politicians or Western diplomats would visit more than Diyarbakir. The Turkish people simply did not realize the extent of the violence, the scale of the village evacuations, or the costs to the Turkish economy. One leftist intellectual in Istanbul commented that "even our own friends do not believe the reports from the Southeast." The thunderous condemnations and disbelief of Professor Doghu Ergil's survey of Kurdish attitudes in 1995 was another indicator of how ignorant both elites and public were.

Those who did try to tell the story were cut down. The fate of *Özgür Ülke* was one such case. In perhaps the most ferocious campaign of village destruction in the mid-1990s, the military demolished in the autumn of 1994 some 137 villages in the province of Tunceli, fully one-third of all the villages in this large area north of Diyarbakir. Vast tracts of forest in one of the last green areas of Turkey were set aflame from helicopters and

F-16s. The press reported the policy of evacuating some of the districts—though it was also reported that villagers would be resettled and some villages rebuilt, neither of which took place. The news media tended to concentrate in that autumn on the skirmishes between the rebels and the military, especially the hunt for one of Öcalan's top lieutenants. But one newspaper did report the evacuations and razing of the villages on a daily basis—*Özgür Ülke*. "We have scanned the Turkish mainstream press but it proved almost useless as a source because of the generally practiced self-censorship where events in southeastern Turkey are concerned," a Dutch human-rights group noted in a lengthy report on the 1994 campaign in Tunceli. The major source of information was instead *Özgür Ülke*. The day-by-day reports, frequently from the region or by interviewing refugees from Tunceli, were an acute embarrassment to the government, and sparked one of Turkey's few public debates about the conduct of the war. "Such is the military's domination of Turkish war policy," one American reported, "that the local military commander would not allow Deputy Prime Minister Murat Karayalçin to visit the area to look into reports that the villages were burned last month." It was the Tunceli campaign, deep in the heart of the province that suffered the most vicious of Atatürk's anti-Kurd pogroms, which stirred the minister for human rights to depict the policy as "state terrorism." This was a daring public utterance by an official, one he was immediately forced to retract. The reports from the field were clearly having an impact.

And so the government acted. In November, Prime Minister Çiller reportedly sent a memo to the General Staff asking, in effect, "Who will rid me of this troublesome priest?" On November 29, the diplomatic correspondent for *Özgür Ülke* disappeared. Four days later, the newspaper's offices in Istanbul were demolished by a bomb. The explosion, at two o'clock on the Saturday morning of December 3, 1994, rocked an entire city block and injured 22 people, but killed just one person. Two other offices of the paper, one in Ankara, the other in Istanbul, were also bombed. The newspaper kept on publishing. The same month, a prominent human-rights attorney investigating the forced evacuations was murdered, purportedly by the death squads that also executed about a hundred journalists and human-rights activists in the Southeast. Unable to stifle the Kurdish voices, the government seized the newspaper on several occasions; the editors responded at times by whiting out large swaths of the six-page daily, writing over the blanks in bold type, "CEN-SORED." Finally, on the first of February, 1995, Çiller closed down the newspaper altogether.

The closing of *Özgür Ülke* was a setback not only for the unique information it gave to its readers, but for the channel it provided into the dissident Kurdish community, for the realistic view of the war it reported, and for its links to the rebels themselves. Öcalan, under a pseudonym, had an occasional column published in the newspaper, for example, and although this established the legal grounds for the government attack, *Özgür Ülke* served as a unique conduit for messages back and forth between the two sides. "It was widely read in government circles," one diplomat remarked at its closing, "every desk seemed to have a copy." If a political dialogue were ever to be created to end the war, *Özgür Ülke* could have been indispensable. Possibly the military realized that and ordered the government to act.

The war raged on unknown to most Americans; the grasp of the situation by the opinion elite consistently misstated the PKK's goals (which, after 1992, no longer included separatism), ignored the millions of displaced Kurds, and repeated the mantra of Turkey's "bad neighborhood." The conflict drew interest only when the Iraqi Kurds acted up and, in the late spring of 1996, when Refah's Erbakan finally was able to form a minority government. The unexpected ascendance of Necmettin Erbakan to the premiership came when the conservative secular coalition formed after the December 1995 election fell apart in acrimony. One of that coalition's partners, Tansu Çiller, bolted and formed a government with Erbakan (some said to avoid a criminal investigation into her finances), an especially ironic turnabout for the woman who had darkly warned Europe of the Islamic tide. Erbakan's limited triumph—Refah held none of the key security portfolios—raised predictable shrieks of alarm about the "fundamentalists," and many in the American press criticized the U.S. government for its "acceptance" of Erbakan. The alarms rang louder when Erbakan promptly cut a deal with Iran (his first foreign trip was to Teheran) to buy natural gas, possibly in violation of the U.S. embargo on Iran. Then, when Saddam Hussein answered Iraqi Kurdish chieftain Barzani's call to help Barzani fight his rival Talabani, Turkey again flouted U.S. policy; Erbakan (and, as foreign minister, Tansu Çiller) declared delight at the prospect that Saddam might gain control over the north of Iraq and help Turkey with its own Kurdish problem.

Erbakan's leadership, to be sure, sent a mixed message. Erbakan said nothing about leaving NATO, for example, or withdrawing from a military agreement with Israel, both of which as candidate he had vowed to do. The war in the southeast intensified anew. Devout Muslims in the military were purged. Still, the military chiefs were restive. The animosity between the Kemalist military and the mildly Islamic premier came to a head in the winter and spring of 1997, when the generals imposed "reforms" on Erbakan to keep Islam out of public life altogether, including measures to ban Koranic study groups and wearing head scarves in government buildings. The climate of panic had rumors of a military coup flying for weeks, and, since Erbakan did fitfully acquiesce to the military's orders, the episode was in effect a "soft coup"—the military openly humiliated the elected government and made unbreachable commands. (The U.S. government coyly said it supported "secular democracy," which some saw as backing the military.) After one year as premier, Erbakan was forced out by the generals.

The crisis also underscored the military's firm control over security policy. The fact that Erbakan could so easily ignore "dual containment" by openly dealing with Iran and Iraq was telling. It was not, as many in Washington charged, his fealty to Islamic brotherhood at work. Rather, it was Turkey's long-standing attitude: Iran and Iraq are neighbors; they have never threatened us, there is no reason not to conduct normal relations.

Dual containment was no more popular with the Turkish military than with Refah, except that the military could wangle more U.S. weapons from Washington by paying lip service to the bad-neighborhood canard. By allowing Erbakan's embrace of Iran and Iraq to go largely unchallenged, the Turkish General Staff, so lavishly supplied and encouraged by Washington for decades, was unambiguously turning its back on the most significant U.S. policy initiative in the region. Dual containment was dead.

But the war against the Kurds was very much alive. The war intensified as Erbakan's flimsy comments about a political settlement went the way of all similar promises of his predecessors. The village-evacuation policy also continued, mocking the condemnations from Europe. Despite some occasional pledges to rebuild the destroyed villages and return the refugees, nothing of the sort occurred. The refugees remained in their camps, in their shantytowns, hidden in crowded apartments in Istanbul and other cities far from their ancestral pastures.

Their sense of betrayal and anger and wariness comes out at every encounter. A group in Diyarbakir shout to a reporter, "We hate the U.S.A.!" A villager in the Southeast carefully explains how they have come to know the words "Sikorsky" and "Cobra": they mean different things, he said, since one would deposit soldiers and the other would simply start shooting. Both were bad.

Two women spoke—among the few brave enough to do so. One was defiant, the other resigned. In their voices were the two ardent feelings which are prototypical of the Kurdish diaspora.

The first, whose village was burned to the ground by the military, spoke with outrage in her voice of all the weapons the state had used to terrorize them, including helicopters, when they were driven from their village. "The burning of the village was one form of oppression. Another is *white genocide:* the children are assimilated into a Turkish identity, Kemalism, and they are denied their own cultural identity."

The second, who fled her village in fear after her husband was murdered, spoke wearily, with the weariness of the perpetual refugee, about her hopes while her seven-year-old son, now the family breadwinner, looked on. "In the village, we had a grapevine and walnut trees and were well off. Now it is harvest time and I would like to return to pick the crop, but I'm scared to go there. We'd like to go home to our village. I had a house and land, and where I stay here is very small.

"I only want the blood to flow no more."

24

THE MORAL EQUATION

Our long, sad tale comes to an end here, though for the players it continues. In Connecticut and the similar venues of Texas, California, and other places, hundreds of thousands of skilled workers whose livelihoods were tied to the Reagan rearmament are ringing cash registers in convenience stores, collecting food stamps, looking for respectable work. Those who remain in the arms factories make weapons likely to be destined for the killing fields of Turkey or the other war grounds of Asia and Africa. At the other end of these lines of fire are the likes of Kurdish peasants, driven from home and village by an American-fed Turkish military that knows no restraint in its desire to eradicate Kurdish dissent. These are the true spoils of war.

How do such disasters unfold? This one was born of a centuries-old Western hostility toward Islam, given urgency by the West's dependence on oil, escalated by radical Muslim challenges to U.S. dominance, and finally driven by America's desperate need to export weapons. So many factors came into play: the plausible need for Turkey's allegiance and its unique geography; Sikorsky's special appeal as a stalwart of the "defense industrial base"; the engine of commerce—"If we don't sell to them, someone else will"—and the locomotion of trade imperatives; persistent U.S. encouragement to its allies to crush leftist politics, driving the dissidents toward more acceptable forms of opposition, such as Islam; and last but far from least, America's nearly total unwillingness to deal with its dependence on foreign oil.

279

Front and center in this drama, however, is the use of military power—surrogate military power in particular—as the first tool of policy. The strategy that originated with Richard Nixon's speech on Guam and that has been eagerly pursued by every administration since has failed so miserably that one can only wonder that it has so resiliently survived to this day. Identify a "friend," a despot or regime who will protect the flow of oil and confront America's enemies, and supply him with a panoply of military goods: weapons, advice, alliances, intelligence, training, infrastructure. While public language will be designed to dignify the relationship—regional gendarme, balance-of-power tilt, container of communism/fundamentalism, stout friend in bad neighborhood—the formula is always the same. And the results, in this crucial part of the world, are nearly always the same—failure, tragedy, "blowback," staggering human costs. Iran, Iraq, and now Turkey. Tomorrow, Saudi Arabia, Egypt. The survival of Israel may be the final victim of a 30-year policy that can most kindly be called amoral.

What successive sets of policymakers have refused to see is the *primary* distorting impact of military assistance on political regimes, whether the country is nominally democratic, like Turkey or Egypt, or clearly despotic, like the Shah's Iran, Saddam's Iraq, or Saudi Arabia. When a former advisor to President Bush told me that military aid to Turkey was "the toe of the elephant" in the U.S.-Turkish relationship, he spoke for the abiding self-delusion of policymakers—that our foreign policy is *really* about principles, and, yes, it includes the exercise of military power, but power projected *only* to back a set of principles, a geostrategic vision.

Foreign policy elites in the United States may see military aid to Turkey as the "toe" of the relationship, even as an afterthought—the necessary payoff to keep Turkey happy and Western-oriented. But the Turks see it differently: it is the fulcrum, the *sine qua non,* of their link to Washington. And the impact on Turkey's people is profound. A small phalanx of scholars has explored the place of the military in "less-developed" societies, and their conclusions are sobering: the generals *can* make positive contributions to nation building, but, over time, the transfer to developing countries of military aid and weapons from the United States (or other major powers) has a deleterious effect on democracy and peace in the recipient nations. The arrival of shiny high-tech weapons, the conveyance of cash, the primacy of military-to-military links in the bilateral relationship—all bolster the military elites, enabling them to exert more political power, draw on more national resources, and, of course, shape national policy. "If one can fly a squadron of advanced fighter planes over the capital on Independence Day, this is (much like a national airline and national palace) a sign of power that commands respect," as one scholar puts it.

These symbolic, budgetary, and international privileges naturally translate into growing fealty to the military outlook: when a state such as Turkey is founded by a military hero; when it spends as much as 25 percent of its national budget on the military and police, as Turkey has for decades; and when its key links to the outside, like Turkey's, are to a military alliance (NATO) and the military of a major power (the Pentagon), then political decision-making will turn first to the General Staff. And the General Staff is likely to see problems as solvable mainly by the organized violence in which they specialize.

Militarizing a society—in effect, encouraging military and police dominance—and then turning a blind eye to the internal consequences of the political hegemony which accrues to the military, was Washington's fundamental mistake in Iran and Turkey. In different ways, this approach also led American policymakers astray in Iraq and Afghanistan.

The fostering of military solutions for political problems now endangers Egypt and Saudi Arabia as well. Egypt's one-party rule has used military supply from the United States to repress dissent, and this repression has fed Islamic militancy, which constantly threatens the government. In 1995 the conservative British weekly *The Economist* described "Egypt's progress towards an Algerian disaster," referring to the bloody civil war between Muslim extremists and the military government in Algiers: "The well-tried strategy of isolating the militants by winning over the moderate majority has been abandoned. Instead moderates and extremists are lumped together as 'terrorists.' In addition, the regime's response to those it suspects of Islamic militancy has moved from repression to something closer to brutality. . . . It is alarming to see Egypt embark on Algeria's path: attempting to defeat a mass movement, rooted in disillusion with a corrupt governing class, by using undiscriminating force." And *Foreign Affairs* adds the poignant observation that "to keep the military on his side, Mubarak will have to preserve access to modern weapons, training and other benefits that come mainly from the United States."

In Saudi Arabia, petrodollars continue to flow into the coffers of U.S.,

British, and French weaponeers to defend a royal family widely believed to be purely self-interested and corrupt. A perverse symbiosis has grown up between the supplier and the supplied, where the Saudi princes, who feed off the arms deals, order more military technology to demonstrate their self-reliance, and American officials urge ever more sales upon the House of Saud. "The acceleration in Saudi arms purchases to guarantee Western political support has not escaped the attention of the Saudi opposition, both the liberal new class and the Islamic fundamentalists," asserts journalist Saïd K. Aburish. "The more arms the West sells to the House of Saud, the fewer friends it has in Saudi Arabia." The country's standard of living has dropped sharply, the government is deeply in debt, and the Muslim radicals—many of them trained in the *jihād* in Afghanistan—are growing bolder.

Should indeed the pro-American regimes in Riyadh and Cairo fall to Muslim extremists, Israel could be another victim of the "Iran precedent." Jordan would come under enormous pressure. Syria would be bolstered by new enemies of the Jewish state. Israel itself, the largest recipient of U.S. military aid for decades past, would feel compelled to arm itself anew. Its own military solutions—invasion of Lebanon, occupation of the West Bank—have cost it dearly, and not until Israel's leaders opted for a political settlement with the PLO did the hostile impasse begin to break.

What is worse is that the militarization of the region was pursued not merely for the sake of geopolitics, but for the benefit of the weapons-making corporations who pressured, lobbied, cajoled, bribed, and extorted political leaders from Nixon onward. In this, the "policy" was not always intentional or rational. Jobs at home were at stake. The trade ledger was out of balance. The home-state politicians, frightened by an angry and anxious electorate, schemed repeatedly to export arms, heedless of the consequences. The managers of the factory lines designed for weapons-making did not have the will or the incentive to change. Like the proverbial balloon, when squeezed at one end the industry had to expand at the other; if it did not burst at home, it frequently exploded abroad.

Ideas and rewards for conversion to peaceful use were scant. Help for the displaced worker—sustained retraining, public works, health insurance—was too little to cushion the blow of the defense drawdown. "Only about 7 percent of workers who qualify for retraining monies get them," a leading expert pointed out, and "much of it is aimed at entry-level inner-city workers and not seasoned blue-collar workers or engineers 40 or 50 years old. Retraining programs are not connected to job-creation efforts. This is causing great levels of demoralization." Far more federal dollars were invested in useless extensions of weapons manufacture, or Pentagon awards for mergers, or financing for exports. Defense workers did not have the luxury of exercising moral concern about how their products were used in alien, faraway places. Cities and towns were left to do special pleading for their weapons plants rather than given the tools to reshape their economies for a post–Cold War world. The tragedy of the "displaced" is— while far, far less severe—every bit as much the story of Connecticut, California, and Texas as it is of Kurdistan.

Chris Dodd, Gene Buckley, Jack Powers, and the many others, past and present, involved in promoting the arms trade are not individually responsible for the tragedy of the Kurds. They are playing out well-worn roles of American politics. As one aerospace analyst close to Sikorsky put it, "We need Turkey as an 'aircraft carrier' more than we need the Kurds." Twenty-five years ago, the same arguments for exports were articulated by their predecessors, with the same foolish results. One can certainly question the sincerity and the energy of their search for alternatives. But American officials typically act as most Americans expect—to protect American jobs and to serve the "consensus" position of U.S. foreign policy. They have all done so with great skill and acumen, legally and for the most part openly. And the result is loathsome.

That is why the think-tank studies and proposals for "restraint" in arms sales (usually very slight restraint) and clever reconfigurations of the defense industrial base are so unsatisfying. Such nibbling at the margins will be overwhelmed by the ingrained habits and shibboleths of the arms business: we're merely supporting a "balance of power," and if we don't sell those weapons, someone else will. In a country now in the grip of a debate over "values," it is astounding that so little heed is given to the values underlying the promiscuous provision of lethal weaponry.

Oscar Arías, the former president of Costa Rica and a Nobel-prize-winning architect of the peace in Central America, frames the matter with a stark comparison: "Some Colombians or Bolivians could argue that exporting mind-altering drugs to the U.S. is justified because the production of cocaine and marijuana creates jobs in their own agricultural, industrial, and commercial sectors. Moreover, it could be claimed that, if these drugs

were not exported from Colombia or Bolivia, they would simply be supplied by other countries. . . . If we are frightened by the extent of drug
trafficking originating from the South and directed toward the North, we
must then also be scandalized by the scope and magnitude of indiscriminate arms sales from the North to the South."

What else could be done? A number of possibilities are at hand, some
quite familiar but still ignored. The most obvious is a no-nonsense
energy policy—*real* conservation and efficiency, taxes on imported oil, a
serious commitment to alternatives—that has been doable for twenty
years. But the will to act is absent in Washington.

A more thoroughgoing revamping of American policy is needed, however, and could profitably take the form of two major—indeed, transfor-
mative—initiatives. The first would be to redirect diplomacy away from its
hidebound protection of state interests toward an outlook that actually sees
peace and stability as primary goals. The second is to stop exporting lethal
weapons. Both suggestions will be seen as utopian, but if the alternative is
the *Realpolitik* of the last three decades, then the utopian ideas surely
should get a hearing.

Halting arms exports can begin with less drastic measures. The proposal for a Code of Conduct in arms sales is a fully formed piece of legislation, nearly passed in Congress in the mid-1990s, which would deny
military assistance to governments that are undemocratic or guilty of a
pattern of massive human-rights violations. A second useful idea is to stop
shipping *offensive* weapons—e.g., fighter-bombers, attack helicopters, and
tanks—and equipment frequently used for internal repression. Applying
either proposal would be troublesome, because some regimes sit on the
margins of the Code of Conduct's proscriptions, and many of the same
weapons used for legitimate defense can be committed to offensive action. But both ideas infuse the arms-export equation with a healthy ration
of ethical standards.

A third idea, while less direct, also deserves a hearing. For governments
purchasing weapons, we should set benchmark standards for social and
military performance: a reasonable balance between military spending and
social spending (education, health, housing, etc.); transparency in and
civilian control of military policy; and a history of nonaggression and stability. And we could go further by persuading the World Bank and the In-

ternational Monetary Fund to withhold financial assistance until such standards are met, which would have the added benefit of "internationalizing" restraint.

Those three ideas alone would go a long way toward slowing down the arms trade. But as we have seen, the trade is driven as much by domestic politics as by hoary notions of national security. The story of Stratford has demonstrated how some early support for conversion at the army engine plant could have averted its closing and saved thousands of good jobs. Lamentably, few clear-cut cases of that sort exist. Conversion of private military firms to commercial products is a far more daunting task than converting U.S. bases to civilian use. But some incentives to diversify can be tried—such as tying some kinds of contracts to investment in civilian enterprises. And the current incentives *not* to diversify (such as the unnecessary U.S. procurement of Black Hawks) could be eliminated, with the savings going into funds to retrain and place defense workers or other programs that reduce the irresistible political pressure on Congress to buy or export weapons.

The sad fact is that a sharp reduction in arms exports will force many white- and blue-collar workers into joblessness. But efforts to save Sikorsky or other firms that fail to diversify are far more costly than alternative programs to employ their workers. Even the overall numbers of defense workers, and those tied to exports (perhaps 100,000), mask the lack of stability in the business, the on-again off-again nature of its employment, and its poor long-term prospects. Its workforce is not a permanent one; many laid-off workers leave the factory area in each down cycle. And military exports are down to 2 percent of all U.S. trade. So an end to exports, even if precipitous, would have a less harsh impact than is often claimed.

The final, cynical argument—that someone else will sell weapons to Turkey, Saudi Arabia, Egypt, et cetera—deserves two rejoinders. The first is simple: So what? There is satisfaction in doing the morally correct thing. We still see moral action as a positive good in global affairs, even when some economic gain is sacrificed. The list of heinous products barred from export is long. The second reply is more complex but still compelling: if the United States stops exporting weapons, the other major suppliers—France, Britain, Russia, Germany, China—will eventually come under pressure to curb their arms trade as well. America's premier position in the world rests not only on military power—which can still be exercised through NATO, the UN, and unilaterally—but on economic dynamism and political leadership. A Washington crusade to end the arms trade as we know it would generate colossal moral and political momentum.

If combined with a new *modus operandi* in U.S. foreign policy that emphasized preventive diplomacy, such a crusade would enhance the prospects for America's global role. Preventive diplomacy, a rather new concept just now generating interest in policy circles, is a mélange of proposals, some old, some new. It includes promoting democracy and openness and fortifying civil society as means to make governments more accountable. It seeks to create mechanisms to address and resolve potential conflicts early in their evolution, and especially for the peaceful redress of ethnic and religious clashes. It promotes economic, sexual, and ethnic equality. It champions collaborative security—e.g., regional security structures, transparency in militaries, confidence-building measures, multilateral cooperation, and arms reduction. It is closely linked to human rights, and sees such rights as the foundation for international politics. To its credit, the Clinton administration has, however fitfully, explored preventive diplomatic action as an adjunct to the power politics of national-security thinking. But we are a long way from making it the centerpiece of American globalism.

Such a new formulation of *interests,* away from a narrow definition of national prerogative and protectionism and toward a broad one of global peace and stability, has been a core value for many Americans and Europeans for many decades. In the post-Soviet world this vision is gaining a fresh impetus. No mortal enemy threatens America or Western Europe. These principal purveyors of weapons have vibrant economies and immense political strength. They can readily turn their diplomacy, technological prowess, and political skills to fostering sustainable economic development, international cooperation, and human rights.

These grand thoughts seem utopian only if we ignore the consequences of the arms trade and the policies that embrace it. Such willful ignorance makes a mockery of the obsessive espousal of "realism" in Washington—that is, the premise that the political world is such a dangerous place that military power must be the primary instrument of American engagement. The consequences of that mindset can be viewed with dreadful clarity in the Middle East. There, the primary instrument of American power has backfired time and again. The costs are incalculable.

Turkey again can provide insight. Sikorsky did not "cause" the war between Kurds and Turks, and the denial of Black Hawks to Turkey would have done little to prevent the horror of that conflict. But the Black Hawk sales not only demonstrated the pitiable machinations of U.S. politicians at home and the wicked use of American weapons abroad—they were part of a much larger frame of mind, a decades-old policy, which thoughtlessly nourished military power in Ankara and sanctioned the use of that power to address a political problem. That there were alternatives for Turkey (and Iran and Iraq) should now be obvious. But the primacy of military "solutions" in Turkey and the region persists, while the other options—political dialogue, economic initiatives, stubborn pressure for human rights—languish in the background.

Turkey is unlikely to follow Iran's path to become a narrow-minded theocracy. But the Iran precedent has been fulfilled all the same, with all the bloodletting, repression, human-rights catastrophe, and alienation from the West that that precedent implies. The plight of the Kurdish people, an unnecessary tragedy in itself, is a symptom of a systemic malfunction in a decrepit and morally vacuous American foreign policy. There must be, and there is, a better way.

Afterword and Acknowledgments

Although I knew when I set out on this research and writing project that some types of information would be difficult to obtain, I was not fully prepared for the number of doors shut in my face. As expected, Sikorsky Aircraft essentially refused to speak to me, and repeated attempts to interview Eugene Buckley failed. (Lockheed and Bell Textron executives were far more cooperative.) Executives of private firms, however beholden to government money, are one thing; being refused information by public servants is another. Senator Christopher Dodd and several of his aides all declined to be interviewed. Many other U.S. government officials, past and present, also declined the opportunity. The State and Defense departments failed to provide a single useful document in response to Freedom of Information Act requests and failed to provide a convincing reason for their action. Fortunately, much of the story told in this book could be pieced together with assiduous research that did not rely on those mute sources. But I am compelled to voice the lament of many journalists: the secrecy that shrouds the government is excessive and shameful. The reason for such non-cooperation, I suspect, has less to do with lack of time or interest than a lack of pride in the actions I wished to explore.

The support and encouragement of the board and staff of the Winston Foundation, where I have happily worked for more than a decade, was indispensable. I am deeply indebted to all, particularly the board of directors, which has always encouraged my writing, and my colleagues Tara Magner, Jean Donnelly Linde, and Monica Dorbandt. The work of the Foundation, which engages many of the topics raised in this book, was enabled by Robert Winston Scrivner, the founder and benefactor, who was an inspiration to many people seeking to build a durable peace.

I benefited from research assistance from my colleagues and particularly from Christopher Weeks. Julie Farb also provided research help. Underfunded but gracious and helpful librarians also aided me; I used public libraries in Stratford, Hartford, and New Haven, Connecticut; Boston, Massachusetts; Fort Worth, Texas; Los Angeles and Palo Alto, California; New York City; Phoenix, Arizona; Providence and Newport, Rhode Island; and Washington, D.C. My editors at The Free Press, Adam Bellow and Mitch Horowitz, and their colleagues were kind, insightful, and encouraging, as was my agent, Robin Straus.

My family was also encouraging throughout. Special thanks are due to Nike, my wife, who served as photographer, booster, news watcher, and traveling companion: this would have been a dreary task without her. With her, Turkey was a place of discovery and intrigue that will long live warmly in our memories.

John Tirman
Washington D.C.
June 1997

Notes and Sources

This book was researched from many different sources, including approximately 120 interviews, dozens of books, and hundreds of articles, reports, and government documents. The notes below, which give references for the more significant assertions in the text and for the direct quotations, reflect the most important sources used. As many of the interviews were conducted on the condition that the person would not be identified by name in the book, sources are often listed simply as "interviews." This "not-for-attribution" condition is common to journalism and is unavoidable in a book dealing with controversial issues. For more information, updates, citations, and discussion of topics in this book, please consult the Winston Foundation Web site, www.wf.org.

CHAPTER 2

On Troy, "where the most famous, most foolish . . . ," comes from Barbara Tuchman, *A Distant Mirror: The Calamitous Fourteenth Century* (Knopf, 1978), p. 565. "On 15 July 1099, amid scenes . . ." comes from John Julius Norwich, *Byzantium: The Decline and Fall* (Knopf, 1995), p. 42. "It is safe to speak evil . . ." comes from Maxime Rodinson, *Europe and the Mystique of Islam*, Roger Veinus, trans. (University of Washington Press, 1991), p. 11. "The West's image of Islam . . ." is from ibid., p. 35. "The famous imposter . . . ," comes from Edward W. Said, *Orientalism* (Vintage, 1979), p. 63. "He raised up the Saracen . . . ," is from Bernard Lewis, *Islam and the West* (Oxford University Press, 1993), p. 89. "Crusaders were not only . . ." comes from Said, p. 172. "As a movement of violence . . ." is in John L. Esposito, *The Islamic Threat: Myth or Reality?* (Oxford University Press, 1992), p. 46. "European powers never seem . . ." comes from Lewis, p. 23.

CHAPTER 3

"For two centuries . . .," comes from Henry Kissinger, *The White House Years* (Little, Brown, 1979), p. 57. "It is only by discussing . . ." is from "Vietnam: the Moral Equation," reprinted in Howard Zinn, *The Politics of History* (Beacon, 1970). On the Nixon Doctrine's evolution, see Lewis Sorley, *Arms Transfers Under Nixon* (University Press of Kentucky, 1983); William Hartung, *And Weapons for All* (Harper Perennial, 1994); Michael Klare, *The Arms Trade Supermarket* (University of Texas Press, 1984); Seymour Hersh, *The Price of Power: Kissinger in the Nixon White House* (Summit, 1983); Tad Szulc, *The Illusion of Peace: Foreign Policy in the Nixon Years* (Viking, 1978); and Anthony Sampson, *The Arms Bazaar: From Lebanon to Lockheed* (Viking, 1977). For FMS numbers, see Sorley, *Arms Transfers;* figures on the defense budget and procurement (current dollars) and for employment are taken from the *U.S. Statistical Abstract* (U.S. Department of Commerce, 1971, 1974, and 1977 editions).

CHAPTER 4

On Iran's history and the role of oil, see David Fromkin, *The Peace to End All Peace* (Avon Books, 1989); Daniel Yergin, *The Prize: The Epic Quest for Oil, Money, and Power* (Touchstone, 1991), among others below. On Nixon's relationship to the Shah, see news stories from the *New York Times;* Hersh, *The Price of Power;* Hartung, *And Weapons for All.* The quotation on the twin pillars strategy from the "policy aide" is found in Howard Teicher and Gayle Radley Teicher, *Twin Pillars to Desert Storm: America's Flawed Vision in the Middle East from Nixon to Bush* (Morrow, 1993), p. 29. "The militarization of Iran . . ." is in Mohsen Milani, *The Making of Iran's Islamic Revolution,* 2nd ed. (Westview, 1994), pp. 96–97. "Recognizing Iran's strategic centrality . . ." comes from Zbigniew Brzezinski, *Power and Principle: Memoirs of the National Security Adviser, 1977–1981* (Farrar Straus & Giroux, 1983), p. 357. Atkins' Teheran experience is described in David Brown, *The Bell Helicopter Textron Story* (Aerofax, 1995). "The decision by President Nixon . . ." is in Gary Sick, *All Fall Down: America's Tragic Encounter with Iran* (Random House, 1985), p. 170. "Iranians see foreign powers . . ." comes from Nikki R. Keddie, *Roots of Revolution: An Interpretive History of Modern Iran* (Yale University Press, 1981), p. 276.

CHAPTER 5

On Connecticut inventors, see Ellsworth Grant, *The Miracle of Connecticut* (Connecticut Historical Society, 1992); Constance Green, *Eli Whitney and the Birth of American Technology* (Random House, 1956); R. L. Wilson, *The Colt Heritage* (Simon & Schuster, 1979). For Igor Sikorsky's life, see Bill Siuru, "Igor Sikorsky," *Mechanical Engineering-CIME* (August 1990); Frank J. Delear, *Igor Sikorsky: His Three Careers in Aviation* (Dodd, Mead [New York], 1969). "The United States seemed to me . . ." is quoted in Curt Wohleber, "Straight Up," *Invention & Technology* (Winter 1993). Material on Stratford comes from Lewis Knapp, *In Pursuit of Paradise* (Phoenix Publishers, 1989); an interview; and Lynn W. Wilson, *History of Fairfield County, 1639–1928,* Vol. I (S. J. Clarke, 1929). On helicopter development, see W. J. Boyne and D. S. Lopez, eds., *The Age of the Helicopter: Vertical Flight* (Smithsonian Institution Press, 1984); Warren R. Young, *The Epic of Flight: The Helicopters* (Time-Life

Books, 1984); Arthur Young, *The Bell Notes* (Robert Briggs Associates, 1979). Material on Sikorsky Aircraft comes from Knapp; from Ronald Fernandez, *Excess Profits: The Rise of United Technologies* (Addison-Wesley, 1983); from Boyne and Lopez; and from interviews.

CHAPTER 6

"Sometimes you get the feeling . . .," and the following quotations, including Aspin's, are from the *New York Times* (Apr. 14, 1975, and Oct. 20, 1975). "The rise of Nader's Raiders . . .," is in Easterbrook, "Ideas Move Nations," *The Atlantic* (Jan. 1986). "The industry argument . . .," is in Hartung, *And Weapons for All,* pp. 56–61. "Production of exports helps maintain . . .," is quoted in Mary Kaldor, *The Baroque Arsenal* (Hill & Wang, 1981), p. 198. "Never since World War II . . .," is quoted in Ronald Steel, "Morality, Reason, and Power," a review of Gaddis Smith's book of the same title in *The Atlantic* (June 1986).

CHAPTER 7

"The catastrophe which Greek restlessness . . ." is quoted in Lord Kinross, *Atatürk* (Morrow, 1964), p 376. Fromkin, in *The Peace to End All Peace* (p. 431), notes that the "Treaty of Sèvres embodied . . . the Liberal dream of triumphant Hellenism and Christianity." Atatürk's 1931 manifesto is quoted in Bernard Lewis, *The Emergence of Modern Turkey* (Oxford University Press, 1966), p. 280. "Our report expressed the seriousness of Russian moves . . .," is from Acheson, *Present at the Creation* (Norton, 1969), p. 195. For Acheson on the Truman Doctrine see ibid., pp. 219–222. "The rally was addressed by Erbakan . . .," is from George E. Gruen, "Turkey's Relations with Israel and its Neighbors," *Middle East Review* (Spring 1985), p. 37. "Officials in Turkish military circles . . ." is from the *New York Times* (Sept. 13, 1980). The State Department denied prior knowledge of the coup, apart from the 75-minute warning. On U.S. encouragement of the coup, see Mehmet Ali Birand, *The Generals' Coup in Turkey* (Brassey's Defence Publishers, 1987), and Feroz Ahmad, *The Making of Modern Turkey* (Routledge, 1994), pp. 173–176. "Turkey under her existing . . .," is in ibid., p. 175. Ahmad, a history professor at the University of Massachusetts, states that the "reason for the generals' intervention was their apprehension and their sense of urgency regarding Turkey's instability now that she had suddenly become strategically important to the West following the revolution in Iran" (p. 174). The "longer pattern" of U.S. encouragement of the coup plotters is also suggested by Ömer Karasapan in "Turkey and US Strategy in the Age of Glasnost," *Middle East Report* (Sept.–Oct. 1989). "The Carter administration would not . . ." is from Henze, *Turkish Democracy and the American Alliance* (RAND, 1993), pp. 45–46. "What lies at the basis . . .," is quoted in Tachau and Heper, "The State, Politics, and the Military in Turkey," in *Comparative Politics* (Oct. 1983), p. 27. Evren said in another speech, "The sole *raison d'être* of the Turkish Armed Forces is to defend this great country as an indivisible whole against internal as well as external enemies," ibid., p. 28.

CHAPTER 8

"Today there seems . . .," is quoted in Michael Klare and Peter Kornbluh, eds., *Low Intensity Warfare* (Pantheon, 1988), p. 4. "Essential element of our global policy . . .," is quoted in

Hartung, *And Weapons for All,* pp. 92–93. On Weinberger's and Haig's visits to Ankara, see the *New York Times* (Dec. 5, Dec. 6, and Dec. 8, 1981; and May 15, 1982). For "is the first Turkish . . .," see the *New York Times* (July 10, 1982). According to Ahmad in *The Making of Modern Turkey* (p. 185), Weinberger's visit "and the promise of more aid strengthened the regime's confidence and resolve."

CHAPTER 9

"Given the proposition . . .," quoted in Klare and Kornbluh, eds., *Low Intensity Warfare,* p. 5. "The reason there's a doctrine . . .," quoted in *Defense News* (June 24–30, 1996). "We were about to go down the tubes . . .," Knapp, interview. On survivability of the Black Hawk, see E. F. Katzenberger and E. S. Carter, "The Technical Evolution of Sikorsky Helicopters, 1950–83," in Boyne and Lopez, eds., *The Age of the Helicopter.* "The army wanted the helicopter . . ." comes from Knapp, in an interview. Tobias "was cheered . . ." per the *New York Times* (Dec. 24, 1976). Data on the UH-60 comes from William Dane, Forecast International, interview; from Boyne and Lopez; and from Paul Pickett, *UH-60 Black Hawk in Action* (Squadron/Signal Publications, 1993). The Army requirement for UH-60 comes from Arneson in an interview. "For some reason . . ." is from Knapp, interview. "When they came back . . .," was stated by Jack Powers in an interview. On the UH-60 in Grenada, see Mark Adkin, *Urgent Fury: The Battle for Grenada* (Lexington Books, 1989); and Lee Russel and Albert Mendez, *Grenada 1983* (Osprey, 1985). "The Black Hawks have . . .," is quoted in Adkin, p. 371. On UH-60s in Delta Force, etc., see the introduction to Klare and Kornbluh, eds., *Low Intensity Warfare* and Stephen Goose, "Low-Intensity Warfare: The Warriors and Their Weapons," therein. On the UH-60 as an attack helicopter, see "Armed/Utility Market Sees Worldwide Growth," *Aviation Week and Space Technology* (Oct. 4, 1993), which quotes Baxter, and *Army Times* (Dec. 21, 1987). "Army aviation stands at . . .," Ostovich, *Military Review* (Feb. 1991). On the Black Hawk as "master weapon," see Major Anthony Coroalles, *Military Review* (Jan. 1991); see also Matthew Allen, *Military Helicopter Doctrines of the Major Powers, 1945–1992* (Greenwood Press, 1993).

CHAPTER 10

"The emergence in Washington of a notion . . ." comes from Teicher and Teicher, *Twin Pillars to Desert Storm,* p. 61. (Brzezinski does not mention this in his memoirs.) The Teichers identify Richard Haass as an early, Reagan-era proponent of the tilt; Haass later became an NSC aide responsible for the Gulf region during the Bush administration and reinvigorated the tilt then; see also Barry Rubin, *Cauldron of Turmoil: America in the Middle East* (Harcourt Brace Jovanovich, 1992), p. 191. Also on the tilt see Dilip Hiro, *The Longest War: The Iran-Iraq Military Conflict* (Routledge, 1991); Phyllis Bennis and Michel Moushabeck, eds., *Beyond the Storm: A Gulf Crisis Reader* (Olive Branch Press, 1991); Murray Waas, "What Washington Gave Saddam for Christmas," in Micah Sifry and Christopher Cerf, eds., *The Gulf War Reader* (Times Books, 1991); and Alan Friedman, *Spider's Web: The Secret History of How the White House Illegally Armed Iraq* (Bantam, 1993). On U.S. sales of military equipment to Iraq, see *United States Export Policy toward Iraq Prior to Iraq's Invasion of Kuwait* (Hearing before the House Banking Committee, Oct. 27, 1992), especially testimony by

Kenneth Timmerman. "There will need to be . . .," is quoted in I. F. Stone, "Weinberger's War," *The Nation* (Oct. 10, 1987). The war "changed Iraq's view . . .," according to Daniel Pipes and Laurie Mylroie in their article, "Back Iraq: it's time for a US tilt," in *The New Republic* (April 27, 1987). On Turkey and the war, see the essay by a prominent American scholar on Turkey, Henri Barkey, "The Silent Victor: Turkey's Role in the Gulf War," in Efraim Karsh, ed., *The Iran-Iraq War: Impact and Implications* (Macmillan, 1989), pp. 133 ff.

CHAPTER 11

"Five years into . . .," Robert Weisman column, *Hartford Courant* (Sept. 12, 1987); he also quotes the others in that paragraph. "Saying the defense budget . . .," *Boston Globe* (Jan. 13, 1987). "The impact of the Cold War's end . . .," *Hartford Courant* (Jan. 28, 1990); "We're in the best niche . . .," ibid.; "I've never seen . . .," ibid. On UH-60 procurement ups and downs: *Army Times* (Dec. 21, 1987; Feb. 8, 1988; Oct. 3, 1988). "International sales are essential . . .," is in Gray's testimony at the Hearing before the House Subcommittee on Arms Control, International Security, and Science, March 5, 1987. "UTC cedes to . . .," comes from the *Hartford Courant* (July 22, 1986). Conversion's "first obstacle has been . . .," according to Bean, "Reconversion in Connecticut," *Social Policy* (Winter 1988).

CHAPTER 12

"We were encouraged . . .," and "We used to view . . .," came from interviews. Charges of corruption in the Turkey deal appeared in the *Fort Worth Star-Telegram* (July 28, 1985); "This will not create . . .," was also in the *Fort Worth Star-Telegram* (Sept 13, 1983). And "We're not here . . .," was in the *Fort Worth Star-Telegram* too (Aug. 31, 1986). "Turkey shares borders . . .," comes from a *Department of State Bulletin* (May 1984). "It was done . . .," was said in an interview. See also a report of Özal's advisors in the *Financial Times* (May 14, 1984). "Is being real generous . . .," was quoted in the *Dallas Morning News* (May 22, 1992). "We've sold the F-16 . . .," and "I cannot determine . . .," were both quoted in David Evans, "We Arm the World," *In These Times* (Nov. 15, 1993). On the FMC deal and warning, see *Middle East Executive Reports* (October 1987). The message was probably delivered by Vahit Erdem, head of DIDA, the agency responsible for such coproduction deals.

CHAPTER 13

"Many here in Turkey . . .," and other observations by Ramazan Ülek were made in an interview. On the 1983 elections, Turgut Özal's party won 45 percent of the vote, the more leftist Populist Party won 30 percent; see John H. McFadden, "Civil-Military Relations in the Third Turkish Republic," *Middle East Journal* (Winter 1985). "The pattern of nominal . . .," comes from David McDowall, *A Modern History of the Kurds* (I. B. Tauris, 1996), p. 21. "Whole villages . . .," is quoted by McDowall, p. 196. "The ban on speaking . . .," is in Kendal, "Kurdistan in Turkey," in Gérard Chaliand, ed., *The Kurds and Kurdistan: A People Without a Country* (Interlink, 1993), p. 74. The "army will not hesitate . . .," is quoted by Kendal, p. 65. On the economic condition of the Kurds, see Gérard Chaliand, *The Kurdish Tragedy*, Philip Black, trans. (Zed Books, 1993), pp. 39–44; and McDowall, pp. 411–412. "Its program was simple . . .,"

Chaliand, *The Kurdish Tragedy,* p. 47. The figures for numbers of persons arrested and jailed after the 1980 coup come from the *Wall Street Journal* (May 8, 1981); from S. Sayari, "The Terrorist Movement in Turkey," *Conflict Quarterly* (Winter 1987); and from McDowall, p. 420. "People who are racially . . ." is taken from McDowall, p. 411. "I went to the Southeast . . .," "The prison situation . . .," and "I lived in a village . . .," are all quoted from interviews.

CHAPTER 14

Figures on Afghan arms are taken from Chris Smith, "Letter from Dara," *New Statesman & Society* (Nov. 11, 1994). "I don't think . . .," is from Anthony Cordesman in the *New York Times* (July 14, 1996). "The Reagan Pentagon . . .," is from Gregg Easterbrook in the *Washington Monthly* (Jan. 1987). On inflation and military spending, see Steve Chan, "The Impact of Defense Spending on Economic Performance: A Survey of Evidence and Problems," *Orbis* (Summer 1985).

CHAPTER 15

Material on Turkey's military modernization plans comes from *Defense News* (Sept. 14, 1987, Jan. 30, 1989, May 8, 1989, July 3, 1989), and from interviews. Accounts of the history of the Dodd amendment come from interviews, Senate and House reports, the *Congressional Record,* and the weekly and year-end editions of *Congressional Quarterly.* On the history of such loans, see J. K. Jackson and L. Q. Nowells, *Export-Import Bank: Financing Commercial Military Sales* (Congressional Research Service, 3 March 1992). "He made it into a jobs issue . . .," was said in an interview. "It was done totally . . .," was said in an interview. The charge that Dodd traded his vote with Kasten was printed in the *Wall Street Journal* (Feb. 9, 1990) in a profile of Dodd by David Rogers, the first to flag the imbroglio; and was echoed in interviews. "According to an industry executive . . .," comes from *Defense News* (April 16, 1990). "We're talking about the universe . . .," comes from the States News Service (June 20, 1990). "It's a liberal delegation . . .," comes from the States News Service (Nov. 23, 1990). The account of the debate in the Banking committee is taken from the official transcript, July 17, 1990. The account of the action on the Dodd amendment in 1990 is taken from the *Congressional Quarterly* (July 21, 1990; Sept. 13, 1990; Nov. 18, 1990) and the year-end *CQ Almanac;* from the *Wall Street Journal* (July 18, 1990); from the *Washington Post* (Jan. 10, 1991); and from interviews. "Public housing advocates . . .," is quoted in the *"Congressional Quarterly* (Nov. 18, 1990). "We had problems . . .," was stated in an interview.

CHAPTER 16

The account of the Arab League action and the Mubarak quote are taken from Saïd K. Aburish, *The Rise, Corruption and Coming Fall of the House of Saud* (St. Martin's Press, 1995). The quotation from NSD 26 and the comment by a "senior administration official" come from Zachary Karabell, "Backfire: U.S. Policy Toward Iraq, 1988–2 August 1990," *Middle East Journal* (Winter 1995), pp. 32–33. NSD 26 is also identified as the source of official decisions in the ill-conceived policy toward Iraq by Rubin and by Teicher and Teicher in *Twin Pillars to Desert Storm.* "It pursued this policy . . .," Karabell, p. 43. "The real victims . . .," comes from Kanan Makiya, *Cruelty and Silence: War, Tyranny, Uprising, and the Arab World* (W. W. Norton, 1993), pp. 203–204. "Our goal is to get rid of Saddam . . .," quoted in Rubin, *Cauldron of Turmoil,* p. 247. Material on post-Gulf-war Turkey is taken from news reports; from Feroz Ahmad, *The Making of Modern Turkey;* and from Tozun Bahcheli, "Turkey, the Gulf Crisis, and the New World Order," in T. Y. Ishmael and J. S. Ishmael, eds., *The Gulf War and the New World Order* (University Press of Florida, 1994). On arms exports to the Middle East see Hartung, *And Weapons for All,* and William Keller, *Arm in Arm: the Political Economy of the Global Arms Trade* (Basic Books, 1995). The description of the Shah as a "confirmed alcoholic" comes from a George Ball interview.

CHAPTER 17

"Desert Storm was a good news . . ." is from *Industry Week* (July 1, 1991). The remarks by the Yale social analyst, Dodd, and Daniells about the January 1992 layoffs are taken from the *Hartford Courant* (Jan. 22, 1992). "It was our first . . ." was said by Jack Powers in an interview. "There was a saying . . .," was said by Mark Barnhart in an interview. Material on the Naugatuck Valley Project and the army engine plant comes from the *Hartford Courant* (Oct. 29, 1989); from *In These Times* (March 28, 1990); from the *New Haven Register* (May 26, 1991); and from Kevin Bean, "From tank work to teamwork," in *The Register Citizen* [Torrington, CT], (July 15, 1991). "As defense budgets shrink . . ." is from Edward Ericson, "Battle-Field Conversion," *Hartford Advocate* (Jan. 30, 1992). "With a long history . . ." is from *Business Week* (Oct. 1, 1990).

CHAPTER 18

"The only way . . ." is from the *Army Times* (July 16, 1990). "He's the driving force . . ." was said by General Chet Rees in an interview. "That's South Korea . . ." is from *Flight International* (Oct. 16, 1991). Material on the Dooley case came from court documents filed by plaintiff and defendants, especially a letter of Aug. 30, 1990, from Dooley's attorney to Robert F. Daniell; from the *Wall Street Journal* (Oct. 7, 1991); from *Flight International* (Oct. 16, 1991); from the *Hartford Courant* (July 14, 1993); and from Paul Lashmar, "Sword of Truth?" *New Statesman & Society* (June 23, 1995). "It helps all their . . ." was said by William Dane in an interview. Material on the August 1990 sale of Black Hawks to Turkey came from the *Wall Street Journal* (Aug. 17, 1990) and from Peter Thomson, "Eximbank's Largest Loan Guarantee," *Kurdish Life* (Winter 1993). "We're getting our clock . . ." and "We think we're . . ." are from the *Hartford Courant* (Aug. 18, 1990). "Defense industry lobbyists . . ." comes from *Defense News* (Aug. 20, 1990). Material on the Fitzwater press conference came from the official transcript. "Cold War thinking . . ." and "I was there . . ." were said in interviews. On the bids for the helicopter deal see *Defense News* (Apr. 13 and 22, 1991; Apr. 10 and July 20, 1992). "We're half the price . . .," and "Build the product . . .," come from *South Magazine* [U.K.] (Nov. 1990). Material on the lobbying for the deal came from interviews. Material on negotiation, awarding of, and reactions to the UH-60 contract came from *Defense News* (Aug. 3, Oct 5, and Dec. 14, 1992); from the *Hartford Courant* (Nov. 29, Dec. 9, and Dec. 11, 1992); from the *Turkish Daily News* (Sept. 22, 23, and 29; Dec. 9 and 24, 1992); and from *Business Wire* (Dec. 8, 1992). "My gut feeling . . .," "As a dealer . . .," and "The offset is . . ." were all said by Alan Urban in an interview. "We never had a problem . . ." came from an interview. "The contract by . . ." is from the *Turkish Daily News* (Dec. 9, 1992). "Most bankers laughed . . ." is from *Bank Letter* (Nov. 2, 1992). "Officials said combat . . ." is from the *Turkish Daily News* (Jan. 16, 1993).

CHAPTER 19

"Why should communities . . ." is from *Fortune* (June 29, 1992); "adequate to handle . . ." is from *Business Economics* (Jan. 1992). "Conversion legislation mandating . . ." was quoted in *Aviation Week and Space Technology* (Aug. 6, 1990). "I've seen guys . . ." and other comments by Olsson were made in an interview. "We were surprised . . ." was in the *Dallas Morning News* (Mar. 9, 1995). "If we don't export . . ." was said in an interview. "They ended up . . ." is from the *Los Angeles Times* (June 8, 1993). "Suddenly, I was Mr. Mom . . ." is also from the *Los Angeles Times* (July 24, 1994). "The companies that I really worry . . ." is from the *Hartford Courant* (Dec. 28, 1991). The comments by Barnhart, Cassidy, and Blodgett were made in interviews. "I love the shop . . ." is from the *US News & World Report* (June 27, 1994). "To the extent . . ." and other comments by Nakamoto were made in an interview. "So much for that . . ." is from the *Los Angeles Times* (Sept. 1, 1994). On offsets see Lora Lumpe, "Sweet deals, stolen jobs," *Bulletin of the Atomic Scientists* (Sept.–Oct. 1994). "History will tell you . . ." is from the *New York Times* (Sept. 20, 1992). "It was all the same crowd . . ." was said in an interview.

CHAPTER 20

"In Turkey, we seek . . ." was in a Department of State dispatch, Mar. 20, 1995 (from testimony before Congress, Mar. 9, 1995). "Our policy toward such states . . ." comes from a speech at the Johns Hopkins School of Advanced International Studies, Washington D.C., Sept. 21, 1993. In a speech to the Council on Foreign Relations nine days earlier, Anthony Lake stated the new policy of dual containment; see *New York Times* (Sept. 23, 1994). "There was an ongoing in-house . . ." comes from a Satloff interview. The Indyk speech was entitled, "Challenges to U.S. Interests in the Middle East: Obstacles and Opportunities" (May 18, 1993); a former colleague of Indyk's says Closson was the main conceptualizer. "Dual containment explicitly disavows . . ." comes from Gregory Gause III, "The Illogic of Dual Containment," *Foreign Affairs* (March/April 1994); also see Edward G. Shirley, "The Iran Policy Trap," *Foreign Policy* (Fall 1994); "Commercial interests . . .," *Arms Trade News* (June 1993); "A critical piece . . .," *Arms Trade Monitor* (Nov. 30, 1993). "Commitment to actively . . ." comes from *Defense Trade News* (State Department, Jan. 1994); "I think it's pretty . . ." is from Reuters (Feb. 17, 1995); "Lacking the courage . . ." and "The most positive . . ." are both taken from *Arms Control Today* (May 1995); "It was discouraging to note . . ." comes from *Report of the U.S. Helsinki Commission Delegation to Bosnia-Herzegovina, Albania, and Turkey* (Nov. 1994). "What do you do . . ." comes from an interview. The quote of a State Department document comes from *Report on Allegations of Human Rights Abuses by the Turkish Military and on the Situation in Cyprus* (June 1995), pp. 18 ff. "The human rights bureau . . ." was said by Steven Goose of Human Rights Watch, in an interview. "Human rights violations have occurred . . ." comes from his testimony (Sept. 19, 1995); he did not read the part regarding the export of U.S. weapons to Turkey, but it was in his prepared statement. "I've been dealing . . ." is from UPI (Sept. 19, 1995). "The support for Turkey . . ." was said by Goose in an interview.

CHAPTER 21

"Turkey was a NATO ally . . .," and other comments by Abramowitz, interview. On the provision of U.S. intelligence data, see Vago Muradian, "Turkish military said to be using U.S. Intelligence to bomb Kurds," *Army Times* (Dec. 12, 1994); see also Carol Migdalovitz, *Turkey: Ally in a Troubled Region* (Congressional Research Service, 14 September 1993), p. 18; and *Turkish Daily News* (June 10, 1997). "Provide Comfort? . . ." and other comments by a senior U.S. diplomat were made in an interview. "The PKK is giving . . ." was said by Öyman in an interview. "The United States should not hurt . . ." is from *Turkish Probe* (May 5, 1995). "Europe and the U.S. condemn . . ." and other comments by Aktan were made in an interview. "It's obvious . . ." was said in an interview.

CHAPTER 22

"The town was on the brink . . ." and "The town, without realizing it . . ." both come from interviews. "There was the expectation . . ." and other comments by Kelly come from an interview. "The BRAC process . . ." and subsequent comments by Barnhart were made in an interview. "Sikorsky, which currently . . ." was quoted in *Defense Daily* (Aug. 10, 1995). "The army orchestrated . . ." was said by Richard Aboulafia of the Teal Group in an interview. "It's a matter of survival . . ." is from the *Washington Post* (Nov. 5, 1994). "People that give away . . ." is from the *Hartford Courant* (Sept. 18, 1994). "Left hanging for six years . . .," is from the *Defense Daily* (May 12, 1994). The December 1995 UTC lobbying scene was described by Michael Remez in the *Hartford Courant* (Dec. 24, 1995). "I have a federal PAC . . ." and other comments by Powers were made in an interview. The figures on the UTC PAC come from Federal Election Commission data; see the Web site, www.tray.com. "We organized the hell . . ." is from *Defense Week* (Feb. 18, 1997). "I can guarantee . . ." is from the *Connecticut Post* (Feb. 20, 1997). "We're all scared . . ." and "Now I'm concerned . . ." were said in interviews (interviewees' names are fictitious). "Big industrial spaces . . ." was stated in an interview.

CHAPTER 23

"The newspaper was accused . . ." and "I met with Öcalan . . ." were said in interviews. Kurds "should be given . . ." was quoted in MacDowell, p. 437. Özal's attitude in 1991–93 did not reverse the harsh measures he proposed to combat terrorism, including the deportations, the village guard system, etc. In a letter to Demirel two months before his death, Özal laid out a strategy for dealing with the Kurdish issue that still relied heavily on military measures, including forced evacuations of the Southeast. The letter was very detailed, e.g., "The purchase of 20 Cobra and 20 to 30 Sikorsky helicopters for the security forces deployed in the area will help create a mobile force that can handle incidents that might occur simultaneously." But Özal suggested not merely evacuating the villages but transferring the villagers, giving them homes and employment elsewhere. And he insisted on other measures not since taken: strong investment in the Southeast; open and free debate on the issue. The full text of the letter and comment can be found in the "Review of 1993," of the *Turkish Daily News* [n.d.]. On U.S. counterinsurgency training, little is documented; one major example is the supergovernor of the Southeast, Ünal Erkan; see Sheri Laizer, *Martyrs, Traitors and Patriots: Kurdistan after the Gulf War* (Zed, 1996). "We have changed the concept . . ." quoted in the Human Rights Watch report, *Forced Displacement of Ethnic Kurds from Southeastern Turkey* (Oct. 1994), written by Christopher Panico, a leading American analyst of Turkey. The report is a succinct and well-documented statement of the Turkish policy. See also the valuable report of the Kurdish Human Rights Project (London), *The Destruction of Villages in South-East Turkey* (June 1996); and a rare, first-hand American account of village destruction by Kevin McKiernan published in the *Santa Barbara Independent* (Aug. 10–17, 1995). "When they burned Kaynak . . ." was said in an interview. "My mother called me . . .," "We had one hundred . . .," and "There was a Jandarma . . ." were all stated in interviews. "Helicopters are the backbone . . .," and other passages are taken from the Human Rights Watch Arms Project report, *Weapons Transfers and Violations of the Laws of War in Turkey* (Nov. 1995). In a grim irony, the Turkish government prosecuted the translator and the publisher of the report for insulting the military; however, the offending passage quoted a U.S. embassy official. "There is no doubt . . .," "I was a shop-keeper . . .," and "In the immigrant populations . . .," were all stated in interviews. Ergil now heads an institute in Ankara dedicated to creating dialogue between Kurds and Turks, with a set of principles to resolve the crisis. "The Turkish state is having . . .," "Yes, the Kurdish refugee crisis . . .," "A structural change in Turkey . . .," and "It is a proto-Islamic party . . ." were all stated in interviews. "We have scanned . . ." comes from *Forced Evacuations* (Netherlands Kurdistan Society, 1995), pp. 16–21. "Such is the military's domination . . .," is quoted from Alan Cowell in the *New York Times* (Nov. 17, 1994). "We hate the U.S.A." is from a report by National Public Radio; the "'Sikorsky' and 'Cobra'" comment is from a film by Kevin McKiernan. "The burning of the village . . ." comes from an interview.

CHAPTER 24

"If one can fly . . ." is quoted from Keith Krause, *Arms and the State: Patterns of Military Production and Trade* (Cambridge University Press, 1992), p. 197. On economic aspects of this argument, see Nicole Ball, *Security and Economy in the Third World* (Princeton, 1988). See also S. Deger and R. West, eds., *Defense, Security and Development* (St. Martin's, 1987). The scholars do not state the case as bluntly as I do. "Egypt's progress . . ." is taken from *The Economist* (Feb. 4, 1995). "To keep the military . . ." is taken from Stanley Reed, "The Battle for Egypt," *Foreign Affairs* (Sept–Oct 1993). "The acceleration in Saudi . . ." is from Aburish, *The Rise, Corruption, and Coming Fall of the House of Saud,* p. 208. "Only about 7 percent . . ." was stated by Ann Markusen before a panel at the United Nations sponsored by the NGO Committee on Disarmament, Oct. 30, 1995. "We need Turkey . . ." was stated by William Dane in an interview. "Some Colombians . . ." comes from Oscar Arias, "Exporting Death and Misery," *Los Angeles Times* (Sept. 19, 1996). On preventive diplomacy see Michael Lund, *Preventing Violent Conflicts* (U.S. Institute of Peace, 1996); V. Volkan, J. Montville, and D. Julius, eds., *The Psychodynamics of International Relationships* (Lexington Books, 1991), 2 vols.; K. Rupesinghe and M. Kuroda, eds., *Early Warning and Conflict Resolution* (St. Martin's, 1992), and the Winston Foundation Web site, www.wf.org.

INDEX